GOOD DESIGN TO HELP YOU . . .

The words you need
All the essential vocab. to deal with every topic

Topic Choice
Each chapter is a
KEY TOPIC in the
GCSE syllabuses

What you need to be able to do
What the examiners are
looking for, carefully
analyzed

Pick off each skill, one by one
Just like the exam,
Listening, Reading,
Speaking and Writing are
practised separately – it's
much easier that way

---

6 GOING ABROAD – TRAVEL

The words you need

Verbs of coming and going

aller	to go	s'arrêter	to stop
arriver	to arrive	descendre	to go down, get off (bus etc.)
entrer	to go in	monter	to go up, get on (bus etc.)
partir	to go away, depart	quitter	to leave
rester	to stay	rentrer	to return (home)
sortir	to go out		

Directions and distances

à droite	on the right/ to the right	à gauche	on the left/ to the left
tout droit	straight on	loin	far
près (d'ici)	near (here)	proche	near

In town

la rue	street	la place	square
le pont	bridge	les feux	traffic lights
une église	church	l'hôtel de ville	town hall
la mairie	town hall	le stade	sports stadium
le Syndicat d'Initiative	information bureau		
le trottoir	pavement	traverser	to cross
un parking	car park	un agent de police	policeman
le commissariat	police station		

Travelling by road

la route	road	l'autoroute	motorway
la gare routière	bus station	l'arrêt	(bus) stop
l'arrivée	arrival	le départ	departure
un (auto)bus	bus	un (auto)car	coach
le billet	ticket	le carnet	book of tickets
le ticket	ticket	l'horaire	timetable
faire de l'autostop	to hitch-hike	un sac à dos	rucksack
le péage	road toll	le voyage	journey
la ceinture de sécurité	safety belt	le conducteur	driver
conduire	to drive	l'essence (sans plomb)	(lead-free) petrol
faire le plein	to fill up	le garage	garage
l'huile	oil	le litre	litre
le mécanicien	mechanic	la moto	motorbike
en panne	broken down	le permis de conduire	driving licence
le pneu	tyre	crevé	punctured
réparer	to repair	la station-service	service station
le piéton	pedestrian	le vélo	bike
le vélomoteur	moped	louer	to hire
la priorité à droite	priority from the right		

What you need to be able to do.

- Understand people giving instructions about finding the way.
- Understand 24-hour clock times.
- Understand spoken and written details to do with different forms of travel, including timetable notes.
- Ask for directions, buy tickets, etc. for travel.
- Talk and write about holidays at home and abroad.
- Know something about transport in France.

A MEG Basic Listening, May 1989.

Exercise 1 Questions 11–15

You are staying with a French family. One afternoon the telephone rings and you take a message from Philippe to give to Michelle.

Look at questions 11–15 below.

Now listen to Philippe and make a note of the information in **English**. You will hear the message **twice**.

11 Where can Philippe not go tonight?
.... [1]

12 Who has had an accident?
.... [1]

13 What happened?
.... [2]

14 Where has Philippe to go?
.... [1]

15 What must Michelle do and when?

(a) .... [1]

(b) .... [2]

[8]

Higher Level
Here you can expect to be tested, as the tasks could include radio broadcasts and telephone messages as well as ordinary conversations. This recent task included two of these types. Read the setting carefully before you attempt the questions. Also, look carefully at Question (a). It is a double-barrelled question with an extra question word tacked on at the end. (L47 on cassette. Answers on p. 181)

TECHNIQUE TIP
Always read to the very end of the question. In reading English we generally have a very good idea before the end of the sentence what is being said, and we tend to skip the last few words, or pay less attention to them.

Technique tips
clearly presented
so you know the
pitfalls, and the
short cuts well in
advance

Over 60 taped exercises fully
transcribed in the
back of the book

*Grammar
Reference* and
pronunciation,
also at the back
of the book, but
no more than you
really need

Listening

Basic Level
You are likely to get simple post-office situations, or situations where people talk about feeling unwell. Most other areas are for Higher Level only. A typical task would be one where you have to understand a chemist's instructions. (L45 on cassette)

You have had a stomach upset while staying in France, and you take a prescription to the chemist's. Can you understand what she tells you about the medicine?

READING

Basic Level
Again, you won't find many tasks at Basic Level on this topic. Notices outside banks, in post offices, simple instructions on medicine, etc. are the most likely tasks.
You have been prescribed some cough medicine while on a skiing holiday in France. The instructions are written on the label.

POSOLOGIE: **Une cuillerée à soupe toutes les quatre heures diluée dans l'eau chaude.**

When and how do you have to take this medicine? (3)

Speaking

Basic Level
Role-plays on this topic are very common. Here are ideas for you to look at and prepare, with a few notes on each to help you.

(a) You are on a camping holiday in France with some friends. You arrive at the camp-site which you wrote to before leaving home in order to make a reservation.
The part of the camp-site owner is played by the examiner.
1. Say you have made a reservation.
2. Say there are four of you.
3. Tell the owner you would like to stay for 5 nights.
4. Ask if there are any showers.
5. Find out if you must pay for the showers. MEG, Autumn 1988

Basic Writing

The only task you are likely to get is a lost-property exercise. Suppose you have lost your wallet or purse and are asked to describe it and mention four things which were in it. This is how you could do such a task.

Mon porte-monnaie.
Description: petit, rouge et noir.
Contenu: 1. 20 livres en argent anglais.
2. Des timbres français.
3. Une photo de ma famille.
4. Les clefs de ma maison et ma valise.

---

14 GRAMMAR REFERENCE SECTION

Grammar Reference Section

Grammar Summary

This summary does not, of course, claim to be a complete grammar of French. It does, however, cover all the grammar normally required for the GCSE examination. The Table of Contents give you a general indication of where to find the information you want about verbs, tenses, adjectives and so on. Many of the examples given have been taken from texts in the book. A reference such as (L4) directs you to Listening text number 4 to find the example given. The reference (10D) means that you will find the example in the Key to the Exercises for Chapter 10, Exercise D.

1. Nouns

Definitions. Nouns are the parts of speech which act as names for objects, actions, feelings, ideas and animate beings. For example, the following words are all nouns: **table** (object), **promenade** (action), **colère** (feeling), **idée** (idea), **cheval** (animate being). There is a special sort of noun called a *proper noun*. These nouns are always written with a capital letter and refer to objects which have their own, individual name, like towns **(Paris)**, countries **(Angleterre)**, people **(Christine)**.

YOUR GUIDE TO GCSE . . .

Check your board

There is variation between exam boards, in the syllabuses and the forms of the exam. For that reason you must be certain which Board's exam you will be taking. Of course, your teacher will tell you, and for any details you should write to the Board. They can send the full syllabus for your exam including word lists.

Be authentic!

The National Criteria, which are a sort of checklist, tell us who the exam is for, and what a French course should do. They ask for the kind of French which you need to understand and use when dealing with French people who are in Britain, or who you meet travelling in France or another French-speaking country.

So the French materials you study must be 'authentic'. When you do a listening or a reading task, the setting and the content are taken from real life, and from the situations where you hear spoken French

and read the language in signs, adverts, articles and public notices.

Skills and Grades

For the exam, language is divided into the four main skills, Listening, Speaking, Reading and Writing. Each of these skills is tested separately. There are also two levels of examination called Basic, and Higher or Extended. You can choose which skills and which levels you want to be examined in, which is another advantage of the new system. *But* you must do the common core. This consists of:

- Basic Listening
- Basic Reading
- Basic Speaking.

In the whole scale of GCSE grades which go from A to G, the common core can gain a maximum of Grade E. As you add on extra elements, your possible maximum grade increases by one each time, as you can see from this table:

GRADE	BASIC LISTENING	BASIC READING	BASIC SPEAKING	BASIC WRITING	HIGHER LISTENING	HIGHER READING	HIGHER SPEAKING	HIGHER WRITING
A	T H E	C O	R E	COMPULSORY	CHOICE OF 2 OF THESE 3 ELEMENTS			COMPULSORY
B	T H E	C O	R E	COMPULSORY	CHOICE OF 1 OF THESE 3 ELEMENTS			COMPULSORY
C	T H E	C O	R E	COMPULSORY	CHOICE OF 1 OF 4 HIGHER ELEMENTS			
D	T H E	C O	R E	CHOICE OF 1 OF 5 NON-CORE ELEMENTS				
E	T H E	C O	R E					
F	T H E	C O	R E					
G	T H E	C O	R E					

YOUR GUIDE TO GCSE . . .

Most people who are aiming at Grades A or B do all 8 elements (Basic Listening, Speaking, Reading and Writing, and the same four skills at Higher Level). Most people aiming at Grade C do all four Basic tests and at least 2 Higher tests, (usually, but not always, Listening and Reading). One Board (MEG) divides the Higher Level papers into Part 1 and Part 2.

The Form of the Exam

The *form* of the exam varies from Board to Board. Some Boards set all the Basic Level papers in one sitting and all the Higher Level papers in another sitting on a different day. Others group papers by skills, and have Basic Level Listening followed by Higher Level Listening, etc. Whichever Board you do, you will only have *one* oral exam, either at Basic, or at Basic + Higher Level. The oral will be conducted by your own teacher. It will be held earlier than the other parts of the exam.

Points and Grades

The last thing to explain is the grading system. For each element of the exam, the marks you score are converted into a number of *points*. The total number of points you get decides your grade. Here is an example of how this works:

Total number of points available for each element

	Listening	Reading	Speaking	Writing
Basic	4	4	4	4
Higher	3	3	3	3

Total = 28 points

Points required for each grade:

Grade	A	B	C	D	E	F	G
Points	24–28	21–23	18–20	14–17	10–13	5–9	1–4

If you are aiming at Grade C you need at least 18 points, so you must take all four Basic elements + at least one Higher element. This would give you a maximum possible score of 19 points *if* you got all the points in each part of the exam. To be sure of your grade it would be better to take at least two if not three Higher elements.

To get all four points in a Basic Level exam, you do *not* have to get full marks, but generally you have to get about 80%. To get at least one point at Higher Level you normally have to get about 35–40%.

The system seems very complicated, doesn't it? Now for the good news! **Because of the points system, it is easier to get a Grade A in French (and other languages) than any other subject.** About 20% got Grade A in the first two years of the exam. So, aim high, take all the elements you have a reasonable chance of scoring a point in. (It doesn't cost more if you take three elements or all eight). And *Good Luck!* or rather, Bonne Chance!

Well done! You chose Work Out for its complete coverage

CONTENTS

WORK OUT
FRENCH
GCSE

Edward Neather and Mike Ounsworth

The authors and publishers wish to thank the following for permission to use copyright material: London East Anglian Group, Midland Examining Group, Northern Examining Association comprised of Associated Lancashire Schools Examining Board, Joint Matriculation Board, North Regional Examinations Board, North West Regional Examinations Board and Yorkshire and Humberside Regional Examinations Board; Northern Ireland Schools Examinations Council and Southern Examining Group for questions from past examination papers.

Worked examples and answers included in the text are the sole responsibility of the authors, and have not been provided or approved by examining boards or groups.

Every effort has been made to trace all the copyright holders, but if any have been inadvertently overlooked the publishers will be pleased to make the necessary arrangement at the first opportunity.

The authors owe a particular debt of gratitude to their two colleagues, Isabelle Rodrigues and Madeleine Davis, who have read the manuscript with care and given the benefit of their knowledge and experience to the final form of the book.

ME, MY FAMILY AND OTHER PEOPLE

What you need to be able to do.

– Understand when someone speaks to you about yourself, your family and friends.
– Talk and write about these subjects.
– Understand details about other people when you hear or read them.

In this topic you should be able to understand when someone speaks to you about yourself, your family and friends, and to talk and write about these subjects. You also need to understand details about other people when you hear or read them.

Perhaps one of the first things you learned in French was to talk about yourself and your family. Things have not changed very much since then, except that you are a bit older. You will still get credit in the exam for saying or writing very simple sentences about, for example, how many brothers and sisters you have, but at Higher Level you should be able to describe in some detail members of your family, your best friend or some other person you know well. You might also be asked to say how well you get on with them or what you feel about them. None of this is difficult if you know the vocabulary and practise it.

A good idea for all the topics which deal with your personal life is to record the details on to a cassette and keep listening to it. Writing a script for this recording can help, too. Use the fact sheet on p. 9 to write in information about yourself, your family and friends. Remember though, that having things written down is not much use by itself. You must also practise listening and speaking often.

The words you need

People you want to talk about

ma famille   my family
ma mère   my mother
mon père   my father
ma soeur   my sister
mon frère   my brother
mes grands-parents   my grandparents
mon oncle   my uncle
ma tante   my aunt
mon cousin   my cousin (boy)
ma cousine   my cousin (girl)
les parents   parents *or* relations
ma belle-soeur   my sister-in-law
                or step-sister
mon beau-frère   my brother-in-law
                or step-brother
son mari   her husband
sa femme   his wife
un enfant (unique)   an (only) child
un bébé   a baby
un fils   a son
une fille   a daughter
mes amis   my friends
mon meilleur ami   my best friend (boy)
ma meilleure amie   my best friend (girl)
un copain   a mate (boy)
une copine   a mate (girl)
son prénom   his/her first name
son nom de famille   his/her surname

Words for describing them

une description   a description

petit(e) small	**grand(e)** tall
de taille moyenne of medium height	**gros(se)** big
mince thin	

aîné(e) elder	**cadet(te)** younger
les cheveux hair	**les yeux** eyes
une barbe a beard	**une moustache** a moustache

gris(e) grey	**blanc(he)** white
blond(e) blond	**brun(e)** brown
noir(e) black	**roux (rousse)** red-haired
bleu(e) blue	**vert(e)** green
marron brown	**noisette** hazel
frisé(e) curly	**raide** straight
long(ue) long	**court(e)** short

marié(e) married	**fiancé(e)** engaged
divorcé(e) divorced	**séparé(e)** separated
célibataire single	**mort(e)** dead

sympa(thique) nice	**aimable** friendly
content(e) happy	**amusant(e)** amusing
fâché(e) cross	**inquiet (inquiète)** worried

drôle funny	**calme** calm, quiet
gentil(le) nice	**joli(e)** pretty
beau (belle) good-looking	
mignon(ne) charming, sweet	**méchant(e)** nasty
vilain(e) naughty	

Pets

le chien dog	**le chat** cat
le poisson (rouge) (gold)fish	**le lapin** rabbit
le cochon d'Inde guinea-pig	**le hamster** hamster
la souris mouse	**un oiseau** bird
le cheval/le poney horse/pony	**la perruche** budgerigar

Fact sheet

Ma famille et moi

Nom de famille: _____

Prénom: _____

Date de naissance _____

Personne	Description	Autres Détails	Mon Opinion
ma mère			
mon père			
ma soeur (mes soeurs)			
mon frère (mes frères)			
autres membres de la famille (grand'mère; chien, etc.)			

Here is an example of how to fill in the fact sheet.

Fact sheet

Ma famille et moi

Nom de famille: _____ Jenkins _____

Prénom: _____ Mary _____

Date de naissance _____ le 3 juillet, 1975 _____

Personne	Description	Autres Détails	Mon Opinion
ma mère	très petite les yeux noisette les cheveux noirs, frisés, assez longs	38 ans	toujours gentille
mon père		je ne le vois pas très souvent; mes parents sont divorcés	c'est dommage
ma soeur (mes soeurs)			
mon frère (mes frères)			
autres membres de la famille (grand'mère; chien, etc.)			

Listening

What you need to be able to do.

At Basic Level you can expect to have to give simple details of what you hear, such as name (including spelling), age, date of birth and simple descriptions of people. The usual idea is that your pen-friend is describing a relative or friend. See how you cope with this task. (L1 on cassette)

A Your pen-friend is telling you about some of her friends whom you will be meeting at her school the next day.

First, read these questions about her best friend.

1. How old is Monique? (1 mark)
2. What does she look like? (Give 2 details) (2 marks)
3. Why does she get on so well with your pen-friend? (1 mark)

Now listen to the cassette. You always hear everything at least twice in an exam, so try to write something down after the first hearing, then play the piece again. (Answers on p. 177)

You should have managed Questions 1 and 2 if you have learned the vocabulary on p. 8. Question 3 might have seemed trickier, but all you needed to recognise was **fille unique** in the last sentence.

A more difficult task would ask you to sort out details about more than one person. Here is a question in grid form. (L2 on cassette)

B Now your friend tells you about the teachers you will be seeing in class tomorrow morning. Fill in the missing details on the plan to help you remember who is who.

(Answers p. 177)

TECHNIQUE TIP

For Question 2 it is a good idea to write all 3 details if you can. That way, if you get 2 correct you should get 2 marks.

TECHNIQUE TIP

Always read all the questions for a task before you listen to it. You can expect the information to come in the same order as the questions. Question 3 looks the most difficult, but there are more marks for No. 2, and you may well have to choose two details from several which are given. *Always* make a sensible guess rather than leave a blank.

Teacher		Description		Character	
Mme Lambert		(i)	(1 mark)	Always nice	
		(ii)	(1 mark)	She laughs a lot	
Mlle Richard		Small		(i)	(1 mark)
		Slim		(ii)	(1 mark)
M.	(1 mark)	(i)	(1 mark)	Very nice usually	
		(ii)	(1 mark)		(1 mark)

In this kind of test you have to select information and put it in the right place. Some of the information is given to you in the table, and this should help you to focus on what is needed, if you listen hard. One or two words are usually enough for each answer.

TECHNIQUE TIP

You can usually answer listening questions in a few words. Do *not* write sentences. The shorter your answer, the sooner you can concentrate on the next one. Facts do not stay in the memory very long! All the examiner wants is the information asked for.

Example

You might have the question: Why didn't John watch the football last night?

The French you hear is: **Non, je n'ai pas regardé le match après le dîner, parce que j'étais trop fatigué.**

You write for your answer: *Too tired.*

You do not need to write. *John didn't watch the match last night because he was too tired.*

Higher Level

The most difficult questions will not always be the longest ones. And although there may be some unfamiliar words in a passage, you can only actually be *tested* on words which are in the syllabus vocabulary list. So it is not the language used which makes a question difficult, but the *task* you have to do. At Higher Level you must always read the questions very carefully and make sure that you understand what is wanted. You may be expected to draw conclusions, or summarise. In other words, the answer may not be a word or phrase in the text; you may have to find your own words.

Here is an example.

You are sitting in a café when you overhear a conversation between two young girls at the next table. (L3 on cassette)

What problem seems to be common to both of them?

Your answer? . . .

This is a situation which you may well recognise! The clues are in the words **sortir; rentrer; 11 heures; téléphoner** and so on. Here you will have to write more than one or two words. *Parents* is not clear enough. *Going out in the evening* does not quite manage to say what the *problem* is. The best answer will be: *When they are allowed to go out,* OR, *How late they can stay out.*

Reading

What you need to be able to do.
At Basic Level you can be expected to recognise simple details about people in letters, magazine articles, requests for pen-friends etc. At Higher Level you will get tasks which ask you to deal with character descriptions and relationships. Again, these are usually from letters and magazines, including problem pages. The more demanding tasks will expect you to draw conclusions from what you read or find a short phrase to sum up what is being said.

Most people are happier with Reading than with Listening. You can choose which questions you do first, how long you spend on each part, and whether you go back and check your answers. (Yes, you should!)

Here is an example of a Basic Level reading task.
C You are interested to see this photo in the paper you are looking through. The item is about a boy who has gone missing. Can you understand the essential information?

AVIS DE RECHERCHE

ON RECHERCHE
ROUSSEL Christophe, né le 3 août 1975, 1,76 m, 62 kg, blond, yeux bleus.
Il était vêtu lors de sa disparition d'un jean bleu, d'un blouson marine et vert, chaussures marron.
Signes particuliers : *bras droit légèrement déformé avec cicatrice d'environ 15 cm*
Contacter le commissariat de Brunoy au 60.46.16.41 ou la brigade des mineurs au 42.60.33.22.

1.   What was Christophe wearing when he disappeared? (3)
2.   He has a 15-centimetre scar which would help to identify him. Whereabouts is this scar? (2)

(Answers p. 177)

TECHNIQUE TIP

Always look carefully for the question word and underline it. You would be surprised how often people misread *when* instead of *where*, or *how* instead of *who*.

TECHNIQUE TIP

You can underline words in the text as well. It is your paper. Make as much use of it as you can. Practise on the extract from a letter on p. 13.

Your new pen-friend Pierre is writing about his family.

Nous sommes cinq dans ma famille et en plus il y a ma grand'mère qui passe six mois chez nous. En septembre elle va chez ma tante Marie jusqu'à Noël. J'aime beaucoup ma grand'mère, elle est toujours très calme, mais quand elle est là, je dois dormir dans la chambre de mon frère aîné, et on se dispute souvent.

The question on this text might be: Give three facts about Pierre's grandma. (3 marks)

It helps if you <u>underline</u> the part of the text which is about grandma. Do it now, before you read any further.

You should have underlined from **il y a ma grandmère** as far as **très calme.**

Now you can focus on the part about grandma and write down three facts.
1.   She is spending six months with the family.
2.   In September she is going to Aunt Marie's until Christmas.
3.   She is always very calm.

The last sentence in the letter could have a more difficult question on it to test you a bit more.

Why do Pierre and his brother argue?

You need to look for the word *argue*. Can you find it in the text? The answer will be in the same sentence, or in the one before or after. Write your own answer here before you read any further.

(Answer: Because they share a room (when grandma is there).)

Here is an example from a recent GCSE paper of a question using a magazine article. How well can you do this one? (Answer on p. 177)

TECHNIQUE TIP

Always put down as much information as you can. If you write 5 or 6 details down and only 3 of them are correct, you may well get 3 marks anyway. BUT:
(i) Never write two things which contradict each other. You will not get a mark;
(ii) Think carefully about the meaning of the English you write. For the first point you could write *She is living with them at the moment.* You should *not* write *She lives with them.*

D   NEA Basic Reading, 1989.

11   Your friend Chantal has sent you a **magazine** cutting about her favourite singer, Jean-Jacques Goldman:

UN DUO AU TOP

GOLDMAN

Carte d'identité

Nom : Goldman

Prénom : Jean-Jacques

Age : Trente-sept ans

Lieu de naissance : Paris

Taille : 1,80 m

Yeux : marron

Cheveux : noirs

Situation de famille :
marié, trois enfants

Apart from his names, give **four** details you find out about him.

(i) ....

(ii) ....

(iii) ....

(iv) ....

E   Problem-page letters are very popular as exam questions – perhaps because we all have problems at one time or another. In the following example you are asked to answer specific questions of detail. Have a go at it.

Mon prénom est Frédérique et à mon tour je vous écris pour vous parler de mon problème. Je suis une fille très complexée et plutôt timide. Je crois que mes complexes viennent du fait que mes parents sont assez pauvtes et ne peuvent m'offrir tout ce dont une jeune fille a envie. Quant à ma timidité elle doit parvenir du fait que mon père est sévère. Mon père veut être au courant de tout ce qui me concerne, si je veux sortir, il faut lui demander la permission et bien souvent c'est un «non» catégorique ou bien un «oui» avec des conditions. Ma mère me reproche quelquefois de ne pas être suffisamment positive. J'ai 15 ans et je ne me sens pas très bien dans ma peau. Pouvez-vous m'aider.
Merci
                                    Frédérique

1.   How does Frédérique describe herself? (1)
2.   She says her father is strict. What is he strict about? (1)
3.   What does Frédérique's mum think about her? (1)

The three answers are in the sentences beginning: **je suis . . . ; mon père . . . ; ma mère. . . .**

Question 1 is straightforward, and you should have spotted the word **timide.**

So, for Question 1, *timid* = 1 mark BUT **timide** might be 0.

Question 2 is the hardest. The sentence is long and a bit complicated. It is important to read the sentence right through to the end, not stopping at the first sign of difficulty. Keep on the lookout for a key word – often a single word will give you the clue you need.

So for Question 2 you will get the mark for *letting Frédérique go out* OR *her going out*.

Question 3 looks fairly easy. **Positive** is spelt the same in English and French. But if you see only the word **positive,** you will get the answer wrong, and you should realise that, because *timid* and *positive* mean the opposite of each other. You have to spot the important **ne . . . pas** in the previous line.

So for Question 3, *She is not positive (enough)* = 1 mark.

Higher Level

Finally in this section of Reading tasks, here is a Higher Level example. (Answers p. 177)

F   NEA Higher Reading, 1989.

TECHNIQUE TIP

Lots of French words are spelt very like English. Sometimes you can write the French spelling without thinking. Be careful, because *you might not get the mark* if you do this.

TECHNIQUE TIP

Do not lose sight of the real world. What sorts of things are parents usually strict about? If you do not recognise **sortir**, you should still be prepared to guess. The word **permission** is an extra clue.

TECHNIQUE TIP

Always be on the lookout for the word **ne** (often shortened to **n'**) which gives the statement a *negative* meaning. (See negatives on p. 200.)

13   Further on, a special feature interests you:

> MÈRE SPÉCIAL
>
> Maman m'énerve et encore je suis polie. Elle n'arrête pas, sur mon dos toute la journée. Il y a toujours un truc qui ne va pas. J'en ai marre, marre, marre. Elle veut toujours savoir ce que je fais, avec qui je sors, à quoi j'ai passé la soirée, pourquoi je suis rentrée si tard. Est-ce que j'ai donné mon adresse à quelqu'un ? Moi je réponds non et je file dans ma chambre. Pardon, mais j'estime qu'à 15 ans je peux avoir ma vie privée.

(a)   How would you describe this girl's relationship with her mother?

....

....

(b)   Mention **two** details to explain your answer.

   (i)   ....

   (ii)   ....

Speaking

The Oral is the first part of the exam which you will have to face, so it is perhaps understandable that you might be a bit nervous about it. Remember that your examiner will usually be your teacher, and also that, although bits of the Oral test are unpredictable, a great deal can be catered for by careful preparation.

Role-play

There are not many possible role-plays on this topic, but you could be asked something which requires you to give your name, age and other personal details, for example if you have to give information about yourself at a camp-site, hotel, hospital, and so on.

 For this, you need to be able to use the French alphabet. It is a very good idea to learn this by heart, because spelling of names sometimes comes up in the listening tasks. To help you, the alphabet is recorded on Cassette No. 1. There are also a few recordings of French names spelt out for you to copy down.

In role-plays at Basic Level, all you need to do is to say in French what is given to you on the card. You do *not* need to understand what the teacher or examiner says to you as a cue. Nearly always the teacher/examiner will speak first.

Role-plays often work out like this. On the other hand, there are sometimes things the instructions do not tell you but which you are expected to do, such as be polite. An example of this is the use of **Monsieur** or **Madame.** The same is true of the use of **merci** and **s'il vous plaît.** Try to include these words whenever possible. It will make your French sound much more natural and is good training for when you want to speak to real French people. Sometimes, as well, it may give you an extra mark in the exam.

Here are two role-plays for you to try. They are both recorded on the tape. (S1 and S2)

1. You are talking to your French pen-friend's father about your family. Your teacher will play the part of the father and will begin the conversation.

    (a)   Tell him there are 4 people in your family.
    (b)   Tell him you have a brother called David.
    (c)   Tell him your brother is 12.

2. You are in a police station giving information about an accident. The policeman asks you for details of yourself to put on a form. Your teacher will play the part of the policeman.

    (a)   Tell the policeman your name.
    (b)   Spell your surname for him.
    (c)   Give him your date of birth (including year).

Conversation

Talking about yourself and your family is a very common task in GCSE French. At Basic Level you will be expected to give facts in answer to questions, so it is very important to recognise the question word, and any other clues to what the examiner is looking for. Here is some advice about asking questions in French.

1. Questions which require the answer **oui** or **non.** Examiners should not use such questions much, because it is too easy for someone to answer **oui** or **non** even if they have not understood the question. You can always recognise questions like this by the way the voice goes up at the end of the sentence. There are three ways of asking such a question.

TECHNIQUE TIP

You are *not* expected to translate the role-play tasks, only to give the information required. Say no more than is necessary. Here is an example:

You are talking to your French correspondent's mother about your family.

Your instructions	*Examiner's questions*
	Il y a combien de personnes dans ta famille?
(a) Tell her there are 5 people in your family.	
	Alors, tu as des frères ou des soeurs?
(b) Tell her you have one brother and one sister.	
	Et qui est l'aîné?
(c) Tell her your sister is the eldest.	

When you get the role-play card a few minutes before the exam, you look at the instructions and perhaps you can't remember the word for *eldest*. Just think for a moment. Almost certainly the examiner is going to ask you who the eldest is, so all you need to say in reply is **ma soeur.** You can probably see that all you need to say for the other answers is (a) **cinq,** (b) **un frère et une soeur.**

(a) The question begins with **est-ce que ...**
     Est-ce que tu as des frères?

(b) Turn the verb and subject round, so instead of **tu as,** you hear **as-tu.**
     As-tu des frères?

(c) There is no change to the sentence, but the voice goes up at the end.
     Tu as des frères?

2. Questions which require other information. Examiners use these all the time! The most common question words are:

quand? *when?*   **quel?** *which/what?*
qui? *who?*   **où?** *where?*
qu'est-ce que? *what?*   **pourquoi?** *why?*
combien? *how much/how many?* **comment?** *how?*

Again, there is more than one way of asking questions using these words. They may be the first word in the sentence or come later. Look at the following examples.

> **Combien de frères as-tu?**
> **Combien de frères est-ce que tu as?**
> **Tu as combien de frères?**

A common technique used by examiners is to ask a question requiring the answer **oui** or **non,** then to follow it up with another question using just the question word.

Example: **Tu as des frères?**
          Oui.
          Combien?

So you have a good chance of recognising the question, and knowing what it means. Now comes the hard part! You have to give the information, and you cannot do that without knowing the vocabulary. That is why it is so important to have learned the words at the beginning of this topic, *and* to have practised them as much as possible.

   The grid on pages 9–10 lets you put down the basic information, and if you know this, you will do well. Listen to the recording on the cassette (S3) of a GCSE candidate talking about her family using the grid.

Higher Level

Here the questions will be more wide-ranging. You will be expected not just to give facts but descriptions, opinions, reasons. You will probably find that your answers are going to be longer, so you need to learn *how* to make them longer. It is not really difficult to do this if you know some vocabulary. Here are some examples of how to improve a description.

(a) Use more than one detail.
     Elle a les cheveux courts et frisés.
     Il a les yeux bleus et il porte des lunettes.

(b) Be as precise as you can.
     Il a les cheveux assez longs.
     Elle n'est pas très grande.

(c) Give an opinion.
     Elle a les cheveux noirs et les yeux bleus. Je pense qu'elle est très jolie.
     Mon petit frère s'appelle Roger. Il est méchant quelquefois.

(d) Give a reason.
     Ma mère est fatiguée quelquefois, parce qu'elle travaille beaucoup.

TECHNIQUE TIP

If you *do* get asked a question which requires **oui** or **non** as an answer, always try to give at least one extra piece of information. This will improve your performance.

Example: Question – **Tu as des frères?**
          Answer – **Oui, j'ai un frère qui s'appelle Paul.**
          Or – **Non, je n'ai pas de frère, mais j'ai une soeur qui s'appelle Tracey.**

TECHNIQUE TIP

Talking is judged more on *communication* than on accuracy. The more you speak on the topic, the better your score, even if you make mistakes.

Basic Writing

We are going to concentrate on Basic Writing in these early chapters. Higher Level writing tasks usually cover more than one topic, so we have written a special chapter (p. 154) which concentrates on Higher Writing.

There are not many tasks you could get on the topic of family or friends. Here is an example of a form-filling exercise which is one possibility.

You are looking for a possible exchange partner and your teacher has given you this form designed by the French school with which your school is linked. Fill in the required details *in French*. (But do not change the spelling of names.)

Nom:
Prénom:
Age:
Date De Naissance:
Nom Du Parent Responsable:
Adresse:

Autres Membres De La Famille:

Description Personnelle: Taille -
          Couleur des cheveux -
          Couleur des yeux -
Ton Caractère: Souligne les trois adjectifs les plus appropriés:
      gentil (le): calme; amical (e); travailleur/euse;
      actif/ve;   paresseux/se; intelligent (e);
      sportif/ve; ouvert (e);   serviable.

The other likely task is a letter. You could be expected to write a short letter describing yourself and your family in 60–70 words. If you have prepared the topic for Speaking, this should be a fairly easy task for you. You may also be given a letter to reply to. Here, the technique is different because you will be supplied with a framework. It is important in this type of exercise to answer all the points you are expected to cover.

Have a look at the following task.

You have just received this letter from your new French pen-friend in which she asks you to tell her about your family and friends. Write a letter of 60–70 words giving all the information she asks for.

Salut,

 J'ai été vraiment heureuse d'avoir ta lettre et la photo de ta famille. C'est ma première lettre d'Angleterre et j'ai compris presque tout ton anglais. Peux-tu m'expliquer exactement qui est sur la photo avec toi? Tu m'as parlé d'une copine – comment s'appelle-t- elle ? Parle moi un peu d'elle dans ta prochaine lettre. Elle est plus âgée que toi ?

Aujourd'hui, je me suis disputée avec ma mère. Elle dit que je suis trop paresseuse. Est-ce que tu t'entends bien avec tes parents, toujours ? Réponds-moi vite, en français cette fois. Avec la prochaine lettre je vais t'envoyer une photo de la maison.

A bientôt

Marie.

There are 2 stages to this task.
1. Find out what information you are being asked for.
2. Write the letter giving all that information. The letter you have to reply to will usually be constructed so that you can write back as yourself rather than pretend to be someone else. Of course, you can make up all the answers, but for most people it is a better idea to give their own details. That is what you are used to talking about.

First, look at the letter and focus on the points you have to reply to.

Tasks: (a)

(b)

(c)

(d)

TECHNIQUE TIP

Underline the sentences which ask for information and jot down a short note in English for each one, saying exactly what the task is. Do this in the space below and then look at the specimen reply which follows.

Chère Marie,
Merci pour ta lettre. (a) Sur la photo il y a ma mère, mon père et mes deux soeurs, Anna (19 ans) et Karen, qui a 17 ans. Karen est à côté de ma mère. (b) Ma meilleure copine s'appelle Liz. (c) Elle a 15 ans, comme moi, mais elle est beaucoup plus grande. Elle a les cheveux longs et blonds et elle porte des lunettes. (d) Normalement mes parents sont gentils – quelquefois il y a un problème, parce que je n'aime pas les devoirs. Et toi?
Ecris-moi vite

The four things you had to do were:
(a) explain who the people on the photo were
(b) give your friend's name
(c) say something about her, including age. Is she older than you?
(d) say whether you get on well with your parents.

TECHNIQUE TIP

Answer the points in the order they are asked for. Then you will not forget any.

How do you spot what you are being asked for?

Obviously, question-marks are the best clues, but there are others. The words **tu, toi, ton, ta, tes** are talking about *you*, and are probably asking for information. So are sentence starters such as:

parle-moi	
dis-moi	tell me
raconte-moi	
explique-moi	explain to me

Next comes the writing of the letter. Again, you need to know the basic vocabulary. Do *not* make up long and complicated sentences in English and try to translate them. If you do this you will make lots of mistakes. Stick to sentence patterns and vocabulary that you know. Do *not* copy sentences from the letter. You cannot usually get marks in this way. Do *not* forget to start and end your letter.

If you have worked all through this chapter and learned all the vocabulary, you have made a good start to your GCSE preparation. You'll find that some of these words come up in later topics. Always go back and check on something if you are not sure.

WHERE I LIVE

What you need to be able to do.

- Understand people talking or writing about where they live (area, town/country, house/flat).
- Understand people giving spoken and written descriptions of their own room.
- Talk and write about your own area, your house or flat, your own room.
- Know a little about the geography of France, the main towns, the rivers, the mountain ranges.
- At Higher Level, express opinions and judgements about your area, your own room etc.

The words you need

Countries

l'Angleterre	England	anglais(e)	English
l'Ecosse	Scotland	écossais(e)	Scottish
l'Irlande du Nord	Northern Ireland	irlandais(e)	Irish
le Pays de Galles	Wales	gallois(e)	Welsh
la Grande Bretagne	Great Britain	britannique	British
le Royaume Uni	United Kingdom		
la France	France	français(e)	French
la Belgique	Belgium	belge	Belgian
la Suisse	Switzerland	suisse	Swiss
l'Allemagne	Germany	allemand(e)	German
l'Italie	Italy	italien(ne)	Italian
l'Espagne	Spain	espagnol(e)	Spanish

Directions, town and country

le nord	north	le sud	south
l'est	east	l'ouest	west
le centre	centre	au centre	in the middle
la montagne	mountain	la campagne	countryside
la côte	coast	la mer	sea
la ville	town	le village	village
le quartier	district	la banlieue	suburb
la rue	street	le centre-ville	town centre
une maison individuelle	detached house	un appartement	flat
un immeuble	block of flats		

In the house

au sous-sol	in the basement	une pièce	room
au rez-de-chaussée	on the ground floor	les meubles	furniture
au premier étage	on the first floor	la cuisine	kitchen
la salle de séjour	sitting room	ma chambre	my bedroom
la salle à manger	dining room	les WC	toilet
la salle de bains	bathroom	à côté de	next to
en face de	opposite	près de	near to
une table	table	une chaise	chair
un fauteuil	armchair	un canapé	sofa
une machine à laver	washing machine	une lampe	lamp/light
une cuisinière à gaz	gas cooker	une porte	door
un frigo/réfrigérateur	fridge	une fenêtre	window
les volets	shutters	un lavabo	washbasin
une baignoire	bath	une douche	shower
un lit	bed	une armoire	wardrobe
une commode	chest of drawers	le tapis/la moquette	carpet
un tableau	picture	un poster	poster

faire le ménage	**passer l'aspirateur**	**mettre le couvert**	**une étagère** set of shelves
do the housework	do the hoovering	lay the table	
ranger la chambre	**la télévision** TV	**faire les courses**	**un placard** cupboard
tidy up the bedroom		do the shopping	
faire la vaisselle	**un ordinateur** computer	**faire la lessive**	
do the washing-up		do the washing	

Use the vocabulary to build up information on the talking grid below. An
example to help you has been given in the first line of the grid.

	maison/appartement	**ville/village/campagne**	**région**	**pays**
j'habite	une petite maison	à Newcastle	au nord-est	de l'Angleterre
	pièces	**situation**	**meubles**	**autres détails**
ma maison **mon appartement**				
	situation	**description**	**mon opinion**	
ma chambre				
	activité	**jour/heure**	**autres détails**	
pour aider à la maison				

Listening

Basic Level

You will have to recognise simple details such as the number and position of rooms in a flat or house, the description of a room, the situation in France where somebody lives, and so on. Here is a fairly easy one to get you started. (L4 on cassette)

 A   Your school's new French Assistant is speaking to you for the first time to introduce herself. Listen to what she says and see if you can give the following pieces of information about her.
(a)   How old is Anne-Marie? (1)
(b)   Does she live in a house or a flat? (1)
(c)   What does she say about Epinal? (3)
(Answers p.177)

This next task gives you a chance to have a go at a group of questions together. Look at these questions. (L5 on cassette)

Your French friend's family have a flat in the Alps and have invited you there to go skiing with them. You have just arrived and the father is showing you round the flat.
(a)   How many rooms are there altogether? (1)
(b)   Whereabouts is your room? (2)
(c)   What special feature does Monsieur Lebrun point out? (2)
(d)   When might you see this? (1)

This task looks a bit tougher and is quite demanding for Basic Level. How can you improve your performance on it? Well, there are clues to help you. The first clue is in the *setting*. That is the bit before the questions which tells you where you are supposed to be. The second clue is the number of marks available for each question. The third clue is in Question 4, and it helps with Question 3. *When might you see this special feature?* implies that you cannot see it all the time. That suggests that it is not inside the room – it's not likely to be a vanishing wardrobe!

One more thing before you have a go at the task. This passage of French is a bit longer than the last one. You will find that there are sentences which have none of the information you are looking for. There will also be little 'fillers', like **alors, tu sais, tu vois.** These make the French more natural and also give you a bit more time to react.

Listen to the passage now and go back to the questions. Try to answer them the first time without stopping the tape. Then listen a second time and use the technique we talked about for *checking*. Listen a third time if necessary. The important thing at this stage is to get something down for each question. Do not read any further until you have attempted the task.

You may have got caught out on Question 1 at first, but if so, we hope you managed to correct it on the second hearing. Here are the answers with some notes to help you.

(a) *5 rooms.* (It is not likely that there would be only 2 rooms. Remember that **chambre** means bedroom. The examiners are testing whether you know **chambre** and **pièce**.)
(b) *on left/opposite bathroom.* (You will not get the second mark if you write *near/next to the bathroom.* A specific word is being tested, **face à**, meaning *opposite* or *facing*.)
(c) *view of the Alps/and Switzerland.* (The word **vue** should remind you of the English word *view*. Of course, it might mean *picture*, but then Question 4 would not make sense.)
(d) *when it is fine.* (Common sense should give you this one, even if you have problems with the French.)

You've spent a long time on this task. There are just a couple of other points to make. In Listening and Reading your best chance of getting right answers

is to know and recognise the French words, but there may always be a word you do not recognise or do not remember. You have two other chances of getting the answer:
(a)   by recognising a word which is like an English word.
(b)   by using common sense and guessing intelligently.

Higher Level

These listening tasks will obviously involve wider vocabulary. So the techniques of recognising similar words and of guessing will be important. You will also find that such points as verb tenses are tested at this level. Recognition of the Perfect Tense (also called **passé composé**) is very important. In this next task, different tenses play an important part. (L6 on cassette)

B   While you are at your pen-friend's home in France, her mum comes in looking rather annoyed. You keep quiet while a rather heated discussion takes place. What *is* going on? Answer the following questions and you will have an idea.
(a)   What is the first thing Marie-Dominique's mum complains about? (2)
(b)   How does Marie-Dominique try to calm her down? (1)
(c)   Does this work? Explain. (2)
(d)   What does her mum say about Jean-Michel? (2)

When different tenses are involved there are often other words which help, for example time words such as **hier** (*yesterday*); **demain** (*tomorrow*); **la semaine prochaine** (*next week*). But you will not always have these to help you, and it is very important to be able to spot (and to use) Perfect and Future Tenses. (See pages 197–198 in the Grammar Section.)
   Listen to the cassette and try this task, following the technique you are getting used to. (Answers p. 177)

Finally for this section, here is a more extended passage from a recent GCSE examination for you to attempt. You will notice that, at times, even the English is quite demanding in this passage. Answers on p. 177. (L7 on cassette)

C   MEG Higher Listening, May 1988.

Whilst staying in France you hear an interview with an artist who lives with his wife in a flat in the *Rue Dauphine* in Paris.

Look at questions 7 to 14.

Now, listen to the interview and answer the questions in **English**. You will hear the interview **twice**.

7   What does the artist particularly appreciate about the flat? Give **two** details.

(i)   . . . .   [1]

(ii)   . . . .   [1]

8   How long have they lived there?

. . . .   [1]

9   How has the atmosphere of the area changed during the time they have been there?

. . . .   [2]

10   What does he say has remained unchanged?

.... [1]

11   What does the artist regret?

.... [1]

12   In what way was it a missed opportunity?

.... [1]

13   Why were they not able to take advantage of the situation?

.... [2]

14   What compensated for this missed opportunity?

.... [1]

Reading

Basic Level

Reading texts will be short letters and notes, or adverts of houses or flats for sale and to let. Here is an example of a short note.

Your French pen-friend has an exam at school so you have stayed home for the day. She leaves a note for you.

Je rentre à une heure, maman aussi. Pourrais-tu mettre le couvert? Comme ça on pourra manger tout de suite. Si tu sors ce matin, n'oublie pas tes clefs.
              Brigitte

(a)   What time will Brigitte get back? (1)
(b)   What has she asked you to do before she gets back? (1)
(c)   What does she remind you about? (2)

You should have coped quite well with the first 2 questions:
   (a)   *1 o'clock.*
   (b)   *Lay the table.*
There are two marks for Question 3, so 2 details are required:
   (c)   *Not to forget your keys/if you go out.*

D Adverts sometimes pose a problem because some words may be shortened. This advert is for flats to let in Tunis in North Africa. (Sometimes you may get reading material from other French-speaking countries.) Can you work out what SB stands for?

A LOUER, banlieue Nord de Tunis à 10 mn de Carthage appartements dans petit immeuble entouré de jardin, 37, Rue Tarek Ibn Ziad, Yasmina, 3 pièces, cuisine, SB, wc, balcon, pour 130 D. avec dépôt et cautionnement. Références morales et professionnelles exigées. Visite sur place tous les jours de 18h à 20h30 Mme Ayachi.

Now see how you get on with the following questions on the advert.

(a) Whereabouts in Tunis are the flats? (2)
(b) How far from Carthage are they? (1)
(c) Apart from the rooms, mention one other feature of the flats. (1)
(d) You may have to pay a deposit. What else do they require? (1)
(e) When can you see the flats? (2)
(Answers p. 178)

Here is another advert for a flat, in France this time. This one uses some words which crop up often in adverts:

neuf = *brand new;* **libre de suite** = *available immediately;* **à partir de** = *from;* **T2** = *a small flat with 2 main rooms;* **50 m²** = *50 square metres, the surface area of the flat.*

LA TURBALLE (Bretagne sud 44), port de pêche, votre appartement vue mer, direct. sur plage. Immeuble neuf standing, libre de suite, T2, 50 m² + terrasse + parking. Studio et T2 à 50 m de la plage et du centre-ville, à partir de 185.000 F.

SIRV GUERANDE
Tél. 40.24.99.47

(a) What do you know from the advert about La Turballe? (3)
(b) How far from the beach are the flats? (1)
(c) How much do they cost? (1)

Question (a) is straightforward. You need to recognise the names for regions of France and give the English equivalent. You will not get a mark for writing **Bretagne**. The full answer is: *a fishing port/in the south/of Brittany.*

Question (b) makes you decide what 50 m means. Remember the metric system. The answer is *50 metres.*

Question (c) requires some care with maths. The French use a decimal point where we use a comma, and a comma where we use a decimal point. The correct answer is *(from) F185,000 (one hundred and eighty-five thousand francs).*

Some adverts will have pictures as well as text. Remember that the questions will always be on the text, not the pictures, and this sometimes means looking at the small print. Here is an example where you have to spot what the last line says.

E   Your friends have seen this advert for a flat in Paris and are planning to visit it this weekend. What piece of advice would you give them about when to visit? (2) (Answers p. 178)

Here is another piece of small print for you to spot.

F   If your friends cannot find a flat in Paris, they are prepared to live just outside. What could you tell them about how near Paris this flat is? (2) (Answers p. 178)

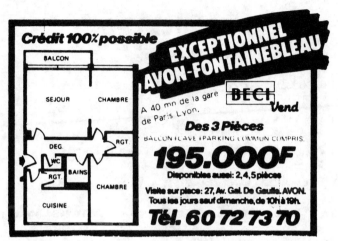

Higher Level

The other most common form of reading material is letters, which could be used at Basic or Higher Level. This Higher Level one goes into quite a lot of detail. Have a go at it and see how long it takes you to complete the task.

G   You are planning to visit a French friend for the first time and have just received this letter in which he tells you about where they live.

Je suis sûr que tu te plairas chez nous. Nous habitons ici depuis deux mois seulement et je trouve que le nouvel immeuble est beaucoup mieux que l'autre. D'abord, l'ascenseur marche toujours – l'autre était souvent en panne. Ensuite, nos voisins sont gentils, et en plus il y a deux camarades de classe qui habitent l'immeuble.

Quand tu viendras, on partagera la chambre. Rassure-toi, il y a beaucoup de place. Il y a un lit pour toi près de la fenêtre, mais tu n'auras pas froid. Le radiateur se trouve tout près. On peut regarder la télé dans la chambre – en ce moment le moniteur est branché sur mon ordinateur, mais on peut changer tout ça très vite.

Ici on est au huitième étage. Tu supportes bien l'altitude, j'espère. On voit toute la ville de chez nous. Il y a aussi beaucoup de bruit quelquefois parce qu'on est en train de construire encore un immeuble à côté de chez nous. Ça va te changer de ta petite maison tranquille! Enfin, tu verras tout ça très bientôt.

Amitiés Richard

(a) How long have Richard and his family been in their new flat? (1)
(b) Give three reasons why he likes it. (3)
(c) Where will you be sleeping when you stay there? (2)
(d) It should be quite cosy. Why? (1)
(e) What 2 things does Richard do in his room? (2)
(f) Apart from being in a flat you will find two big differences staying with Richard. What are they? Give as many details as possible. (4)

You should not spend much more than 6–7 minutes on a passage of this length, so it helps to have the technique right.

Check your answers on p. 178 to see how well you did. A total of 6–7 marks on this task is a reasonable score, the kind of mark you should be getting if you are aiming at a Grade C pass or better.

TECHNIQUE TIP

Always read all the questions first before you start to read the passage. This has two advantages – it gives you an outline of what the passage is about and it means that when you read the French you know immediately what you are looking for.

Speaking

TECHNIQUE TIP

Role-play

In this topic, the role-plays you might get are showing someone to their room or finding out about household routine, etc. Here is a straightforward Basic Level role-play from a recent GCSE exam. (S4 on cassette)

You are staying with a French family. Your teacher will play the part of your French friend and will start the conversation.
(i) Say you will do the washing-up.
(ii) Ask if your friend works in the garden.
(iii) Say you prefer shopping.

NEA, May 1989

The first thing to decide in a role-play is whether you have to use **tu** or **vous** to the person you are addressing. In this case, the **tu** form is correct. Where the examiner opens the role-play, he or she will use the **tu** or **vous** form. You should use the same form.

Listen to the example on cassette. You could practise saying the candidate's part yourself in answer to the examiner, once you are sure of it.

Here is another role-play for you to look at, also from a recent exam.

You have just arrived at your pen-friend's flat. Your teacher will play the part of your pen-friend and will start the conversation.
(i)   Say you have no toothpaste.
(ii)   Ask where the bathroom is.
(iii) Ask if you can have a shower.

NEA, May 1989

Conversation

Talking about where you live is one of the most popular tasks at GCSE because it can lead on quite naturally to talking about yourself and your likes and dislikes. Again, your speaking grid, if you have prepared it properly, will be a very good basis. Remember, though, however well you have prepared, you must be ready for the examiner to intervene and perhaps change the direction of the conversation. Listen to the candidate on the cassette (S5).

Basic Writing

Here again you might get a form-filling exercise such as the following.

H Your family have decided to do a house exchange for the summer after seeing an advert in a French magazine. The company have sent a form for you to fill in, and your parents get you to do it for them. Fill in the required details. (Answers on p. 178)

Échange de domiciles

Nom:

Adresse exacte (avec pays si à l' étranger):

Type de domicile:

Nombre de pièces:

Détail des pièces:

Avez-vous un jardin?

Situation du domicile - campagne/ville/côte/montagne

(soulignez les mentions utiles)

(this means *underline whatever is appropriate to you.*)

Again in this topic you could quite easily get a letter to reply to. Rather than giving you a full letter this time, we are giving you some extracts which you are expected to write replies to. Aim at writing 15–20 words of French in reply each time. This may mean giving more details than seem obvious. For instance, a very common question would be:
On m'a dit que tout le monde a un jardin en Angleterre. Est-ce que c'est vrai?
And you could write:
Il y a des appartements sans jardin, mais nous habitons une maison avec un grand jardin derrière où il y a beaucoup de fleurs.

I Extract (a): **Est-ce que ton quartier est calme? Chez nous il y a toujours beaucoup de bruit.**

TECHNIQUE TIP

There is always a vocabulary problem with role-plays. In this example, if you do not know the word for *toothpaste*, what can you do? If you ask the examiner (in French) for the word, or if you say the word in English, you will not get marks for that part, though it is probably better to do that than to say nothing and lose confidence. A lot of people come out of exams really upset because they did not know one or two words, which can cost only 1 or 2 marks at the most. The first piece of advice therefore is **pas de panique** – do not worry over a couple of words. Confidence is all-important in the Oral. The second piece of advice is think of another way of communicating your message in French. Here, words like **machin** (*thingamajig*), **objet** (*object*), **produit** (*product*) can be very useful. So you could say for task (i), **je n'ai pas de produit pour les dents.** This gets the message across and should get you full marks for that task.

J   Extract (b): **Notre appartement est très petit, hélas! Je suppose que tu as une très grande maison comme tous les Anglais!**

K   Extract (c): **Parle-moi un peu de ta chambre. Il y aura de la place pour moi aussi?**

The other kind of letter is one where you are given an outline in English, as in this example from a recent GCSE paper.

L   You have received a letter from your French pen-friend asking about your home. Write a letter in French in reply and make sure you say:
–   if you live in a house or a flat
–   what rooms there are
–   what your room is like
–   if you have a garden or not.
You will probably need to write about 60 words. There is no need to count the number of words.

NEA, June 1988

You will notice that there are 4 points to cover and you are expected to write about 60 words. This tells you that some details are required, e.g. for point 2 you should mention at least 3 different rooms if you want to get a mark. For point 4 you must say whether *or not* you have a garden. The time expected for such a letter is about 15 minutes, which is long enough for you to give quite a few details. You can also try to vary what you write. The obvious verb to use in descriptions is **il y a.** Here are some alternatives you could try to use sometimes.

il y a form	alternative
En face de ma chambre il y a la salle de bains.	**La salle de bains se trouve en face de ma chambre.**
Dans le jardin il y a beaucoup de fleurs	**Dans le jardin on voit beaucoup de fleurs.**
A gauche, il y a une grande bibliothèque.	**A gauche, on trouve une grande bibliothèque.**

It would be good practice for you to allow yourself 15 minutes to have a go at this letter. Remember to answer each point in turn, and do not forget to start and end your letter. A simple beginning would be:
>   **Cher ami,**
>   **Je vais te parler de ma maison.**
And to finish, all you need to write is:
>   **Amitiés**
followed by your name. There will often be marks given for the beginning and end of letters, and it is easy to forget them when you are following an outline. (Model answer p. 178)

To end this unit here is a slightly different task, also taken from a recent GCSE exam. You see that this one covers 2 topics, shopping as well as household chores, and that it is open – you choose what you write, which is fine if you have learned some vocabulary. The time allowance for this one is quite generous. You get 15 minutes for it. (Model answer p. 178)

M   You are staying with a French friend. One day you are alone in the house. Your friend's mother telephones and you have to take a message. She explains that she will be late home from work and wants her daughter to do some shopping and household chores. You write down her instructions. She asks for 7 things to be done. TWO HAVE BEEN WRITTEN DOWN FOR YOU – GIVE 5 MORE. Write 25–30 words.
Aller à l'épicerie acheter du sucre et du café.
Donner à manger et à boire au chien et au chat.

NISEC, June 1988

3

SCHOOL, WORK AND FUTURE CAREER

What you need to be able to do.
- Recognise the numbers for telling the time.
- Understand people talking and writing about school, work and their daily routine.
- Talk and write about school and your daily routine and express opinions about school subjects (Higher Level).
- Talk and write about your future plans (i.e. use Future Tense).
- Know a little about the French school system.

The words you need

School

l'école school	**le collège** comprehensive school
le lycée sixth-form college	**mon emploi du temps** my timetable
les matières subjects	**la gym(nastique)** gymnastics/PE
l'éducation physique PE	**l'art dramatique** drama
les sciences science	
la chimie chemistry	**la biologie** biology
le dessin drawing	**la musique** music
l'art art	**la géographie** geography
l'histoire history	**la physique** physics
les math(ématique)s maths	**le français** French
l'anglais English	**l'allemand** German
le professeur teacher	**la récréation** break
un cours lesson	**le travail manuel** craft
les arts ménagers home economics	**la salle de classe** classroom
l'informatique computer science	**la cantine** dining hall
intéressant interesting	**important** important
difficile difficult	**facile** easy
ennuyeux boring	**affreux** awful
fort(e) en maths good at maths	**nul(le) en gym** useless at PE
travailler to work	**étudier** to study

faire les devoirs to do your homework
avoir une bonne note to have a good mark
le bulletin scolaire school report
passer un examen to take an exam
être reçu(e) à un examen to pass an exam
rater un examen to fail an exam

Days of the week

lundi, mardi, mercredi, jeudi, vendredi, samedi, dimanche.

School years

sixième (1st year); **cinquième** (2nd year); **quatrième** (3rd year); **troisième** (4th year); **seconde** (5th year); **première** (1st-year sixth).

Daily routine

se lever to get up	**se laver** to wash
déjeuner to have breakfast	**commencer** to begin
quitter la maison to leave the house	**finir** to finish

Jobs

un poste	job	**un emploi**	job
la carrière	career	**le chômage**	unemployment
employé de bureau	office worker	**devenir**	to become
ouvrier/ère en usine	factory worker	**sténo-dactylo**	typist
médecin	doctor	**avocat**	lawyer
ingénieur	engineer	**mécanicien(ne)**	mechanic
infirmier/ère	nurse	**technicien(ne)**	technician
agriculteur	farmer	**agent de police**	policeman/woman
vendeur	salesman	**vendeuse**	saleswoman

Use this vocabulary to fill in the talking grid below and on p. 33. Here is an example of how you might fill in this grid.

Je me lève à 7 heures 30.
Je me lave dans la salle de bains. Je prends une douche.
Je m'habille dans ma chambre.
Je mets l'uniforme d'école. Je n'aime pas ça du tout! Je déteste la cravate. Je prends le petit déjeuner dans la cuisine avec ma mère.

L'Ecole – Ma Routine

Je me lève à   heures.
Je me lave dans
Je m'habille dans
Je mets l'uniforme./Je ne mets pas l'uniforme.
Je prends le petit déjeuner dans
Je prends

Je quitte la maison à   heures.
Je vais à l'école à   /en
J'arrive à   heures.

Mon Emploi du Temps

lundi	mardi	mercredi	jeudi	vendredi

Pendant la récréation je

A midi je

Mes Opinions sur les Matières	
L'anglais	
Les maths	
Le français	
Les sciences	
Ma matière préférée, c'est	**parce que**
L'année prochaine je vais	

Listening

What you need to be able to do.

Both at Basic and at Higher Level, recognition of numbers is essential. You must learn them off by heart. On the cassette we have recorded all the numbers up to 100, plus the hundreds up to 1000. You can use these for Listening and Speaking practice. For Listening practice you could fast-forward the tape and stop every so often, then write down the next number you hear (L8 on cassette)

But numbers do not always come up by themselves. You need to be able to recognise numbers in other contexts, for example when they are used to tell the time. L9 on the cassette has some recorded times. The first few are done for you below. Write out the rest in the spaces provided. These are all 12-hour clock times; 24-hour clock times will come later. (Answers p. 178).

A

(a)	1.05	(f)	6.30	(k)		(p)	
(b)	2.10	(g)	9.35	(l)		(q)	
(c)	3.20	(h)	20 to 9	(m)		(r)	
(d)	4.25	(i)	half past 10	(n)		(s)	
(e)	5.15	(j)	quarter to 12	(o)		(t)	

A common task is to fill in part of a school timetable. Here is a fairly easy example. Notice that the times are not tested here, but you do have to understand them to complete the task.

It is your first day in your French partner's school and she is telling you what lessons she has and when she has them. Fill in the grid to help you remember what you will be doing. Leave blank any times she does not mention. (L10 on cassette)

Read the advice below before you attempt the grid.

There are 9 spaces on the grid, so there could be as many as 9 marks for this task, which is a lot. The difficulty is not understanding the French for the different subjects, it is keeping track of what happens when. Technique is very important here. Rule 1: **pas de panique!** Remember, the facts will come up in order, so all you have to do is start in the right place and work down the list.

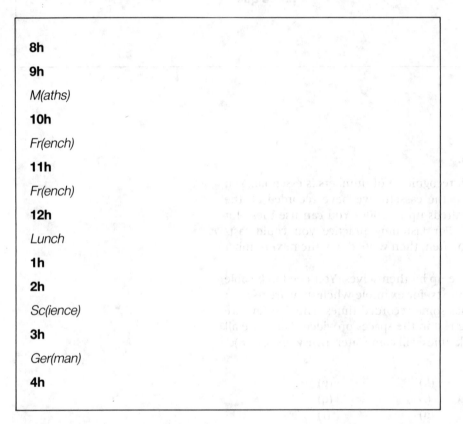

| 8 heures |
| 9h |
| 10h |
| 11h |
| 12h |
| 1h |
| 2h |
| 3h |
| 4h |

Now try the task before you look at the completed grid below.

| 8h |
| 9h |
| M(aths) |
| 10h |
| Fr(ench) |
| 11h |
| Fr(ench) |
| 12h |
| Lunch |
| 1h |
| 2h |
| Sc(ience) |
| 3h |
| Ger(man) |
| 4h |

Suppose you got everything wrong by 1 hour because you started at 8 rather than 9. Don't worry! Examiners are not that mean. You would still get most of the marks if you got the sequence right.

Talking more generally about school will come up as a fairly difficult task for Basic Level. Look at this recent example from a GCSE paper which has got a slightly different format. This looks quite demanding at first because there is a lot to take in at the beginning. You can help yourself by underlining key words that you must listen out for: the subject names, the words *homework, this afternoon,* etc. On the first hearing, write letters *next to* the boxes, and decide finally on the second hearing. Never leave a box blank.

Have a go at this one now. (L11 on the cassette. You will find the answers on p. 178.)

B   You are visiting a French school during an exchange visit. In the canteen you hear some 16/17-year-old students discussing their work.

Look at the comments A–F.

Now listen to the conversations and, next to each student's name, write a letter to show which comment applies to him or her. You will not need all the comments.

A finds the day too long
B prefers sciences
C had a difficult Maths homework
D does not like History
E thinks there is too much homework
F has a German lesson this afternoon

(i)	Christian	☐	(1)
(ii)	Vincent	☐	(1)
(iii)	Christel	☐	(1)
(iv)	Philippe	☐	(1)
(v)	Françoise	☐	(1)

(MEG Basic Listening, May 1988)

Higher Level

Listening tasks will focus less on facts and more on opinions and attitudes to school life. There might possibly also be discussions about the future or about part-time or temporary jobs. Both of these topics came up recently in the same GCSE Higher Listening paper. They are both included below for you to do. And we want you to do these two tasks straight off to give you practice in concentrating over a slightly longer time span. With Listening especially, building up concentration is very important and you really have to work at it. It does not help that the more difficult texts come towards the end of the exam when you are starting to get tired.

As you do these two passages, remember all the points of technique you have learned so far. (L12 on cassette. Answers on p. 178)

C LEAG Higher Listening, June 1988.

TECHNIQUE TIP

A good way to keep concentrating is to try to predict what the answers are likely to be. This gets you more involved with the task. The better your preparation, the more easily you will cope.

A – YOUNG PEOPLE TALKING
Part 1

While staying in France you meet a French teenager called Christophe who tells you about his school life. What he says is divided into two parts.

Listen to the first part and then answer questions 1 and 2.

Question 1

What exactly does Christophe want to do at University?

....

Question 2

What is his weak subject?

....

Now listen to the second part of what Christophe says. Then answer questions 3, 4 and 5.

Question 3

State **two** things about his school which he does not like.

....

....

Question 4

Why does he find it difficult to study in the evenings?

....

Explain your answer fully.

....

....

Question 5

How does he feel about this?

....

D   LEAG Higher Listening, June 1988.

Part 2

You are listening on French radio to a series about young people and their problems.

Listen to the first part of the talk, then answer questions 6 and 7.

Question 6

Three groups of young people who take summer jobs are mentioned. Name **two** of the groups.

....

....

Question 7

Why must you be careful if you take this type of job?

....

Now listen to the second part of the talk, and then answer questions 8, 9 and 10.

Question 8

How many hours a day did Michelle work?

....

Question 9

What had not been included in her month's wages?

....

Question 10

After speaking to her boss, how did she feel about the job?

....

....

Reading

Basic Level

You will get timetables, short letters and notes. For jobs, adverts are common tasks.

Here is a straightforward timetable question with just a small catch in it. Can you spot the catch? Do the question first before you look at the answer below.

7. You are looking at your French friend's homework timetable.

Lundi	mardi	mercredi	jeudi	vendredi	samedi
maths	français	physique	français	chimie	physique
anglais	chimie	histoire	dessin	maths	espagnol
géo			anglais		

(a) What **two** foreign languages does your French friend learn?

(i) ....

(ii) ....

(2 marks)

(b) Which day does your friend have Art homework?

....
                                                                                              (1 mark)

(c) Which sciences is your friend studying?

(i) ....

(ii) ....
                                                                                              (2 marks)

LEAG Basic Reading, May 1989

You probably got it all right without even realising there was a little trap, which is in the word *foreign*, i.e. *not* French. *English* is obvious, but did you spot *Spanish* tucked right over in the corner?

The other answers were easy, weren't they? (b) = *Thursday*, and (c) = *Chemistry and Physics*. Remember to change the spelling to English, otherwise you will not get marks. If you have been careful you could count on 5 marks here.

This next task is a short note, still on the topic of school.

You find this note from your French friend whilst staying with her and her family. You were expecting her to be at home when you got back from a shopping trip.

Je suis au collège cet après-midi. Il y a un cours supplémentaire d'allemand avant l'oral demain. Je rentre vers 5 heures et quart.

P.S Marie a téléphoné – peux-tu aller l'aider ce soir ? Elle passe l'examen d'anglais vendredi.

Hélène.

(a) Why has Hélène gone to school this afternoon? (2)
(b) When does she expect to get back? (1)
(c) What is happening tomorrow? (1)
(d) Why did Marie phone up? (3)

Notes are a bit different from letters. They usually contain only the essential information. You will probably need to use all of it in your answers. Two things about this note are rather unusual. First, the questions do not appear in the expected order. Secondly, there is a problem over what to write for Answer (d). Let us look at the expected answers in detail.

(a) The key word for the second mark is *extra*. You get 2 marks for *extra German (lesson)*; 1 mark for *(a) German (lesson)*. **Supplémentaire** might not be in the vocabulary list for the Board whose exam you are taking, but it is one of those words which looks enough like its English equivalent to be allowed for an exam question. So you need to know that *supplementary* means *extra*. You could write *a supplementary German lesson* as a correct answer.

(b) Remember always to read the *end* of a sentence before writing down your answer. **5 heures** is on one line, **quart** on the next. You could overlook it. The other point about this question is that there is often confusion between **quart** = *quarter*, and **quatre** = *four*. A moment's thought will tell you that people do not usually write *I'll be home at about four minutes past 5*! You would get 1 mark for *5.15* or *quarter past 5*.

(c) You have to go back to the previous sentence for this answer. It is also worth remembering that your answer needs to be clear. You might get away with *an oral*, but you can be much more sure of the mark if you write *a German oral exam*. Neither word is in the French, but in the context it is quite clear that that is what Hélène means.

(d) Remember the note is supposed to be addressed to you. It does not really matter whether you write *she wants you to . . .* or *she wants me to . . .* in your answer. But be consistent. Do not write *she wants her/him to. . . .* You will find that this gets confusing, and even if you know whom you mean, the examiner will not. There are quite a few points in this answer and you really need to get them all to obtain all 3 marks: *She wants me to help her this evening with her English. She is taking the English exam on Friday.*

There are not all that many sources of material for tasks about young people and work, partly because fewer young French people have part-time jobs than British youngsters. Here is one we've managed to find for you to do.

You notice your French friend browsing through a brochure, and you look at the front page.

(a)   Whom is the brochure aimed at? (1)
(b)   What sort of job is it advertising? (2)

jeunes de 17/18 ans
qui cherchez
un emploi temporaire
pour un service
avec
des jeunes

You should cope with that one fairly easily.

(a) *It is aimed at young people of 17/18.* (You must include both details for the mark.)

(b) *It is offering temporary work with young people.* (Not part-time work, which is different.)

The task could then be developed further as follows (see the next part of the brochure on the following page).

E Being interested in the brochure, you look further into it and find it is offering to give you training leading to a diploma. There are 4 different possibilities listed. For each of the statements below write down the *number* of the possibility (1, 2, 3 or 4). Choose only one number for each statement.

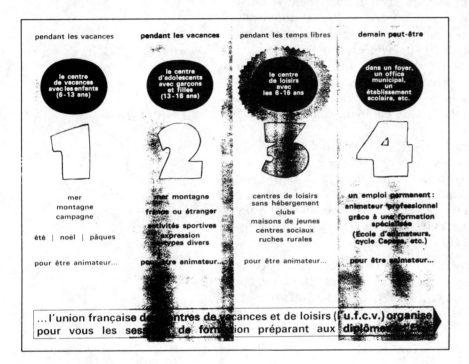

	Statement	Number
(a)	Working abroad	2
(b)	Working at weekends	
(c)	Working in a school	
(d)	Working full-time	
(e)	Working in the countryside	
(f)	Working at Easter	
(g)	Working only with secondary age children	
(h)	Work which involves sports	

(8 marks)

This is a genuine multiple-choice activity, and is worth quite a few marks. Remember that a multiple-choice question can have only one answer, so if you can see 2 possibilities, think hard and try to see which is the more likely. Generally speaking, the key word or an equivalent should be somewhere in the text. For example, numbers 1 and 2 both talk about holidays, so you need to look for the word which means *Easter*. In number 1, even if you do not know the word for *abroad*, you can *deduce* it (i.e. work it out) because of its position after the words **France ou. . . .** Deduction is a commonly used skill to improve reading comprehension. We have done Question (a) for you. Do the rest and check the answers on p. 178.

Higher Level

The last example was fairly difficult for Basic Level. This one is clearly a Higher Level task, although it is quite a short text. When you attempt it, think about what **notre** means.

F You are looking for books to take back to England with you to improve your French. You find this catalogue of a series of books for young French readers.

For what 3 reasons might people buy these books?   (3 marks) (Answers p. 178)

Probably the most likely text type for Higher Reading on the topic of school is a letter from a French friend. Here is a fairly long letter with several questions on it (not all of them on the topic of school), and you will need to work through it very carefully. Notice that it has paragraphs, which generally indicate a change of subject.

TECHNIQUE TIP

Remember to read through all the questions *before* you start reading the letter.

G Your friend John shows you a letter he has just received from his correspondent, Mathieu. How much of it can you understand?

(a) Mathieu seems to be having a hard time at school at the moment. Give 2 reasons why. (2)

(b) What kind of subjects does Mathieu seem to prefer? (1)

(c) Why is Mathieu excused PE and games at the moment? (1)

(d) What was the doctor's advice? (2)

(e) How can you tell Mathieu is keen on tennis? (2)

(f) What 2 important things are happening within the next week? (2)

(g) Would you say Mathieu is a serious-minded young man? Explain. (1)

You can probably afford to spend only about 8–10 minutes on this text. See how long it takes you to do and check your answers on p. 00. If you are getting 5–6 marks out of 11, you are on target to score at least 1 point in Higher Reading.

Lannion, le 13/03/89

Salut John,

Cela fait longtemps que je n'ai pas eu de tes nouvelles, par conséquent, je t'écris cette petite lettre.

Ici, la vie n'est pas toujours facile, car les devoirs sont nombreux au lycée et les professeurs sont parfois sévères avec les élèves. Comme tu sais, je ne suis pas trop attiré par les maths et la physique, mais par contre j'aime beaucoup les cours d'anglais et d'espagnol, je trouve que ces leçons sont beaucoup plus vivantes, plus intéressantes.

Depuis peu de temps, je suis dispensé de sport car je souffre énormément d'un mal de dos et lorsque j'ai rencontré le médecin, il m'a recommandé de ne plus pratiquer de sport durant environ deux mois. Je trouve que c'est dommage d'être dispensé d'activités sportives lorsque l'on adore le tennis, tout comme moi, j'avais l'habitude de m'entraîner quatre fois par semaine.

Les vacances se terminent dans trois jours, et dans moins d'une semaine il va falloir que je passe un examen très important: le baccalauréat blanc. Cet examen est relativement important et c'est pourquoi, ces derniers jours, j'ai beaucoup travaillé dans le but d'être reçu à l'examen.

Bon, je crois que je vais te quitter en espérant que tu m'écrives bientôt.

Salut,

Mathieu.

Speaking

Role-play

Most exam boards do not often test talking about school as a role-play. However, it does sometimes occur, as in this example from a recent exam.

You are staying with a French family and are discussing school with your exchange partner. Your teacher will play the part of your French friend and will start the conversation.
(a)   Say that lessons begin at 9.15.
(b)   Say you like French.
(c)   Ask if your friend has a lot of homework.

NEA, May 1988

There are 2 points to remember here. First, how much are you likely to have to say for (a)? Secondly, remember you are speaking *to* your friend, so what do you say for (c)? You say, **Tu as beaucoup de devoirs?**, *not* **Est-ce que ton ami a beaucoup de devoirs?**

 Look at this next example, also from a GCSE exam. Spend a few minutes preparing it, and then listen to the cassette, where it is recorded (S6).

You are visiting a French school with your correspondent. Your teacher will play the part of your correspondent and will start the conversation.
(a)   Say lessons last 35 minutes usually.
(b)   Say you prefer Art and Games.
(c)   Ask what your friend does in his holidays.

NEA, May 1989

You could also get a Higher Level role-play, and on this topic it is likely to be more testing in terms of vocabulary and structures, perhaps expecting you to use the Future Tense. Here is a recent example, recorded on the cassette for you with comments (S7).

Your French friend is staying with you and you are chatting about school and careers. Your teacher will play the part of your friend and will start the conversation.
(a)   Say you will spend two years in the sixth form.
(b)   Say you are not sure.
(c)   Say you would perhaps like to work abroad.

                                                                    NEA, May 1988

Conversation

All exam boards make sure that school and future plans come up in the conversation part of the Oral, because you are expected to have some ideas and opinions on both areas. The speaking grid will be very useful if you have filled it out. Remember to keep looking over it because, if you filled it in early in the year, you may well have changed your mind about what subjects you like, or perhaps you have decided on a different career.

Listen to the candidate on tape talking about school at Higher Level (S8).

Basic Writing

You could get a timetable blank to fill in, perhaps with an outline in English. Your speaking grid should help you with this. Another possibility is a note for your French friend such as the one below.

Your French friend had a late night at a disco while staying with you and is still fast asleep when you have to go to school in the morning. Leave a note for your friend with the following messages.
(a)   You are coming home at lunch-time.
(b)   You will buy some chips for you both.
(c)   You have a maths exam this afternoon.
(d)   You are going to watch a football match afterwards. Your friend can come too.

Do you notice that even short Writing tasks can cover more than one topic area?

Here is an example of how you could do this task.

> **Marie**
> **Je rentre à midi.**
> **Je vais acheter des frites pour nous deux.**
> **Il y a un examen de maths cet après-midi.**
> **Après je vais regarder un match de football. Tu peux venir aussi.**

Here are some examples of how you could get round problems of vocabulary.
(a)   *Lunch-time:* You could write **à 12h,** or **à 12h 30.**
(b)   *Chips:* You should know this really! If not, write **quelque chose à manger.**
        Buy: If you cannot remember **acheter, prendre** is a very useful verb – it can replace lots of words.
(c)   *This afternoon:* Just write a time, e.g. **à 2h.**
(d)   *Afterwards:* You could say **à 4 heures.**
        Your friend can come too: This is an invitation, so you could do it with **Toi aussi?,** or **Ça t'intéresse?** But do *not* forget the question-mark.

H   Here is a letter for you to try. It comes from a recent GCSE exam. Notice that you could do this task without using the attached timetable. So why do you think it is there?

Give yourself 20 minutes and try to do this task without looking back at your speaking grid. You could show this letter to your French teacher and ask for comments on it. Most teachers are pleased to help pupils who are doing extra work, but be careful to choose the right moment! (Model answers p. 178)

---

2.   *Imagine that you have received the following school timetable in a letter from your French penfriend who has asked you to tell him/her about life in* **your** *school.*
Write a letter of 70/80 words **in French** *to your penfriend, including the points below.*

Mon Emploi du Temps

Heure	Lundi	Mardi	Mercredi	Jeudi	Vendredi	Samedi
08H15	Français	—	Math.	Anglais	Physique	Anglais
09H15	Math.	Français	Chimie	Français	Allemand	Français
			RECREATION			
10H30	Anglais	Histoire	Education	Allemand	Education Civique	Dessin
11H30	Biologie	Français	Physique	Math.	Géographie	—
			DEJEUNER			
14H00	Allemand	Math.	—	Travaux Manuels	—	—
15H00	Education Physique	Musique	—		—	—

(a)   Thank him/her for the letter.

(b)   What time your school day starts and finishes.

(c)   How long you have for lunch, and where you eat.

(d)   Which lessons you like.

(e)   Which lessons you dislike.

(f)   Who your favourite teacher is and what he/she is like.

(g)   How much homework you have each evening.

(h)   What you hope to do when you leave school.

Remember to start, date and end the letter in a suitable manner.   *(20 marks)*

FREE TIME

What you need to be able to do.
– Recognise and use weather expressions
– Understand people talking and writing about their free time.
– Talk and write about your own free time.
– Know the months of the year.

The words you need

Leisure

les loisirs leisure activities
le temps libre free time
une activité sportive a sporting activity
une activité artistique an artistic activity
le théâtre theatre
une pièce de théâtre play
le disco disco
faire du lèche-vitrine to go window-shopping

Music

la musique music
jouer de la guitare play the guitar
jouer de la trompette play the trumpet
jouer du piano play the piano
jouer du violon play the violin
écouter des disques listen to records
écouter la radio listen to the radio
un transistor radio
un électrophone record-player
une chaîne hi-fi hi-fi equipment
chanter sing
danser dance

Sports

le sport sport	**un jeu** game
jouer au foot(ball)	**jouer au hockey**
jouer au basket	**jouer au rugby**
jouer au tennis	**jouer au ping-pong**

s'entraîner to train
faire des promenades to go for walks
faire des randonnées to go for long walks/hikes
faire de la natation to go swimming
une Auberge de Jeunesse youth hostel
la patinoire skating rink
la piscine swimming pool
le stade sports stadium
faire de l'équitation to go horse-riding
faire du cyclisme/du vélo to go cycling
faire de la voile to go sailing
faire de la pêche to go fishing
faire du ski to go skiing
faire partie d'un groupe to be part of a group
faire partie d'une équipe to be part of a team
le terrain de jeu games field
une salle omnisports sports hall
ouvert open
fermé closed
gratuit free
jouer aux cartes to play cards
jouer aux échecs to play chess
jouer au babyfoot to play miniature football
jouer au flipper to play a pinball machine

Cinema and television

le cinéma   cinema
la télé   TV
regarder un film   to watch a film
regarder un vidéo   to watch a video
un magnétoscope   video-recorder
un feuilleton   soap opera
un documentaire   documentary
un film d'amour   love film
un film comique   comedy film
un film de guerre   war film
un western   cowboy film
un dessin animé   cartoon
une vedette   film star
un comédien   actor

Reading

la bibliothèque   library
la lecture   reading
faire de la lecture/lire   to read
un livre   book
un roman   novel
un magazine   magazine
un journal   newspaper

In the house

à la maison   at home
s'amuser   to amuse oneself
jouer avec l'ordinateur   play with the computer
un jouet   toy/plaything
une boum   party   **une fête**   celebration
les jeux de société   board games
une surprise-party   party

Weather

le temps   weather
la météo   weather forecast
beau temps   fine weather
mauvais temps   bad weather
il pleut   it's raining
il neige   it's snowing
il fait du soleil   it's sunny
il fait beau   it's fine
il fait mauvais   it's bad weather
il fait du vent   it's windy
il fait du brouillard   it's foggy
il fait froid   it's cold
il fait chaud   it's hot
il fait frais   it's cool
il fait gris   it's gloomy/grey
c'est couvert   it's cloudy
pluvieux   rainy   **orageux**   stormy
brumeux   misty   **neigeux**   snowy
humide   wet   **sec**   dry
une averse   shower   **un orage**   thunderstorm
une tempête   storm   **la pluie**   rain

Months and seasons

les mois   months
janvier; février; mars; avril; mai; juin; juillet; août;
septembre; octobre; novembre; décembre.
les saisons   seasons
le printemps   spring   **au printemps**   in spring
l'été   summer   **en été**   in summer
l'automne   autumn   **en automne**   in autumn
l'hiver   winter   **en hiver**   in winter
à Pâques   at Easter   **la Pentecôte**   Whitsun
les grandes vacances   the summer holidays
à Noël   at Christmas   **le Nouvel An**   the New Year
le réveillon   **le congé**   holiday, leave
                New Year's Eve
la Toussaint   All Saints' Day

Mes Loisirs				
heure/jour	activités	où	avec qui	pourquoi/ autres détails
Après l'école				
Le soir				
Le weekend				
Le dimanche				
Le samedi				
Pendant les vacances				

Mes Préférences

j'aime	parce que
la télévision	
le cinéma	
la musique	
les magazines et les livres	
le sport	

There are so many different leisure possibilities available now that the ones you enjoy most may not be in the list of vocabulary. Remember that the GCSE vocabularies cover only the most common things and you are expected to add your own items of vocabulary to suit your circumstances. The grids give you the basis for talking about this important area. Here is an example of how you might fill them in.

Mes Loisirs

heure/jour	activités	où	avec qui	pourquoi/ autres détails
Après l'école	j'écoute des disques	dans ma chambre		pour me reposer.
Le vendredi soir	je sors	dans un disco	avec mes amis	pour danser et rencontrer beaucoup d'amis.
Le dimanche matin	je reste au lit et je lis des magazines sur la mode ou sur les sports.			

Mes Préférences

J'aime les films comiques parce que j'aime beaucoup rire avec mes amis.

J'aime les feuilletons comme *Eastenders* parce qu'il est intéressant de suivre l'histoire des personnages.

Listening

Basic Level

You can expect to get something about the weather, including temperatures in various cities or parts of France. (Remember that temperatures will be in degrees Celsius.) Here is a short task in grid form. (L13 on cassette)

You are listening to the weather forecast before going away for the weekend. Brittany and Normandy are both possibilities. Fill in the forecast on the grid. (6 marks)

	Saturday	*Sunday*
Normandy		
Brittany		

This should have been a quite straightforward task, but did you get all 6 marks? Obviously, there will be more than one detail in some cases. The marks are given as follows:

	Saturday	*Sunday*
Normandy	fine (1), 21 degrees (1)	wind (1)
Brittany	rain (1)	cloudy (1), fog on coast (1)

In the area of leisure and free time you can expect to get conversations about arrangements (so times and days are important) and announcements about events, programmes etc. Here is a recent GCSE exam task (L14 on cassette). You should find you can cope with this one quite well if you have learned the numbers properly. (Answers on p. 179)

A   You are with a French friend and hear this conversation.
(a)   Where is the disco being held? (1)
(b)   When is it being held? (1)
(c)   What time does it begin? (1)
(d)   How long has Pierre held a driving licence? (1)

SEG, November 1988

Higher Level

Here, possibilities are very varied. This recent example shows how much information can be packed into one short sentence, and emphasises how important it is for you to have your technique correct. Listen twice only and see how you cope. (L15 on cassette)

You are watching television when the announcer tells you about a programme the family is planning to watch.
   Give *three* details about it.

Answer: 1 ....

             2 ....

             3 ....

NEA, June 1988

In fact, there are 6 details given. If you can get more than 3 down in the time, you are doing very well. The trickiest one is the 24-hour clock time, so it is worth writing three others as well as that one. You need to be familiar with the French TV channels, of which there are 6 at the moment, as follows: TF1; A(ntenne)2; FR3; Canal Plus; LA5; M6.

The 6 details were:
(a) this evening; (b) on TF1; (c) at 18.30; (d) serial; (e) for all the family; (f) *Dynasty*.

It would be easy to miss out *this evening* because you think it is given in the question or because it is too obvious. Look carefully at the text and you will see that *this evening* is not mentioned.

TECHNIQUE TIP

As far as being too obvious is concerned, the rule is *always* put the obvious things in your answer – they are often what is being tested.

Examiners' ideas of young people's leisure interests are not always the same as yours might be. Visits to museums and châteaux are quite popular with them. On the other hand, you are quite likely to visit such places during an exchange trip, and even, maybe, enjoy the excursions. Here is a recent GCSE question based on such a visit. Notice again how many details involve numbers, days, etc. This information will come up in sequence, and there are quite a few details, so remember to keep listening as you write. Check that you are sure what Questions 2, 3 and 4 mean. With Question 1, concentrate on the last half of the number. Questions 5 and 6 ask for more than one day and date. It is a good idea to underline the *-s* on the end of these words. Question 7 is almost certainly going to involve a reduction for students. Remember that the more carefully you look at the details before you listen the first time, the better you will do. Your work does not start when the recording plays; it must start beforehand. (L16 on cassette. Answers on p. 179)

B Exercise 1: Questions 1–7

Look at the pad below.

There are four exercises in this test. You will hear all recordings **twice**. You should answer **all** the questions in this test. The intended marks for each exercise are given in brackets.

Exercise 1: Questions 1–7

During a visit to Normandy you go to the Post Office Museum in Caen. You make notes about the museum to tell your friend.

Look at the pad overleaf

Post Office Museum

1   *Year of opening*   : . . . . [1]

2   *Theme of present exhibition* : . . . . [1]

3   *Source of stamps*   : . . . . [1]

4   *Additional feature*   : . . . . [1]

5   *Days open in winter*   : . . . . [2]

6   *Dates of summer season*   : . . . . [2]

7   *Entry charges*   : *(i)* . . . . . . *for* . . . . [1]

                                 : *(ii)* . . . . . . *for* . . . . [1]

                                      and . . . . [1]

                                                      [11]

MEG Higher Listening Part I, May 1988

Now, listen to the guide and make a note of the information in *English*. You will hear the guide *twice*.

Reading

Basic Level

There is a greater variety of possibilities for this topic than for almost any other. Adverts, notices, posters, notes, letters and brochures are all possible. You are likely to have visual material to cope with as well, as in the example below, which has quite a lot of information on it. Here are some questions for you to have a go at.

You have seen this advert for a roller disco and you are thinking about going with a group of friends.

(a)   What time does the roller disco close? (1)

(b)   How do you get there? (1)
(c)   Why is Friday a good night to go? (2)
(d)   What do you do about roller skates? (1)

There are two or three words here which crop up all the time in Basic
Reading: **jusqu'à** = *until;* **location** = *hire* (remember this one; it looks like
an English word but means something very different); **gratuit(e)** = *free.*

Answers: (a)   4 in the morning
              (b)   bus (no. 28)
              (c)   girls (1) get in free (1)
              (d)   hire them there

An alternative way of testing the material in this text is by a true/false
format, as follows: (Answers p. 179)

C   Put a tick in the correct column.

	True	False
You can get there by bus.		
It is open in the afternoons.		
You have to bring roller skates.		
Girls get in free in the evenings.		
It is open every evening.		

This sort of task is quite a lot more difficult and probably made you think,
even if you understand the French. It might therefore be a Higher Level task.

Here is a task taken from a newspaper, in two parts.

D You are in Switzerland on holiday when you see this advert for a competition.

(a)   What is the competition about?

Concours « Informatique »

A vos ordinateurs Inventez un jeu!

(b)   If you wanted to take part, when would you have to get your entry in by?

(c)   What is the last piece of information they require after your address?

BULLETIN DE PARTICIPATION

Ce bulletin est à retourner, en même temps que votre jeu, à la *Tribune de Genève*, Concours informatique, case postale 434, 1211 Genève 11, jusqu'au 30 août.

Nom (Groupe) : _____   **Prénom** : _____

Profession : _____   **Catégorie** :   Juniors   ☐

                                                            Seniors   ☐

                                                            Groupes   ☐

Age : _____

Adresse : rue _____

         ville : _____   No postal _____

Ordinateur utilisé : _____

Notice that for Question (a) you have to identify a verb – not just its meaning, but which part of the verb is being used. (Answers p. 179)

We have already said that leisure activities can be very varied, so sometimes you can come across the unexpected in Reading Comprehension tasks. The following are all taken from the year's programme of a social club in Caen in Normandy. Although you will not recognise all the vocabulary, there are enough clues in each extract for you to find the necessary information. (Answers p. 179)

E   (a)

JE JOUE EN ANGLAIS (enfants de 7 à 11 ans)

Dominique COSSARD

Mercredi: 14h 15 - 15h 15

Tarif saison: 550 F.

What does this activity give children the chance to do? Remember that your answer must make sense. (1)

(b)

> ## COUPE ET COUTURE
>
> Martine PAGNY
> Stages offrant la possibilité de confectionner ses propres vêtements (10 séances de 2h 30) débutante et confirmée
> Lundi: 17h 30 - 20h
> Mardi: 17h 30 - 20h
> Jeudi: 13h 30 - 16h
>
> **Tarif: 470 F. le stage.**

What could you learn to do on this course? (1)

(c)

> ## BEBE NAGEUR (à partir de 6 mois)
>
> Encadrement pluri-disciplinaire (M.N.S., Médecins,...)
> • Activités de découverte de l'eau pour les tout petits
> • Piscine chauffée à Hermanvillé sur Mer
>
> Samedi: 13h 30 à 16h (par demi-heure, suivant l'âge)
> **Tarif au trimestre: 410 F.**
> **Tarif saison: 1.100 F.**

If you went to the swimming pool on Saturday afternoon, whom would you see in the water? (1)

(d)

> ## CAEN MINI-BOLIDES
> Le premier vendredi de chaque mois à partir de 20h 30
> • L'Association regroupe des possesseurs de voiture radio commandées

When do the people in this group meet? (2)
What is their common interest? (1)

F   Another longer extract from the same leaflet gives you an insight into how highly organised life in France sometimes needs to be. What you know about France can help you understand the text better and so complete the task more successfully. In this case, it helps to know that in many parts of France Wednesday is a day off for schoolchildren.

The **Ile aux enfants** is a children's centre which helps parents who work.
(a)   Mention 3 ways in which it provides a service for parents on school days. (3)
(b)   What age children does it cater for? (1)
(c)   What extra services does it provide on Wednesdays? (2)
(d)   The **Ludothèque** is a kind of library. What does it lend and to whom? (3)

"L'Ile aux Enfants"

L'accueil des enfants avant et après l'école

Les parents déposent les enfants à l'"Ile aux enfants", où une anima-trice les accueille, puis les conduit à l'école; à 16 h 30, ils sont repris en charge à l'école.

Dans un espace adapté, les animateurs proposent aux enfants différents "coins d'activités :

• Ludothèque
• Dessin et peinture
• Lecture
• Jeux électroniques...

Pour ceux qui le souhaiteraient, un "coin devoirs" fonctionnera régu-lièrement. Les enfants sont accueillis à l'âge de la scolarité maternelle et primaire.

Jours et heures d'ouverture :
Lundi, Mardi, Jeudi et Vendredi
7 h 30/8 h 30 - 16 h 30/18 h 30

Tarifs pour le matin plus le soir à l'année scolaire
• Allocataire :   560 F.
• Non-allocataire : 1.350 F.

Possibilité d'accueil le matin ou le soir uniquement avec des tarifs spéci-fiques.

Les mercredis de l'île aux enfants

Tous les mercredis, des animatrices et des animateurs accueilleront les enfants dans le Centre de Loisirs de l'"Ile aux enfants".

Le fonctionnement, prévu pour des enfants de 4 à 11 ans, leur permettra de vivre des activités d'intérieur et d'extérieur.

Possibilité de repas. Accueil à la journée ou demi-journée.

Horaires :
8 h - 12 h / 14 h - 18 h

Tarifs pour l'année scolaire (sans repas)
• Allocataire :   648 F.
• Non-Allocataire : 1.048 F.
• Repas :   20 F.

Ludothèque

Plus de 300 jouets sont à la disposition des enfants, des jeunes et des adultes ; pour jouer seul, à plusieurs, en famille. La ludothèque fonc-tionne avec un système de prêt de jeux et de jouets ; elle est aussi un lieu d'échange et d'information.

Horaires :
- Mardi : 17 h 30 à 18 h 30
- Mercredi : 16 h à 18 h

Tarifs pour l'année scolaire : 80 F.
(tarifs dégressifs pour plusieurs enfants d'une même famille)

Realisation maquette : Francine HAELTERS · Caen Repro ·

There is a lot of text to work through here, perhaps with some words you will not understand but do not need. Here you need to start with an idea of what services would be useful for working parents with young children. Do not forget that the headlines often give help, in this case with Question 1, and they show you where to look for the different answers. This task also involves the topic of school and work which we have already covered. Allow yourself a maximum of 10 minutes for the task, then check your answers on p. 179.

Higher Level

Finally for this topic, here is another letter which covers some other areas as well as leisure-time activities. It is a fairly long text so you could expect a fair number of questions on it. Letters are usually quite straightforward because people write as they talk, and by now you are used to French people talking!

G

(a)   What is the weather like in Exeter? (1)
(b)   Why is Anne thanking Françoise? (1)
(c)   How has Anne been spending her spare time? (2)
(d)   What else is she hoping to do? (1)
(e)   What are Anne's plans for Easter? (4)
(f)   How does she get to school? (1)
(g)   Mention one new experience she has had since coming to England. (1)
(h)   What kind of weather does she seem to be expecting? Explain. (2)

There are 13 marks for this task, and 8 would be a good score. Allow a maximum of 10 minutes for it. Be careful with (d) and (g) and also think hard about Questions (f) and (h). These are *inferential* questions, i.e. the answer is not given directly, you have to work it out from what is being said. For example, if Anne said in the letter, **Demain je vais acheter un parapluie** (*Tomorrow I'm going to buy an umbrella*), you would *infer* that she was expecting rain. (Answers p. 179)

Exeter le 12. 9. 86

Chère Françoise,

Je suis bien arrivée à Exeter et je commence à m'organiser. Exeter est une très jolie ville. La Cathédrale est merveilleuse. Il fait très beau et il y a même du soleil!

Je te remercie pour le paquet que tu m'as envoyé. Les biscuits sont très bons. J'espère que tu vas bien et que tu viendras me voir en Angleterre pendant l'année.

Je suis allée à la piscine et j'ai fait de l'équitation.

J'aimerais apprendre à jouer au golf mais je n'aurai pas assez de temps pour tout faire!

J'ai reçu une lettre de Sylvie. Elle est à Glasgow et elle m'a invitée à passer les vacances en Écosse. J'irai la voir à Pâques. J'espère pouvoir visiter plusieurs châteaux hantés et voir le monstre du Loch Ness!

Pour le moment, j'ai peu de temps libre car je travaille à l'école du lundi au vendredi. L'école n'est pas très loin de chez moi et je ne suis pas obligée de prendre l'autobus pour y aller.

A midi, j'ai mangé dans un pub pour la première fois et j'aime beaucoup l'ambiance.

J'espère que tu viendras me rejoindre très bientôt

Je t'embrasse!

Anne

PS: pense à emporter des vêtements chauds!

Speaking

Role-play

Tasks will involve making arrangements, fixing times and places, inviting or accepting invitations, finding out what is on, etc. Sometimes this topic can involve phone calls. Tasks could also involve talking about leisure activities, as in the following example.

 You are discussing with a French family what you do in the evenings. Your teacher will play the part of your French friend and will start the conversation.
(a)   Say you stay at home.
(b)   Say you prefer listening to records.
(c)   Ask what your friend does at the weekend.

NEA, May 1988

Listen to the recording (S9), and see how well the candidate gets the three messages across.

The second role-play for this unit is another simple one, involving an invitation and a time. Just prepare this one. It is not on the cassette. Tasks (a) and (c) are typical model sentences which you learn as patterns so you can change parts of the sentence. That means that once you can say *There is a bus at 3 o'clock*, you ought to be able to say *There is a train at 10 o'clock*, and so on. This is how you learn to extend the range of language you can produce, by learning patterns which you can alter. The more role-play practice you get at school or with a friend who is doing French too, the more confident you will be.

You are discussing plans for the day with your French exchange partner. Your teacher will play the part of your friend and will start the conversation.
(a)   Ask if your friend would like to go to the swimming pool.
(b)   Say it is in the town.
(c)   Say there is a bus at three o'clock.

NEA, November 1988

You need to feel very secure about Basic Level role-plays if you are planning to do Higher Level ones as well. Some exam boards have three tasks at Basic Level, some have more, such as the recent one on the next page, which is very specifically tied to one topic. If you have learned your cinema vocabulary you should cope, but it requires concentration and memory.

The things you can do to get round a problem of vocabulary are, in order of value:
(a)   Say something which explains what you want. For example, for task 2, if you forget the word for *ticket* you could say **Je voudrais voir le film.** For task 3 you could say **Je voudrais une place près de la porte.** This technique will often get you a mark. It is a good idea to try to put yourself in the situation and visualise yourself doing the various things that you are required to do by the task.
(b)   The next best technique is to guess the word, if necessary using the English word. Sometimes, perhaps not very often, you will be right. Even if you are not right, the point is to decide beforehand and just say it. The worst that can happen is that you lose the mark you would have lost anyway, *but* you have kept up your confidence by not pausing and stumbling, and you can always have a laugh about it with your friends afterwards. If you have prepared for the exam properly, there will only be the occasional word which will throw you anyway.
(c)   The other technique you can use is to say *less* than required but still a sentence. For example, for task 3 you could say **Je voudrais une place.** It is important to say *something* to keep the exchange going between you and the examiner.

TECHNIQUE TIP

You also need to decide what you are going to say for the tasks which you cannot do properly. It is very important to do this during your preparation, not to wait for the actual Oral exam and hope for inspiration.

Look at the following role-play for 5 minutes and decide what you are going to say for each task, remembering what we said about asking questions. The role-play has been performed on the cassette (S10).

Whilst in France you decide to go to the cinema to see *The Masters of the Universe*, though you first want to know if it is the English version. The role of the cashier will be played by the examiner.

(a)   Find out if the film is in English.
(b)   Say you would like a ticket.
(c)   Tell the cashier you would like a place at the back.
(d)   Ask how much it costs.
(e)   Ask when the film starts.

MEG, May 1988

Higher Level

Finally in this section, here is an example of a different type of Speaking task required at Higher Level by one exam board (MEG). Here you have to tell a story, supported by pictures and notes in French. The task is called *Candidate as Narrator*, and is intended for 'good' candidates, by which the examiners mean those aiming for a grade A or B. It is assessed on communication (out of 15) and on quality of language, which in this case means pronunciation and how fluent you are.

Look at the example from a recent exam which deals with the topic of free time, then read the notes which follow.

HIGHER PART TWO

CANDIDATE AS NARRATOR – CARD FIVE

The photographs and notes below give details of some people the candidate met during a recent touring holiday in South West France.

The candidate will tell you about these people in the first person.

You play the role of the French Assistant(e) to whom the candidate is relating his/her holiday.

The exercise is not intended to be a monologue and you are encouraged to take part at your discretion in the narrative in the following ways:

　　　　as a cue for the candidate to begin
　　　　to prompt and help where necessary
　　　　to elucidate a point where necessary
　　　　to encourage the candidate to expand a point
　　　　to guide the candidate through the narrative at a suitable pace.

Royan le 16 août	Arcachon le 19 août	Cognac le 23 août	Saintes le 29 août

Marc 16 ans Parisien	Annick 15 ans Bordelaise	Sylvie 17 ans Canadienne	Bruno 18 ans Grenoblois
– sports nautiques – disco – invitation chez lui	– restaurant chinois – partie de tennis – concert	– travaille au camping – cinéma, le soir – visite aux caves (jour de congé)	– visite à la forêt – photos d'animaux – promenades à vélo

---

MEG, May 1988

There is a setting in English, as usual. The important facts to remember are:

(a) This story will almost certainly all be in the *Past Tense*. Therefore you need to be very confident in using the Perfect and the Imperfect Tenses. These are explained for you in the Grammar Section, p. 197.

(b) It is called a conversation because you will be asked questions by the examiner, and invited to expand on your answers.

(c) The part printed in **bold** is the task, and you *must* get this part across. In the example there are 4 tasks, one for each picture, and you must get across date, place and person.

(d) The approximate time allowed for this part of the exam is 5 minutes, which is a *very long time* when you are talking in a foreign language, so you need to be well prepared. You can't write anything down either, so you need to have a good memory.

(e) You are also expected to include phrases such as **Bonjour monsieur/ madame/mademoiselle; merci,** etc., if it seems right to do so.

To do well on this exercise you need to be sure you do all the tasks and that you *expand* on the notes. You also need to listen to (and understand!) what the examiner says and be able to reply, so you should have thought through the story-line you are going to put across. To avoid hesitation, be as certain as you can be about the verbs you are going to use, their tenses and how they will sound. It helps some people to work out the Perfect Tenses first. These are the ones which talk about completed actions – what you did first, what you did next, and so on, in sequence.

Once you've got the basic sequence right, fill in the extra details and *always* include somewhere:

Time ⎱
Weather ⎮ which will
Reasons ⎬ all be in
Descriptions ⎮ the
Opinions ⎰ Imperfect.

If you can include extra tenses such as Pluperfect, it will all help to improve your grade.

Here is an example of how a good candidate might complete the first task.

Candidate: **Alors, je suis allé en vacances dans le sud-ouest de la France en août avec mes parents. On y est allés en voiture.**

Examiner: **Pourquoi en voiture?**

Candidate: **Parce que c'est beaucoup plus pratique en vacances. On peut s'arrêter quand on veut. Alors, on est arrivés à Royan le 16 août. Je suis allé sur la plage pour me baigner et là j'ai rencontré un jeune Parisien qui s'appelait Marc.**

Examiner: **Il nageait aussi?**

Candidate: **Non, il se bronzait sur la plage tout près. On a parlé ensemble. Il m'a dit qu'il était en vacances avec son frère. Ce soir-là, on est allés à un disco ensemble, mais je ne l'ai pas aimé, parce que c'était trop petit et très cher.**

Examiner: **Vous allez revoir Marc?**

Candidate: **Oui, il m'a invité à Paris pour Noël et j'espère y aller.**

You see that there is a lot of detail expanding on the suggestions, but lots of other things that could have been said – a description of Marc, something about the weather, what you did at the disco.

Notice also that for *we* the candidate used **on.** This is very common in spoken French, but there is another reason. When you have to choose between **avoir** and **être** for your Perfect Tense, you have to say **on a . . .** or **on est . . .** when using **on,** which are easier than **nous avons** or **nous sommes** to get your tongue round. It will make you sound more French, more fluent, and if you get it wrong it won't be so obvious.

TECHNIQUE TIP

If you are not sure whether a verb should be in the Perfect or not, try the *and next* test. If it sounds all right, the verb should be in the Perfect.
Example: I went to the disco *and next* he invited me home. This sounds all right. You use Perfect for both verbs.
Example: He invited me home *and next* he was called Marc. This sounds completely wrong, so your second verb will *not* be Perfect. This means it will nearly always be Imperfect.

TECHNIQUE TIP

Use **on** rather than **nous** when speaking. (See Grammar Section, p. 187.)

There has been a lot for you to take in about this task, but it's worth reading through carefully, working out for yourself how you would carry on for the rest of the task. Remember also, if you are doing this kind of task in GCSE Speaking, the exam board concerned also has a story in Higher Writing. Preparation for this Higher Speaking task will also help you more than anything else with the Higher Writing. (See Chapter 10 for more about Higher Writing.)

Conversation

This topic is very popular with examiners because it gives candidates a chance to talk about what really interests them. It is important in conversation to be able to give reasons why you like certain activities. Long lists of groups or TV programmes will not impress, because of course you are not producing any French.

Listen to the conversation on the cassette and the comments afterwards (S11). If you have your speaking grid filled out and memorised, you could expect to do well in conversation on this topic.

Basic Writing

You are likely to get a note, or a short letter or perhaps a postcard to write on this topic. It is important to have some confidence about tenses here because there is a good chance you will need the Perfect or the Future Tense, or perhaps both, even in a short task. The following provides an example.

H While staying with your correspondent in France, you get a phone call from an English school-friend also on the French trip, who wants you to go into town with her to help her buy clothes to take back to England and impress her friends. Leave a note for the French family telling them the following things:
(a) Your English friend Claire phoned.
(b) You are going to town together to look at clothes.
(c) You will be back by 6 p.m.
(d) There is a programme on English pop music tonight on TV that you would like to watch.

Notes on tasks
(a) You might think it is enough to write *Claire*, without the French for *your English friend*. But make sure you include this as well, as there will almost certainly be a mark for it.
(b) What do you do if you forget *clothes*? Put down the words for some items of clothing that you can remember, e.g. **des jupes.**
(c) For *6 p.m.,* either use the 24-hour clock if you are *sure,* or write **six heures du soir.**
(d) This is a long sentence. Break it into two sentences in French.

Write the message in the space below and check with a correct version on p. 179. But remember that there is more than one way of writing these tasks.

A common idea at Basic Level is a postcard which you have to reply to, as in the example on p. 60.

I You have just received this postcard from a French friend you met last year on holiday.

E.9.2160 - FOUESNANT BEG-MEIL (Finistère)
La pointe de Beg-Meil et les plages
jusqu'à la pointe de Moustertin.

TREGUNC

— Editions Le Doaré, Châteaulin
Fabrication française - Reprod interdite

Bonjour,

Je suis en vacances avec des copains à Nice. Il fait très chaud et on se baigne tous les jours. Hier on est allés en Italie ! Le soir il y a toujours un disco ici. C'est super ! Bonnes vacances à toi aussi.

Marc

....

....

....

....

....

You decide to send Marc a card of your home town, saying:
(a)   You are staying at home this year.
(b)   You are playing tennis in the afternoons.
(c)   It is raining today, so you are going to the library.
(d)   You are going skiing in France at Christmas.

Do you notice how many expressions of time come into this task? These are important fillers at Basic Level Writing and Speaking and you should always try to include them even when they are not actually required. It makes your French sound far more interesting.

Have a go at this task in the space below and check with a correct version on p. 179.

Finally for this unit, here is another slightly more straightforward postcard from a recent GCSE paper. One thing that needs pointing out is that, in this case, a lot of vocabulary is supplied for you in the postcard you are replying to. You can feel free to use as much of this text as possible. There is no need to find different expressions where the words are the same. Allow yourself only 8 minutes for this task and then check with p. 179.

J Your French friend is on holiday and has sent you this postcard

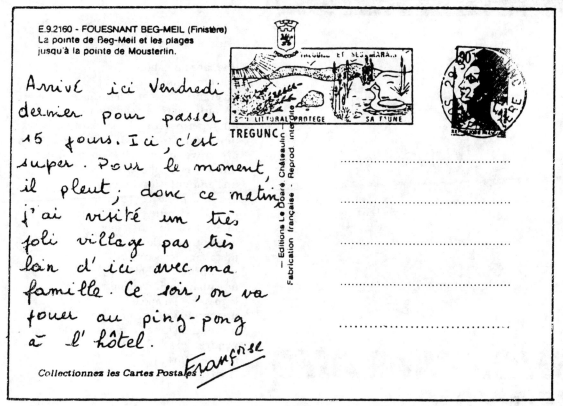

When you go on holiday, you write a similar postcard, **in French**, telling your French friend that:

— you arrived on Thursday evening.
— you are staying for one week.
— at the moment, the weather is hot.
— this morning, you swam in the sea.
— tonight, you are going to a concert.

SHOPPING AND MONEY

What you need to be able to do.

- Understand French money, weights and measures.
- Understand and use names of shops.
- Understand people talking and writing about shopping.
- Perform shopping tasks.
- Talk and write about your shopping habits.

The words you need

Shops

un magasin shop
une boutique shop
un grand magasin department store
un supermarché supermarket
un hypermarché hypermarket
une grande surface hypermarket
un centre commercial shopping centre
une épicerie grocer's
une alimentation grocer's
une boucherie butcher's
une charcuterie pork butcher's
une pâtisserie cake shop
une boulangerie baker's
un tabac tobacconists's
une librairie bookshop
une pharmacie chemist's
le marché market
un marchand/une marchande shopkeeper; stallholder
un vendeur/une vendeuse salesman/woman
vendre to sell
acheter to buy
la vitrine shop window

Shopping

faire les courses/les achats/du shopping to go shopping
l'argent money
la monnaie small change
un billet note
une pièce coin
une carte postale postcard
une enveloppe envelope
un stylo (ball-point) pen
un timbre stamp
du papier paper
des bonbons sweets
un paquet de a packet of
une boîte de a box/tin of
une bouteille de a bottle of
un litre de a litre of
une tranche de a slice of
un pot de a jar/pot of
un kilo de a kilo of
une livre de a pound of
un demi-kilo de half a kilo of
un quart de a quarter kilo of
100 grammes de 100 grams of
un tube de a tube of
le dentifrice toothpaste
le shampooing shampoo
le rayon de . . . the . . . department
payer to pay
la caisse cash desk
un chariot trolley
un sac en plastique plastic bag
soldes sale
offre spécial special offer
un souvenir souvenir
un cadeau present
un paquet-cadeau gift-wrapped parcel

emballer   to wrap up
dépenser   to spend
gagner   to earn
cher   expensive
bon marché   cheap

Clothes

les vêtements   clothes
la taille   size

une robe dress	**un chemisier** blouse
une jupe skirt	**un pull** pullover
un gilet cardigan	**un tricot** jumper
un pantalon trousers	**un jean** jeans
une chemise skirt	**une veste** jacket
une cravate tie	**un T-shirt** T-shirt

un maillot de bain   swimming trunks,
   bathing costume

un slip pants	**un collant** tights
des chaussettes socks	**des chaussures** shoes
des sandales sandals	**des baskets** trainers
un manteau topcoat	**un imperméable**

raincoat

un anorak anorak	**essayer** to try on
un blouson	**un survêtement**

bomber jacket   tracksuit

un maillot   sports shirt

laine wool	**coton** cotton
cuir leather	**nylon** nylon
soie silk	**bois** wood

This is the last speaking grid you will be doing, so try to make a good job of filling it up. There is an example on the page after the grid of how you might do this. The 5 grids you have should give you the main basis for talking and writing about yourself directly in French without translating, once you have learned the material. This is probably the most valuable use you can make of revision time.

les magasins près de chez moi	situation exacte	on peut y acheter

je fais des courses pour ma mère	quand, exactement?	une raison pourquoi

je vais en ville (où?)	quand?	pour acheter

les derniers vêtements que j'ai achetés	description	prix

les magasins près de chez moi	situation exacte	on peut y acheter
un tabac	à 200 mètres de chez moi	des cigarettes (je ne fume pas) des journaux des magazines des bonbons
une épicerie	à côté du tabac	les provisions
une boulangerie	en face de l'épicerie	du pain des gâteaux

je fais des courses pour ma mère	quand, exactement?	une raison pourquoi
quelquefois	après l'école	elle travaille jusqu'à 5h30

je vais en ville (où?)	quand?	pour acheter
aux magasins de disques avec mes amis	le samedi matin	des cassettes et pour écouter de la musique
aux magasins de vêtements avec une amie	après l'école	pour essayer des vêtements

Listening

The most important thing to be able to do, both for the exam and, even more importantly, when you go to France, is to understand French prices when you hear them. You need to know that some numbers sound *different* when followed by the word **francs.** Listen to the tape-recording (L17 on cassette) of prices from **1 franc** to **10 francs** and you will notice that **5F, 6F, 8F,** and **10F** sound different from the numbers 5, 6, 8, 10 alone. The next thing is to calculate approximate equivalents in English money so that you have an idea of what the price is in English and can check whether it seems right. This is especially necessary when the word **francs** is missed out of the price, just as in English the word **pounds** may be missed out. So, in English someone may say *five sixty* when they mean *£5.60*, and in French you might hear **deux cinquante** instead of **deux francs cinquante (2F50)**.

You often get individual exam questions with a price in the answer, as in this example from a recent GCSE paper. (L18 on cassette. Answer on p. 179)

A You are on holiday in the south of France and you go to the market for some fruit. You buy some peaches. The stallholder tells you how much they are.

How much are the peaches? (1)

MEG Basic Listening, May 1989

Individual questions to do with payment are also popular with examiners. Look at this one from the same paper as the last example. Remember to *predict* what kind of question you could be asked when paying, and to guess if necessary. Write your answer in the space provided. (L19 on cassette Answer on p. 179)

B You go to pay at the **caisse** and the lady asks you a question.

What does the cashier ask you? (1)

MEG Basic Listening, May 1989

Details about items you are buying are common questions at Basic Level. This one asks you to give 3 details for one item. Probably there will be more than 3 to choose from. Remember the technique tips we have covered so far.

You are in a souvenir shop trying to find a suitable present for your elder sister. You like the look of a necklace and ask the shop assistant how much it costs. She starts telling you about the necklace. Write down *three* details about it in the space provided. (L20 on cassette)

(a)

(b)

(c)

Probably you expected a price to be quoted. Did you get it right? You should also have expected something about what it is made of and where it comes from. The first detail was *(very) pretty*. You may have thought this would not count, but it is part of how she describes the necklace, so it scores a mark. The other details were: *Spanish* (easy); *plastic* (easy); *5 (different) colours* (quite easy); *on sale* (well done if you got that); *75 francs*. The word **seulement** at the end can be ignored for this task.

Announcements in supermarkets and hypermarkets are a popular test. They can be difficult at Basic Level because sometimes there is an introductory chime which can put you off. This GCSE example is a very typical one. If you can get 4 marks out of 6 on this one, you are doing well. Fill in the details on the grid and check your answers on p. 179. (L21 on cassette)

TECHNIQUE TIP

How did you cope with the number? The technique is to keep saying it over and over in your head until you have worked it out. In this case, if you were pretty sure of 3 or 4 other details, you did not need to worry about getting the number wrong.

C At the hypermarket you hear some announcements on the loudspeaker system. Say what is being advertised each time and give *one* extra detail for *each* item (e.g. which department/price/special offer etc.).

ITEM ADVERTISED	EXTRA DETAIL
(a)	
(b)	
(c)	

NEA Basic Listening, June 1988

Higher Level

There are not many examples of Higher Listening on the topic of shopping, probably because it is usually seen as a fairly simple and straightforward task. Therefore, what tasks there are will probably involve several questions, as in the example below on shopping for clothes. Do this one straight off and see how you cope. (L22 on cassette. Answers on p. 179)

D LEAG Higher Listening, June 1988.

B — SHOPPING

Questions 11-17 *are based on a longer passage. This passage is sub-divided into two sections, Questions 11-13 and Questions 14-17. You will hear the whole passage once. Each section will then be heard twice.*

While you are staying in France your French friend wants to buy a shirt, and you go with him to the shop.

Listen to the first part and answer questions 11, 12 and 13.

Question 11

State **two** things about the appearance of the shirt he wants.

....

....

Question 12

Why is he not sure what size he needs?

....

Question 13

Explain why he decides he needs a size 40.

....

....

Now listen to the second part of the dialogue and answer questions 14, 15, 16 and 17.

Question 14

What is the price of the shirt?

....

Question 15

Why is it good value?

....

Question 16

Why does he choose a brown tie?

....

Question 17

What does he ask the assistant to do?

....

Another and more challenging task will consist of looking at visual material, such as adverts, and perhaps making a choice. This generally means doing some reading as well, spotting differences, etc. Look carefully at the four computers advertised before you play the tape for this task. Remember that it is very unlikely you would be expected to write the same answer for two different questions. (L23 on cassette. Answers on p. 179)

TECHNIQUE TIP

Do not be afraid to indicate, by circling or underlining on the photograph, any differences you notice before you start listening. The more closely you concentrate on the task, the better, and marking the pictures helps your concentration.

E Your pen-friend's mum and sister are discussing which computer to buy your friend. The four adverts they are discussing are shown on p. 68. Look at them carefully.

(i) They decide on computer D.
      Give *two* reasons for that choice.

      1 ....

      2 ....

(ii) Why do they reject the others?

      (a) Computer A ....

      (b) Computer B ....

      (c) Computer C ....

NEA Higher Listening, June 1988

THOMSON
MICRO-INFORMATIQUE

A

**T07.70 + BASIC MICROSOFT®
+ LECTEUR DE CASSETTES + 2 JEUX
+ UN BON DE RÉDUCTION DE 50%
SUR 3 LOGICIELS ÉDUCATIFS
POUR 3390 F**

B

**Le micro-ordinateur
le crayon optique
le lecteur de cassettes**

2990 F

C

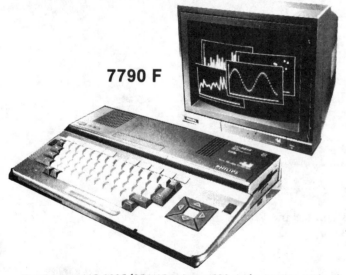

7790 F

– L'ordinateur VG 8235 (256 K RAM dont 128 vidéo, lecteur intégré de disquettes),
– Un moniteur couleur (VS 0070) haute résolution,
– 4 logiciels sur disquettes

D

CPC 6128 COMPLET 4490 F

Reading

At Basic Level you will always get some fairly simple tasks to do with signs in shops. These are often just one word, so it is very important to learn all the shopping vocabulary. Another possibility is a multiple-choice test where you have to choose between four signs.

Here are five such items for you to try. (Answers below)

(a)   In a shop window you see the following sign:

> **VETEMENTS EN SOLDE**

What is on sale? (1)

(b)   You are about to enter a department store when you see the following notice on the door:

> **FERME**

What does it mean? (1)

(c)   In the books section of a supermarket you see the following sign:

> **PAYEZ A LA CAISSE**

What does it ask you to do? (1)

(d)   You are trying to buy some bread in a hypermarket. Which sign should you look for? Tick the correct box.

> **BOUCHERIE**

> **CHARCUTERIE**

> **BOULANGERIE**

> **EPICERIE**

(e)   In a department store you want to buy some food for a picnic. You look at the information board to see which floor the food department is on.

2e étage	MAISON ET JARDIN
1er étage	CONFECTION-HOMMES
rez de chaussée	PAPETERIE/PARFUMS
sous-sol	ALIMENTATION

Which floor did you choose?
2nd floor   1st floor
ground floor   basement

You should have coped with this successfully. The answers should be:
(a) *clothes;* (b) closed; (c) *pay at cash-desk/checkout/till* (d) **boulangerie;** (e) *basement.*
(Remember that capital letters do not normally carry accents.)

Sometimes the sign may be a little unexpected, like this recent GCSE one.

You are shopping in a supermarket. Above the cheese counter you see a sign:

PRENEZ UN TICKET

What is it telling you to do?

MEG, May 1989

But the French is very simple, and the answer is, *Take a ticket.* This probably has something to do with the system of queueing.
    This one is a bit trickier, but the examiner helps you with the *setting.* The setting is the part before the questions which explains where you are supposed to be, and what you are supposed to be doing.

F   4.   *This is an advertisement in a shop window, for tights.*

What is the special offer?   (2 marks)

SEG, November 1988

Occasionally you have more text to get through but still have to find only one or two key words. This question came from the same paper as the last one. (Answers p. 179)

G   6.   *You are planning a shopping expedition, and find the following advertisements in a town guide.*
    (a)   Which firm will hire you things for the beach?   (1 mark)
    (b)   Which firm will sell you fishing tackle?   (1 mark)
    (c)   You need to buy clothes. Which shop should
          you choose?   (1 mark)
    (d)   At which shop can you buy groceries?

                                                                (1 mark)

Note: To answer this question write the appropriate letter (A, B, C, D, or E) on your answer paper.

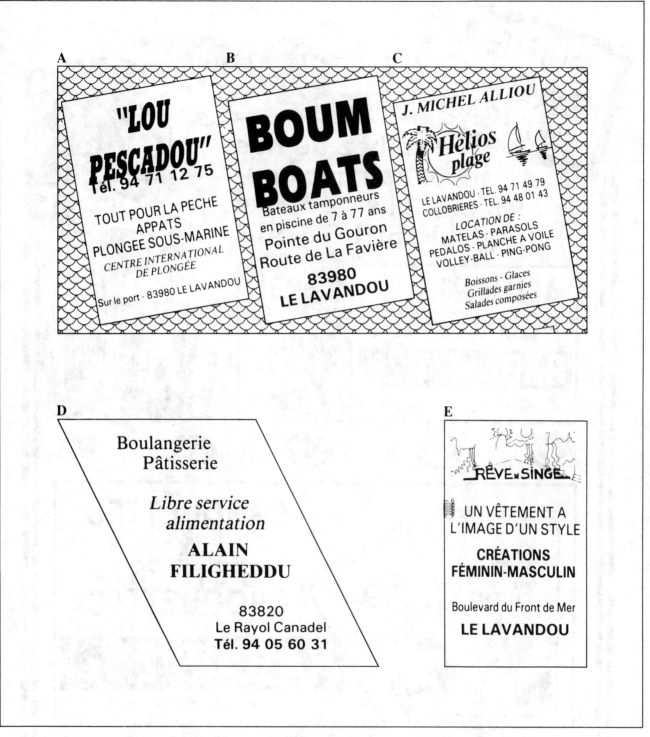

A

"LOU PESCADOU"
Tél. 94 71 12 75
TOUT POUR LA PECHE
APPATS
PLONGEE SOUS-MARINE
CENTRE INTERNATIONAL
DE PLONGÉE
Sur le port - 83980 LE LAVANDOU

B

BOUM BOATS
Bateaux tamponneurs
en piscine de 7 à 77 ans
Pointe du Gouron
Route de La Favière
83980
LE LAVANDOU

C

J. MICHEL ALLIOU
Hélios plage
LE LAVANDOU - TEL. 94 71 49 79
COLLOBRIERES - TEL. 94 48 01 43
LOCATION DE :
MATELAS - PARASOLS
PEDALOS - PLANCHE A VOILE
VOLLEY-BALL - PING-PONG
Boissons - Glaces
Grillades garnies
Salades composées

D

Boulangerie
Pâtisserie

*Libre service
alimentation*
**ALAIN
FILIGHEDDU**

83820
Le Rayol Canadel
Tél. 94 05 60 31

E

RÊVE ᴅᴇ SINGE
UN VÊTEMENT A
L'IMAGE D'UN STYLE
CRÉATIONS
FÉMININ-MASCULIN
Boulevard du Front de Mer
LE LAVANDOU

SEG General Reading, November 1988

Below is another example, taken from a Canadian magazine, which is why the prices are in Canadian dollars.

What are they offering price cuts on? (1)

*Answer*_____

There was only one mark for this and to get it you must write either *cat and dog food*, OR *pet food*. If you wrote *cat food* OR *dog food* alone, this would not be a correct answer.

Higher Level

In the GCSE papers which have been set so far, there are not many examples of the shopping topic set as a task for Higher Reading. Here are three examples from a recent paper, with notes on the answers.

1   You are looking at some jars of chocolate spread in a supermarket. On the label are these words.

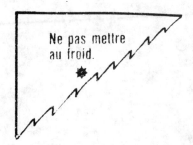

    What do they mean?

    .... *(1)*

2   In the same supermarket your pen-friend points to a notice at the check-out.

> VEUILLEZ PRESENTER
>
> VOS SACS OUVERTS
>
> A LA CAISSE
>
> S. V. P.

(a) What must you do?

    .... *(1)*

(b) Why do you think you must do this?

    .... *(1)*

3   Further down the street, in a small shopping precinct, you see this sign outside a shop.

(i)   Name **two** items you can buy here.

1   ....

2   .... *(2)*

(ii)   What is special about them?

NEA Higher Reading, June 1988

Answer 1: Do not put in a cold place/fridge.
A lot of people answer this one *do not freeze/put in the freezer*. This is wrong, because you have to exclude the idea of putting it in the *fridge*. The point is that the chocolate spread will not spread if it has been kept in the fridge. So you could write *keep at room temperature*, and it would be correct because it gets the right idea across.

Answer 2(a): Open your bags at the checkout. (**Veuillez** = *please*; worth remembering for reading comprehension.)
    2(b): This is an example of *inference*. You have to work out why, as the French does not tell you. You rely on your knowledge of the real world. The point about this one is that there is more than one possible answer, and if it seems reasonable, you will get the mark. Most people write: *for security reasons* OR *to stop shoplifting/stealing*. Some write: *because of bomb scares*. One person (who probably had a Saturday job in Sainsbury's) wrote: *so they can help you pack your shopping*. All of these are fine as answers.

Answer 3(i): Toys; gifts/presents; games. (Any 2 = 2 marks)
A lot of people went for *drinks*, because they misunderstood **bois**.
    3(ii): They are made of wood.
Again, a lot of people opted for *exclusive*. If they had thought a little bit about the word **exclusivement,** they might have remember that the ending meant it was *exclusively*, and that it came after another phrase **en bois,** which must mean *in* something OR *made of* something.

In this question, the fact that the shop sign was in the shape of a tree could have helped, but most people perhaps did not have time to take this into account.

TECHNIQUE TIP

For Higher Reading especially, do not look at a word in isolation. Look also at the words it is linked to.

Here are a few more Higher Reading tasks with more text to work through. The first one is straightforward, the rest become more demanding. You will see lots of vocabulary which is recognisable because of your knowledge of English. This *should* help as long as you *think* about what you write and do not lose sight of common-sense. (Answers on p. 179)

H   (a)   You pick up this piece of paper in a hypermarket. What is it asking you to do? (1)

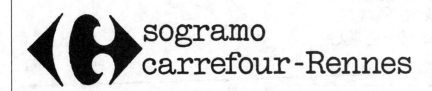

sogramo
carrefour-Rennes

MERCI DE NOUS AIDER
A MIEUX VOUS SERVIR
et améliorer notre magasin par vos
SUGGESTIONS

Je suggère : ....

(b)   You are looking at radio cassettes and notice this one on special offer. What is the special offer? (1)

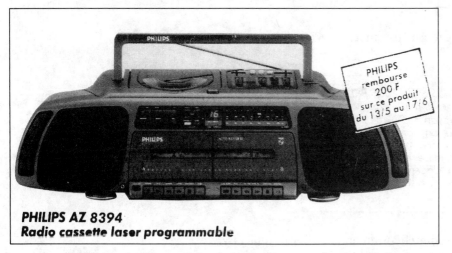

PHILIPS
rembourse
200 F
sur ce produit
du 13/5 au 17/6

PHILIPS AZ 8394
Radio cassette laser programmable

(c)   You are thinking of buying a shirt to take home for your 6-year-old brother. Give three details about the one advertised. (3)

85 F CHEMISE MANCHES LONGUES
*impression cachemire, 100% coton,
divers coloris, du 2 au 8 ans
du 10 au 16 ans **90,00 F***

(d)   In the Prisunic store you notice an advert for **Messager** products.
       What kind of product is the **Messager** range? (1)

> *Mais oui,* MESSAGER
> *c'est la plus grande marque*
> *française de papeterie. Toute*
> *l'année, le tout pour écrire est chez*
> *Prisunic et s'appelle* MESSAGER
> *De l'école au bureau,* MESSAGER
> *c'est toute une vie.*

(e)   A hypermarket chain is making a big effort to attract customers.
       What promises is it making in this advert? Give any three. (3)

LE SERMENT

Nous nous engageons:

- A pratiquer les prix les plus bas.
- A vous garantir la qualité et la fraîcheur.
- A vous assurer un large choix.
- A vous apporter une information claire et loyale.
- A vous recevoir dans un Intermarché accueillant.

(f)   A competitor is also trying to get customers in. What guarantee is
       it making?

GARANTIES MEILLEURS PRIX
Si vous trouvez moins cher ailleurs dans un rayon de 30 km et dans les 30 jours suivant votre achat (pour tout article portant la même référence et bénéficiant des mêmes conditions de services), nos magasins vous remboursent la différence.

We have given you a lot of reading comprehension practice in this topic. By
now you should be building up your technique and finding it easier to cope
with more demanding tasks as well as handling the simple ones confidently.
Remember, the essentials for reading comprehension are:
(a)   Know the vocabulary.
(b)   Use your common sense.

Speaking

Role-plays

At Basic Level, shopping role-plays are very popular, as you might expect,
and the language needed will usually include asking for something and
finding out the price. Here is a simple example from a recent paper.

You are in a French store. Your teacher will play the part of the sales assistant and will start the conversation.

(a) Say you would like some shoes.
(b) Say grey or blue.
(c) Ask how much they are.

NEA, May 1988

As long as you can pronounce the word **chaussures,** you should get full marks for this, but in fact a lot of people are unsure or careless about the word which goes before **chaussures.** The correct thing to say is **des chaussures** OR **une paire de chaussures.** It would not be a very bad mistake to say **de chaussures,** but if you said **une chaussure(s),** you could imagine that a shop assistant would be rather puzzled, so you could drop a mark.

On the second task, some candidates were unsure whether to say just *grey* or just *blue* or both. When in doubt, say all of it.

 The next task is a 5-task role-play again. This one is recorded on the cassette (S12), but prepare the role yourself before you listen to it.

You are on a short holiday in Paris. Before coming home you want to buy some souvenirs. You have just entered a shop where you think you may be able to buy what you need. You have seen, for example, a little model ornament of the Eiffel Tower.

The role of the shop assistant will be played by the examiner.

(a) Buy three postcards.
(b) Ask if they sell stamps.
(c) Say you would like a book on Paris.
(d) Ask how much the little Eiffel Tower costs.
(e) Say it is too expensive.

MEG, November 1988

Shopping role-plays at Higher Level are often used to test the unexpected, to see how you can cope with problems. This means that, unlike other role-plays, you have to listen very carefully to what the examiner says and react to it. Look at this example, which you can see is set out differently.

SITUATION	You go into a shop to buy a pair of shoes. You have seen a pair of grey shoes at 200 francs in the window. Your teacher will play the part of the shop assistant and will start the conversation.
ESSENTIAL INFORMATION	You have only 250 francs with you.
YOU MUST	1. Ask to try on the shoes you have seen. 2. Say they are too big and ask if there are any others. 3. Respond appropriately to what the shop assistant says. 4. Say you will come back on Friday.

NEA Higher Role Play, May 1988

Conversation

 Shopping fits in with a lot of other topics and therefore often comes up in the exam. Listen to the example on cassette of a candidate talking at Higher Level using the speaking grid (S13). As we have already said, this is the last speaking grid, and the last conversation recorded for you on the cassette. The remaining topics deal largely with you in France and we shall be covering different techniques for Higher Level Speaking especially.

TECHNIQUE TIP

Technique is really important here if you want to score marks. The first point is the *situation*, which tells you something about the shoes. You must include details from this situation in doing task 1. The information *grey* and *200 francs* are essential, and if you do not mention this information, the examiner will ask you a question in French to get those details from you.

The second point is the *essential information* box. You must give this information at an appropriate moment. If you look carefully at the tasks, you will see that task 3 is likely to be the place where you will have to say this. Some candidates try to solve the problem by giving the essential information as part of task 1. Usually this will *not* work because the examiner *has* to ask you the question to see if you can understand and respond. So you can lose out by saying it too soon. The best technique is to do the tasks in order, then you will not confuse yourself (or the examiner!) by missing anything out.

In Higher Level Speaking, you may have 10–12 minutes to prepare 5 role-plays (this is true of NEA, for example), and you will need to think carefully about how this one might develop. Also, a role-play like this one will always be the last one you do, so you really need to be sure about it and do it confidently. There will be other examples coming up in the later topics for you to practise and listen to.

Basic Writing

The most likely task at Basic Writing is a shopping list or note. This recent one was quite easy but it shows the importance of knowing vocabulary.

You are staying in France with a friend. Her mother has asked you if you need anything.

    You give her a note asking for the following items:
- 2 postcards
- 2 stamps for England
- an English newspaper
- a map of the town.

NEA, Summer 1988

Here are a few comments on the tasks.

(a) **2 cartes postales.** Always write the number as a figure unless *told* not to do so on the exam paper. Do not write just **2 cartes,** as that might mean birthday cards, Christmas cards, etc.

(b) **2 timbres pour l'Angleterre.** *Not* **2 timbres anglais,** which is something different.

(c) **un journal anglais.** *Not* **le** *Sun,* or **le** *Telegraph* or any other *name* of a paper. A French person would not know what they mean.

(d) **un plan de la ville. Plan** is the word used for a town map, *not* **une carte,** which is a road map or the sort of map you would find in an atlas.

There is no need to write any more than these 15 or so words. Nothing else will be marked and you can only afford 5 minutes on this task.

The only other type of task you might get would be in a letter asking you to answer certain questions. How would you respond to the following questions? Try to write one or two sentences in answer to each one, if possible without referring back to your speaking grid. Aim to write 15–20 words each time, in the space after the question.

I   (a)   **Est-ce qu'il y a beaucoup de magasins près de chez toi?**

    (b)   **Tu vas en ville faire des courses quelquefois?**

    (c)   **Est-ce que tu achètes souvent des vêtements?**

Again, you could show your teacher, or someone else who can help, what you have written and get their view on it. We have given possible answers on p. 179.

6

GOING ABROAD – TRAVEL

What you need to be able to do.

– Understand people giving instructions about finding the way.
– Understand 24-hour clock times.
– Understand spoken and written details to do with different forms of travel, including timetable notes.
– Ask for directions, buy tickets, etc. for travel.
– Talk and write about holidays at home and abroad.
– Know something about transport in France.

The words you need

Verbs of coming and going

aller	to go	**s'arrêter**	to stop
arriver	to arrive	**descendre**	to go down, get off (bus etc.)
entrer	to go in	**monter**	to go up, get on (bus etc.)
partir	to go away, depart	**quitter**	to leave
rester	to stay	**rentrer**	to return (home)
sortir	to go out		

Directions and distances

à droite	on the right/ to the right	**à gauche**	on the left/ to the left
tout droit	straight on	**loin**	far
près (d'ici)	near (here)	**proche**	near

In town

la rue	street	**la place**	square
le pont	bridge	**les feux**	traffic lights
une église	church	**l'hôtel de ville**	town hall
la mairie	town hall	**le stade**	sports stadium
le Syndicat d'Initiative	information bureau		
le trottoir	pavement	**traverser**	to cross
un parking	car park	**un agent de police**	policeman
le commissariat	police station		

Travelling by road

la route	road	**l'autoroute**	motorway
la gare routière	bus station	**l'arrêt**	(bus) stop
l'arrivée	arrival	**le départ**	departure
un (auto)bus	bus	**un (auto)car**	coach
le billet	ticket	**le carnet**	book of tickets
le ticket	ticket	**l'horaire**	timetable
faire de l'autostop	to hitch-hike	**un sac à dos**	rucksack
le péage	road toll	**le voyage**	journey
la ceinture de sécurité	safety belt	**le conducteur**	driver
conduire	to drive	**l'essence (sans plomb)**	(lead-free) petrol
faire le plein	to fill up	**le garage**	garage
l'huile	oil	**le litre**	litre
le mécanicien	mechanic	**la moto**	motorbike
en panne	broken down	**le permis de conduire**	driving licence
le pneu	tyre	**crevé**	punctured
réparer	to repair	**la station-service**	service station
le piéton	pedestrian	**le vélo**	bike
le vélomoteur	moped	**louer**	to hire
la priorité à droite	priority from the right		

Travelling by rail and underground

la gare SNCF railway station	**le train** train
le guichet ticket window	**les bagages** luggage
le buffet buffet	**les toilettes** toilets
libre free	**occupé** engaged
le compartiment compartment	**(non)fumeur** (non)smoker
la portière train door	**composter un billet** punch a ticket
le wagon-restaurant restaurant car	
le wagon-lit sleeper	**la consigne** left luggage
la valise suitcase	**la correspondance** connection
prochain next	**durer** to last
le quai platform	**la voie** railway line
le métro underground	**la station** metro station
les renseignements information	
la salle d'attente waiting room	

Holidays

l'avion aeroplane	**l'aéroport** airport
l'agence de voyages travel agency	**le ferry** cross-channel ferry
le bureau de tourisme tourist office	**le douanier** customs official
au bord de la mer at the sea-side	**la douane** customs
à l'étranger abroad	
les grandes vacances summer holidays	
une semaine week	**une quinzaine** fortnight
quinze jours fortnight	**le week-end** weekend
Noël Christmas	**Pâques** Easter
congé holiday, leave	**la pellicule** film
l'appareil-photo camera	

Listening

Basic Level

By the time your French exams are over you will probably feel like forgetting about French altogether. But remember that the real reason for learning a language is to be able to speak it and visit the country. Even travelling by car on the way to Spain, you will notice lots of differences between travelling in France and travelling in Great Britain. If you decide to visit France by bike or train with a few friends, you will really come into contact with the French and get a chance to use your French a lot. This topic is very popular with examiners, because it is one of the most useful ones, and there is plenty of material available.

At Basic Level you will get short announcements about times, platforms, flight numbers etc., as well as instructions for finding the way. These items are often quite short and are sometimes a bit tricky because of the quality of the sound. They may be played through a loudspeaker or over the radio (in the case of traffic conditions, for example). The setting should give you a clue about this. Try not to let it put you off. The sound should still be OK.

To start with, here is a fairly simple finding-the-way item. Write in the answers before checking below. (L24 on cassette)

Your family have just driven off the ferry in France and are trying to get to the motorway. It is not signposted very clearly and you end up in the middle of the town. You have to ask a passer-by for directions. How do you get to the motorway? (3)

You should have got 1 mark out of 3 almost before you heard the tape. It is a pretty safe bet that you will have to turn right or left in most items about finding the way. As long as you do not get them mixed up, that is one safe mark. How did you get on with the other 2 marks though? Both rely on common words which you could easily miss because they are so short. This is where learning pronunciation is so important – and learning how it *sounds* by using the Pronunciation Guide on pp. 166–169. The 3 marks are for:

(a) *cross the bridge* ⎫
(b) *at the second traffic light* ⎬ these could be the other way round
(c) *turn right* ⎭

Here is an example with a similar setting from a recent GCSE exam. Notice that these questions are quite open-ended. You have to do some hard thinking before you hear this item. Which officials would you come across at a port? Customs, immigration (which deals with passports), and just possibly police for other reasons. Be prepared to guess sensibly on this one. Do not leave it blank. Have a go at it and then check your answers on p. 179. (L25 on cassette)

A   You are going on a camping holiday in France with your family. You are travelling by car and you are acting as interpreter. When you arrive at the port an official stops you.
(a)   What does he ask?

Answer_____

He then asks for information.
(b)   What does he want to know?

Answer_____

NEA, November 1988

Railway items are very popular exam questions. This one goes for 6 pieces of information, which is quite a lot, but it has been made fairly straightforward – you will need to write only very brief answers. Notice that the question tells you to fill in the details in *English*. You can write figures. You do not have to write out the numbers in full.

Notice also that the question about price of ticket states *2nd class*. This may mean the first-class price will also be quoted and you will have to ignore that piece of information.

As you do this question, try as hard as you can to put something down for each item the first time you hear it. By now your technique should be quite sound enough for you to do this. Then you can use the second hearing for checking. (Answers on p. 180. L26 on cassette)

B   MEG Basic Listening, November 1988

TECHNIQUE TIP

Always write numbers as figures and always make sure your figures are clear.

You are on holiday in Dieppe and you decide to take the train to Rouen for the day. You telephone a recorded message about the Dieppe to Rouen train service. This message provides you with the information you require, shown on the note-pad below.

Look at the note-pad below for the information you require.

Now listen to the message, which you will hear twice, and fill in the details in English.

Dieppe – Rouen (trains)

35   *Number of trains in morning:* . . . .

36   *First train leaves at:* . . . .

37   *Platform number:* . . . .

38   *Price of ticket (2nd class):* . . . .

39   *Last morning train leaves at:* . . . .

40   *Service provided on the train:* . . . .

24-hour clock times are always used for train, bus and air timetables and come up very often in Listening tests as they test 2 numbers at once. We have recorded 5 on the cassette for you to write in below. (Answers on p. 179. L27 on cassette)

C   Times: (a)
             (b)
             (c)
             (d)
             (e)

Numbers come up quite often in road travel, too. You need to know that French roads, like English ones, have a letter and then numbers. The letters are **A** (for **Autoroute**), **N** (for **Route Nationale,** like our A roads), and **D** (for **Route Départementale,** like our B roads). Here is a recent question using a map. In such questions it is vital to focus on the numbers, but because you have to circle the right one you cannot use the underlining technique we mentioned earlier. Here is an alternative technique for this situation.

The second part of this question seems much less predictable, but the setting and the name of the museum should give you some ideas. Do this question now and then check your answers on p. 180. You should be getting 3 out of 4 at least on a question like this, if you are aiming at Grade C or better. (L28 on cassette)

TECHNIQUE TIP

Never try to change 24-hour times to 12-hour times. Leave them as they are.
   Some people find it easier to concentrate on the hours the first time they hear the tape, and the minutes the second time.

TECHNIQUE TIP

While looking at the map, *write down* the road numbers in the margin or somewhere they will not interfere with your answer. Writing them down will focus your mind on them much more.

D   The following day you go the the Tourist Information office in Chantonnay and ask what there is to do and see in the region.

You are handed a leaflet about the Musée de la Nature.

(a)   Put a circle around the number of the road you would take to get to this place.

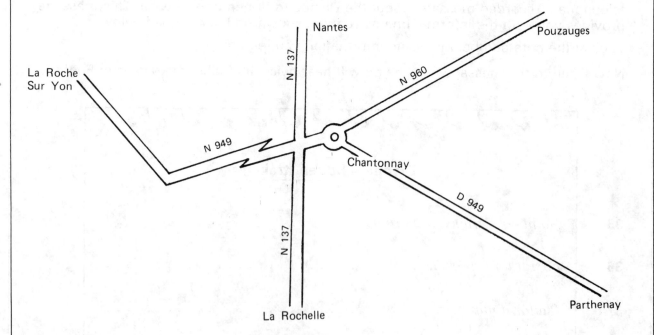

(b)   What **three** things does he say about it?

Answer: 1 ....

        2 ....

        3 ....

Higher Level

At Higher Level questions will be longer and more varied as well as less straightforward. Sometimes also they are linked together, as in the following case. Notice how many marks there are for this series. You will need to write short answers, especially for Question 3. Do this group together and then see how well you did by checking on p. 180. If you are getting 8 or more marks out of 16 you are on target for at least 1 point at Higher Level. (L29 on cassette)

E NISEC Higher Listening, May 1988.

---

1. At the Charles de Gaulle airport in France you hear this announcement.

   (a) Why can the London flight not leave?

   .... **(1)**

   (b) When is it expected to leave?

   .... **(1)**

2. A French person standing beside you in the airport departure lounge asks you some questions.

   (a) What does this person want you to do?

   .... **(3)**

   (b) What does he intend doing?

   .... **(2)**

3. You hear two people near you discussing the delay of the flight.

   (a) Where are the male passenger's friends coming from?

   .... **(2)**

   (b) What have they arranged for him in London?

   .... **(3)**

   (c) What does the lady passenger have to do immediately she arrives in London?

   .... **(2)**

   (d) If she arrives late what will happen?

   .... **(2)**

Remember that at this level, attitudes and opinions often crop up. In the next example, about hitch-hiking in France, the first question is straightforward but 2 and 3 are more testing. You may well find that there is not a specific answer stated for 2 and you have to sum it up. (Answers p. 180. L30 on cassette)

F   You are touring France with a friend. One day you decide to hitch a lift to Poitiers. A car-driver stops for you.

Before getting into the car you have a conversation with the driver. Listen to what the driver says and then answer Question 1.

Question 1
How near to Poitiers can the driver take you?

_____ (1)

After you have got into his car the driver continues talking. Listen to what he says and answer Questions 2 and 3.

Question 2
What is his general attitude now towards hitch-hiking?

_____ (1)

Question 3
Why did he stop to offer you a lift?

_____ (1)

LEAG, May 1989

Another recent example tested the same kind of question and linked it to holidays. You need to concentrate a lot on this one because there are 2 people speaking, and remember that you are writing reasons for *rejecting* the first 4 places. Do *not* put anything down which is in their favour. *Do* think beforehand about the kinds of reasons why people would *not* go somewhere on holiday. (Answers p. 180. L31 on cassette)

TECHNIQUE TIP

When answering a question about attitudes, try to answer in one word or a short phrase. Do *not* write a sentence explaining your reasons – you have not got time.

G   NEA Higher Listening, November 1988.

4   Your pen-friend's parents are discussing a proposed holiday. They produce arguments for and against each place, then finally agree where to go.

Give **one** reason why they reject each of the following places.
Write your answer in the box below.

(a)

	REASONS FOR REJECTING
Spain	
Edinburgh	
Côte d'Azur	
Switzerland	

(b)   Where do they finally decide to go instead?

Answer: ....

(c)   Give **two** reasons for their choice.

Answer: 1   ....

2   ....

Finally in this section (thank goodness, you'll probably say!), here is another question involving a map. This one came right at the end of a GCSE Higher Listening paper and was a demanding question. More than 4 marks on this would be a good score. There is a lot of reading to do, for both the setting and the questions. A quick look at the map tells you that you won't need to concentrate on it. You are better off focusing on the questions as you listen to the text. Again, short answers will help you to keep up. With question 31, you can expect the answer to be in metres – do not forget the M for metres. Remember to guess for any question you can't get. (L32 on cassette. Answers p. 180)

H   You are travelling by car with your parents on the A7 motorway nearing Lyon and heading for Aix-en-Provence, where you are about to spend a week's holiday.

As you approach Lyon you turn on the car radio and hear a road report about conditions on the A7. You jot down the details quickly, but you miss some of them. Fortunately the report is repeated shortly after, so you have the chance to complete your notes.

Study the map and questions 27–33 below.

Now listen to the report (you will hear it twice) and insert the remaining details in English.

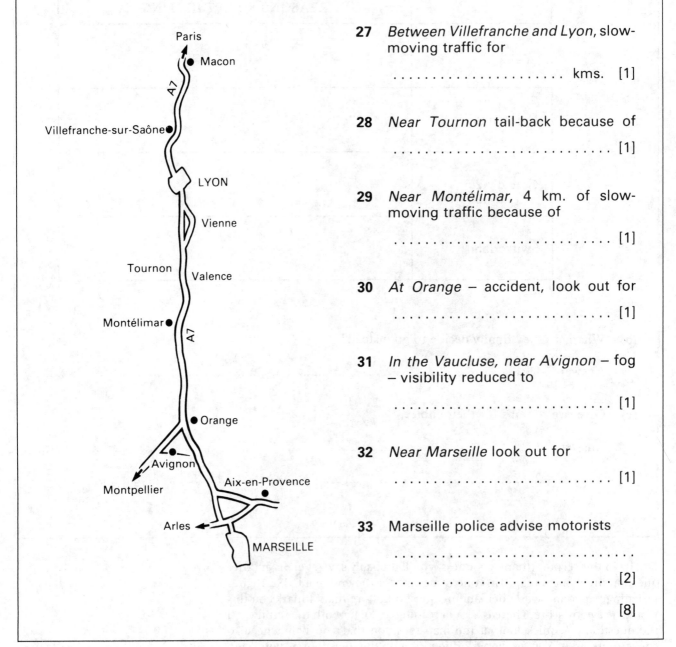

27   *Between Villefranche and Lyon*, slow-moving traffic for

.... kms. [1]

28   *Near Tournon* tail-back because of

.... [1]

29   *Near Montélimar*, 4 km. of slow-moving traffic because of

.... [1]

30   *At Orange* – accident, look out for

.... [1]

31   *In the Vaucluse, near Avignon* – fog – visibility reduced to

.... [1]

32   *Near Marseille* look out for

.... [1]

33   Marseille police advise motorists

....

.... [2]

[8]

MEG Higher Listening 2, November 1988

Reading

Basic Level

You will always get some tasks on this topic in the GCSE exam because there is so much material available. Three things are very important if you want to do well in this part of the exam.

(a)   You must know all the basic vocabulary.

(b)   You must remember the words which look as though they mean one thing but actually mean something else. There are quite a few of these words in this topic. Without looking back at the vocabulary lists, give the meanings of the following words:

> **le conducteur** –
> **la correspondance** –
> **la station** –

(c)   You must remember facts about the French transport system. In the exam, people can forget even the most obvious things such as driving on the right, as well as other differences such as getting a reduction if you buy ten tickets, having tolls on motorways, giving priority to traffic from the right, and so on.

   Remembering such facts can help you with questions such as these.

Whilst driving through a town you see this sign at a roundabout.

NEA Basic Reading, June 1988

What should you do? (1)

The answer is *Give way* or *Stop if there is traffic coming.* Three possible wrong answers would be:

(a)   *Stop*, by itself. You do not have to stop if there is no traffic on the roundabout.

(b)   *Give way to traffic from the right.* You might write this if you just remembered **priorité** and did not look at the traffic sign (or did not know left from right).

(c)   *Give priorité*, using French spelling.

While on the ferry to France, you pick up an interesting brochure. Its title is:

> **Autoroutes**
> **Cartes et Tarifs 1989**

What will it be about? (2)

Note that there are 2 marks for three pieces of information.
1st mark – *Motorways* (not *roads*).
2nd mark – *Maps and prices (for 1989).* Remember, you pay tolls for most motorway driving in France.

Parking signs are very popular questions, too. This recent one caused problems. Do it first and see how you cope.

TECHNIQUE TIP

1. With traffic signs, look at the *sign* as well as the *language.*
2. Be careful not to write *too short* an answer in these cases.

14   You are driving through a French **town** with your friend's family. You see this sign.

(a)   Which day are you not allowed to park?

.... *(1)*

(b)   Why not?

.... *(1)*

NEA Basic Reading, June 1988

(a)   is no problem. *Tuesday* = 1 mark.
(b)   relies on your knowing that the key word is **marché** (with an accent)
        and *not* **marche** (without an accent). *Market day* = 1 mark.

Remember that capital letters often do not have the accents printed. In this case you could have been misled into thinking the answer was something to do with a *march* or a *walk*. (But use your common sense. Why hold one every Tuesday for 12 hours?)

Here are a number of practice questions for you to work your way through, all from GCSE exams. Notice that there are the usual types of task – single words, notices, multiple choice, lists, etc. (Answers p. 180)

I **(a)**   MEG Basic Reading, November 1988.

4   You have heard that internal flights with Air Inter are reasonably priced for young people. You consult their advertisement and find a list of prices under the heading

> **TARIFS**
> **ALLER SIMPLE**

What does **ALLER SIMPLE** mean?

.... [1]

(b)   MEG Basic Reading, November 1988.

5   You are consulting a local bus timetable for a journey from Boulogne to Le Touquet on a Sunday. You notice this warning

> **ATTENTION**
> A partir de 13 heures les dimanches et jours de fête, un seul arrêt au Touquet: La Gare Routière.

Where will you have to get off the bus in Le Touquet?

.... [1]

(c)   SEG, June 1988.

1.   *At the station in Marseille, the ticket clerk writes down some journey details.*

(a)   How do you get from Toulon to Le Lavandou?   *(1 mark)*

(b)   Where will you find this transport?   *(1 mark)*

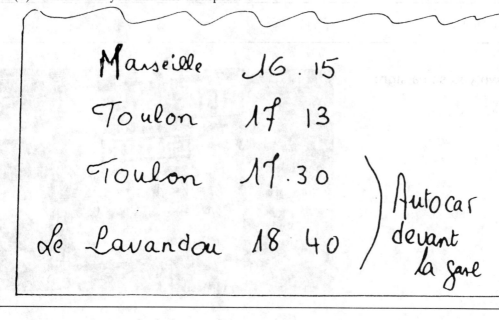

Marseille 16.15
Toulon 17 13
Toulon 17.30
Le Lavandou 18 40) Autocar devant la gare

(d)   MEG Basic Reading, May 1989.

---

10   In the Paris underground you get off one train, wanting to change trains. Which sign should you follow? (Tick one)   [1]

SORTIE   ☐   GARE   ☐

CORRESPONDANCE   ☐   POSTE DE SECOURS   ☐

(e)   MEG Basic Reading, May 1989.

---

7   In town you see four signs at the roadside. Which one means you can park on this side? (Tick one)   [1]

DEFENSE DE STATIONNER   ☐   POIDS LOURDS   ☐

COTE DE STATIONNEMENT   ☐   FEU DE CIRCULATION   ☐

(f)   MEG Basic Reading, June 1988.

---

7   When you return to your car you find some leaflets tucked under the windscreen wiper. One says:

> AUX AUTOMOBILISTES.
>
> M. LE MAIRE RAPPELLE QUE LE STATIONNEMENT DES VÉHICULES EST INTERDIT SUR LES TROTTOIRS

Where does it tell you not to park? .... [1]

(g)   MEG Basic Reading, May 1989.

---

2   In town you see a sign:

What can you hire here? .... [1]

(h)   MEG Basic Reading, May 1989.

8   While driving along a French road you see a sign:

ATTENTION – VIRAGE DANGEREUX

What danger is it warning you of?

.... [1]

(i)   NISEC Basic Reading, June 1988.

7.   This is an extract from an article published by the French equivalent of the AA (Automobile Association). It contains advice for people intending to go off on a long journey by car. Read the article, and then answer the questions.

EN ROUTE

• **Comportement :**
Dormez une nuit complète avant le départ. Mangez légèrement des mets faciles à digérer. Buvez beaucoup... d'eau pure pour éliminer les toxines. Ne vous fiez pas à une impression de récupération après un bref arrêt. **Vous êtes aussi fatigué qu'avant !**

Au bout de 4 heures sur route ou 400 km sur autoroute, reposez-vous au moins 2 heures... mangez léger. Après 8 heures sur route ou 800 km sur autoroute, **allez vous coucher !** ■

Cet article a été écrit par "Auto Défense", hebdomadaire consacré aux conseils et à la défense de l'automobiliste.

(a)   What should you do before setting out?

Answer: ....

....   **(2)**

(b)   What advice are you given about drinking?

Answer: ....

....   **(2)**

(c)   What should you do after 4 hours' driving?

Answer: ....

....

....   **(4)**

(d)   What should you do after 8 hours' driving?

Answer: ....

....   **(1)**

(j)   MEG Basic Reading, November 1988.

> You are at the Gare de l'Est in Paris. You consult a plan of the station at the entrance. The key to the plan lists various places. e.g.
>
> 1   OBJETS TROUVES
>
> 2   BILLETS–GRANDES LIGNES
>
> 3   BILLETS–BANLIEUE
>
> 4   CONSIGNE
>
> 5   BAGAGES, EXPRESS (EXPEDITIONS)
>
> 6   SALLES D'ATTENTE
>
> 7   POSTE DE SECOURS
>
> 8   BUREAU MILITAIRE
>
> 9   DEPARTS–GRANDES LIGNES
>
> 10   DEPARTS–BANLIEUE
>
> Which number on the plan will show where you must go to
>
> 19   leave your suitcase?   [1]
>
> 20   obtain a ticket for a local train?   [1]
>
> 21   the waiting room?   [1]
>
> 22   catch a mainline train?   [1]
>
> 23   the lost property office?   [1]

Higher Level

Brace yourselves! You will probably have more small print to read through on this topic than on any other at Higher Level, and information given is often very detailed, about times, prices, dates, ages (for fare reductions), etc. You have to have your technique right to be able to cope with an example like this one. It was worth 8 marks out of 50 in an exam lasting 40 minutes, which meant that you could afford to spend 6 minutes or so on it. How do you deal with such a task? Remember your technique.

Give yourself 6 minutes for the following task and then look at the notes underneath.

TECHNIQUE TIP

1. Read the setting first, then the questions. Note the marks available.
2. Underline key question words.
3. Mark areas of the text to help yourself.
4. Always read to the end of a sentence before you answer a question, and look carefully at information in brackets.

7   Your friend's family wants to visit the city of Bordeaux and has obtained a brochure from the Tourist Office. Your friend's father turns to this page of the brochure.

Comment se déplacer à Bordeaux.

Avec votre voiture.
La plupart des rues du centre de Bordeaux sont à stationnement limité. (parcmètres individuels ou horodateurs) - Utilisez de préférence les Parcs Autos (payants).
- Allées d'Orléans (D 3), non couvert.
- Allées de Chartres (E 3) non couvert.
- Qu. Louis XVIII (D3 - E3), couvert.
- Quai Richelieu (C 4) - non couvert.
- Gambetta (C 2) - couvert.
- Cours du Maréchal Juin (B 1) - couvert.
- Place de la République (B 2) - couvert.
- Palais des Sports (B 3) - couvert.
Dépannage : Des services de dépannage automobile fonctionnent jour et nuit. Tél. : 56 86 61 70 et 56 91 45 22. L'Office de Tourisme tient à votre disposition la liste des représentants des marques françaises et étrangères.
Automobile Club : 8, place des Quinconces (D 3) — Tél. : 56 44 22 92.
Etat des routes : C.R.I.R. — Tél. : 56 96 33 33.

En autobus.
Ils vous permettront de vous déplacer facilement dans Bordeaux et la Communauté Urbaine.
A chaque arrêt, un panneau vous indique le parcours de la ligne et les différents arrêts. Vous payez au conducteur en montant à l'avant de l'autobus. Indiquez lui votre destination, il vous délivrera les billets nécessaires. Des carnets de réduction (10 billets) peuvent être achetés dans les bureaux de transports situées Place Gambetta (C 2) et à la Gare Saint Jean, face à la sortie de la Gare, ainsi que chez des commerçants près des arrêts d'autobus.
Des plans complets du réseau sont à votre disposition à l'Office de Tourisme.

Taxis.
Plusieurs stations à Bordeaux et en Banlieue. 2 stations fonctionnent jour et nuit. A la gare Saint-Jean (Tél. : 56 91 48 11) et Pl. Gambetta (Tél. : 56 48 00 79). Il est également possible d'appeler un Radio-Taxi (Tél. : 56 96 00 34-56 86 80 30).

Les tarifs sont affichés dans les voitures. Attention : suppléments pour l'Aéroport, le Lac et le service de nuit.

Service spécial Aéroport.
Un autobus spécial (toutes les 1/2 heures en semaine, service réduit le dimanche) relie l'Aéroport à la Gare et à l'Office de Tourisme. Durée du trajet 20 à 30 minutes. On paie au conducteur.
Location de vélos
Gare Saint-Jean, tél. : 56 91 34 20, rue Domercq — Bordeaux.
Ecocycle, tél. : 56 96 07 50, avenue Aristide-Briand — Mérignac.
GO, tél. : 56 34 47 54, avenue Kennedy — Mérignac.

He asks you these questions.

(a)   If we take the car, what's it like for parking in the city centre?

.... (1)

(b) It might be easier not to use the car. Tell me how to use the bus.

....

....

.... (3)

(c) What does it say about taxi fares?

....

.... (2)

(d) If we decide to fly to Bordeaux, what does it say about connections between the airport and the city?

....

.... (2)

NEA Higher Reading, June 1988

Notes

(a)   Only 1 mark available. Underline **voiture** and **centre de Bordeaux.** As you read through you find the word **limité** which you could also underline, but look at the bracket. **Parcmètres individuels** must mean *parking meters*. This tells you that there is a *time* limit, not limited *space*. As you read on, you find a list of car parks and again a bracket **(payant).** This is also important information for anyone driving in Bordeaux. So the points for the answer are: *time limit; parking meters; pay car parks*. Any one fact should give you the mark.

(b)   3 marks here, and there are lots of facts available. Remember to mention as many as you can to give yourself a better chance of 3 marks. Apart from the first sentence the French is fairly straightforward if you are careful. Read to the end of each sentence, including brackets, etc. There are 9 points made which could gain the 3 marks.
      Each stop *shows bus route; it lists all the stops; you pay the driver* (NOT *conductor*); *you get on at the front* (this may seem obvious to you, but it is there so put it down); *tell him your destination; you can buy reduced books of tickets* (*reduced* is the key word); *in transport offices* (NOT *at station*); *and in shops near stops; you can get route maps at the tourist office.*
      If you realised that the whole paragraph was relevant and if you worked through carefully, you should have got at least 2 out of 3.

(c)   The key word is *fares*, so you can ignore the first paragraph and find the French word **tarifs** which you can underline. Then you come to the word **affichés,** which you may not know (it means *displayed*). In this case you could just leave this out and write: *prices are in cabs*. (This technique does not always work!)
      There are another three facts. *You pay extra* (or *more*) *for the airport; for the lake; at night.*
      Remember what *supplement* means in English. Do not write: *it is expensive at night*. Write: *it is more expensive at night*. Any two of the four facts will give you 2 marks.

(d)   To cope with this question, you need first of all to ignore anything to do with bike hire, which has a different heading. There are seven pieces of information:
      There is a special bus. (Do not miss out the word *special*.); *every half hour; reduced service on Sunday; from airport to station; from airport to tourist office; journey takes 20–30 minutes; pay the driver.*

Now use the same technique on these two questions from recent exams and see how you cope. (Answers p. 180)

J   NEA Higher Reading, November 1988.

PAQUES A ROME

8 JOURS DE TOULOUSE 4 950 F
du 27 mars au 3 avril

Place St-Pierre à Rome

1er jour - Jeudi : Toulouse - Nice
● TOULOUSE : Rendez-vous des participants à 9 h à la Gare Routière Matabiau, Quai FRAM. Départ à 9 h 15 par l'autoroute vers Montpellier pour NIMES. Déjeuner. Continuation par Arles, Salon et l'autoroute jusqu'à NICE. Dîner et logement.

2e jour - Vendredi : Nice - Rome
● NICE : Rendez-vous à 7 h 45 devant l'hôtel. Départ à 8 h par Vintimille. Passage de la frontière. Autoroute de la RIVIERA du LEVANT pour PISE. Déjeuner. L'après-midi, continuation par l'autoroute et arrivée à ROME. Dîner et logement.

3e jour - Samedi : Rome
Découverte guidée de la Ville Eternelle. Le matin, visite de la Basilique St-Pierre et la Chapelle Sixtine. Déjeuner. L'après-midi : le Forum, le Colisée et St-Pierre aux Liens. Journée en pension complète.

4e jour - Dimanche (Pâques) : Rome
Matinée libre ou vers 10 h, départ pour St-Pierre afin d'assister à la Messe et recevoir la bénédiction Papale. Déjeuner. Après-midi libre. Vers 20 h 30, départ pour dîner à la Taverne 800 Da Méo Patacca.

5e jour - Lundi : Rome - Florence
Matinée libre. Déjeuner. L'après-midi, par l'autoroute pour FLORENCE. Dîner et logement.

6e jour - Mardi : Florence
Le matin, visite guidée à pied du centre ville : le Dôme, la Cathédrale, le Baptistère, le Ponte Vecchio. Déjeuner. Après-midi libre pour la découverte personnelle ou les achats. Dîner et logement.

7e jour - Mercredi : Florence - Nice
Départ par l'autoroute vers RAPALLO. Déjeuner.
Continuation pour NICE. *(Fin des services pour les participants de Nice).* Dîner et logement.

8e jour - Jeudi : Nice - Toulouse
Départ par l'autoroute jusqu'à Salon, Arles et NIMES. Déjeuner. Continuation par l'autoroute. Arrivée à TOULOUSE, gare routière, vers 18 h 30.

VILLES de DÉPART	PRIX
TOULOUSE BORDEAUX ou LIMOGES	4950 F (billet SNCF inclus)
PARIS	4500 F (+ billet SNCF nous consulter)
NICE	4200 F

Carte nationale d'identité obligatoire. *Nota : 20 participants minimum.*

6 You are staying in the town of Toulouse. Some people who do not understand French want to go to Italy. They show you this brochure.

Answer their questions.

(a) How do we travel?

....
.... *(1)*

(b) When exactly will we cross over into Italy?

....
.... *(1)*

(c) What's the programme for the full day in Florence?

....
....
....
.... *(2)*

(d) Is there anything special we have to take with us?

....
.... *(1)*

K   MEG Higher Reading 2, June 1988.

You are finding out for some friends, how their young children can travel by rail in France. Read this extract from a leaflet published by SNCF and answer the questions as fully as possible in English.

Votre enfant voyage en train

PAGES

LE VOYAGE DE L'ENFANT

VOUS NE POUVEZ PAS ACCOMPAGNER VOTRE ENFANT EN VOYAGE ?

Confiez-le à une hôtesse JVS (Jeune Voyageur Service) : elle est chargée de l'accompagner et d'assurer l'animation de son voyage.
Ce service s'adresse aux enfants âgés de 4 à moins de 14 ans.
JVS plaît aux enfants et rend service aux parents.

COMMENT ORGANISER SON VOYAGE ?

La réservation est indispensable : vous pouvez formuler votre demande dans les gares ouvertes à la réservation et dans les agences de voyages, du lundi au vendredi inclus (sauf les jours de fête) de 8 heures à 18 heures et le samedi de 9 heures à 13 heures et de 14 heures à 18 heures.
La réservation est close la veille du départ à 12 heures, et le vendredi à la même heure pour les départs des dimanche et lundi.

Le prix du voyage JVS comprend :
• le billet de 2e classe : faites valoir les réductions auxquelles votre enfant a éventuellement droit ;
• le supplément JVS (157 F)*, réservation comprise, pour les voyages de jour ;
• le supplément JVS (215 F)*, réservation en place couchée pour les voyages de nuit.

Les bagages : L'enfant peut avoir un bagage à main qu'il doit impérativement pouvoir porter. Son poids, variable suivant l'âge de l'enfant, ne doit pas excéder 10 kg, sous peine de le voir refuser par l'hôtesse au moment du départ.
• Si plusieurs enfants d'une même famille voyagent ensemble, chaque enfant aura son propre bagage afin de ne pas dépasser le poids autorisé.
• L'excédent peut être expédié en bagages enregistrés.

Au départ. Vérifiez que l'enfant est en possession de son billet et du supplément JVS compostés et de ses titres de réduction éventuels.

• L'hôtesse prend en charge les enfants 1 heure au plus tôt et 30 minutes au plus tard avant le départ du train, dans les conditions et aux lieux indiqués au moment de la réservation

Dans le train. L'hôtesse veille à la sécurité de votre enfant et assure l'animation de son voyage. Le nombre d'enfants qui lui sont confiés est limité à 10 maximum.
• Votre enfant voyagera plus agréablement si vous pensez à le munir d'un **repas** et d'une boisson.

A l'arrivée. Demandez aux personnes qui attendent l'enfant d'être présentes au point de rendez-vous 15 minutes avant l'heure d'arrivée du train.
Elles auront à justifier de leur identité et à signer le formulaire de décharge de responsabilité.
• Précisez à ces personnes qu'en cas de retard elles doivent prévenir en temps utile le Service JVS de la gare d'arrivée (vous trouverez les numéros de téléphone des gares concernées en pages 19 à 21 de cette brochure).
Le Service JVS est assuré dans les deux sens entre Paris et de nombreuses gares, et sur certaines relations transversales, ainsi que sur certains parcours intermédiaires (consultez les tableaux des pages 22 à 31).

14 For children of what age is this service applicable?

....

.... [1]

15 What twofold advantage is claimed for the service?

....

.... [2]

16 Where can one book?

....

.... [2]

17 When is the latest booking accepted for a journey on a Monday?

....

.... [2]

18 What does the price include for a night-time journey?

....

.... [3]

19 What limitation is placed on the luggage a child may take?

....

.... [2]

20 What should have been done to the child's tickets on departure?

....

.... [1]

21 How can a parent help a child to have a more pleasant journey?

....

.... [2]

22 When should those responsible for meeting the child arrive?

....

.... [1]

23 What should they do if they are delayed?

....

.... [2]

[18]

Finally for this section, here is a recent leaflet advertising reductions for bus travel. Choose any 3 of the 6 categories and give details as required. (Answers p. 180)

L   TYPE OF TRAVELLER   TYPE OF TICKET   REDUCTION

(9 marks)

ROULEZ MOINS CHER AVEC
LE CARNET DE 5 BILLETS
UTILISABLE SUR TOUTES LES LIGNES ET A TOUS MOMENTS, à durée de validité illimitée.
Il est pratique pour tous ceux qui utilisent les BUS VERTS par intermittence et qui désirent quand même avoir un PRIX DE TRANSPORT ECONOMIQUE
près de **25%** de réduction sur le billet de base

ROULEZ MOINS CHER AVEC
LA GRATUITÉ :   NOUVEAU
Les enfants de moins de 10 ans accompagnés d'un parent voyagent gratuitement sur les lignes des BUS VERTS.
Très agréable pour toutes les mères de famille qui peuvent ainsi se déplacer avec leurs jeunes enfants sans dépenses supplémentaires.

ROULEZ MOINS CHER AVEC
LE CARNET HEBDOMADAIRE
Le carnet qui comprend 10 Billets utilisables par 1 seule personne au cours d'une même semaine (dimanche compris) est particulièrement recommandé aux voyageurs qui se rendent quotidiennement à leur travail EN BUS VERTS.
près de **50%** de réduction sur le billet de base

ROULEZ MOINS CHER AVEC
LES PLACES VERTES
Le même trajet à moitié prix. Vendus en carnets de 5 Billets d'une durée de validité illimitée, ces billets sont **utilisables sur les services colorés en vert sur l'horaire.** Intéressants dès que l'on peut voyager en "heure creuse".
50% de réduction sur le tarif de base

ROULEZ MOINS CHER AVEC
LA CARTE PLUS   NOUVEAU
C'est une carte offrant un nombre **illimité** de voyages, SUR UN PARCOURS DONNÉ. Le prix du coupon mensuel est égal au prix du carnet hebdomadaire x par 4. Simple et pratique la CARTE PLUS est idéale pour tous ceux qui voyagent souvent.
près de **50%** de réduction sur le billet de base

ROULEZ MOINS CHER AVEC
LE BILLET DE GROUPE
Utilisable par un groupe d'au moins 10 personnes voyageant ensemble. Très économique pour tous les déplacements de loisirs dans le Calvados.
près de **55%** de réduction sur le tarif de base

RENSEIGNEMENTS VOYAGEURS : téléphoner au (31) 86.55.30 à Caen - (31) 62.49.95 à Lisieux
ECRIRE AU SERVICE COMMERCIAL - BUS VERTS - STDC - Place du Canada - 14000 Caen

Speaking

Basic Level

You are quite likely to get a role-play involving travel at Basic Level in one of the following areas: finding the way; travelling by car; travelling by bus/coach; travelling by train. Remember that at Basic Level, getting your message across is the important thing. For instance, as far as finding the way is concerned, a common task would be:

Ask how to get to the railway station.
The text-book answer would be:

Pour aller à la gare, s'il vous plaît?
But you would get the same mark for:

La gare, s'il vous plaît?
You would probably also get your mark for:

Pour le train, s'il vous plaît?

This is an extreme example, as everyone knows the word for *railway station*. But suppose you had to ask for the *police station* (**le commissariat**), a long and difficult word for some people to remember. You could cope by asking for **la police, s'il vous plaît.**

A word which often comes up when finding the way is *far* (**loin**), and people often forget this word or are unsure about pronouncing it. Remember that you will get the same answer by asking if something is *near*, or by using the phrase **à quelle distance d'ici?** or **combien de kilomètres d'ici?** Look at this recent GCSE role-play and see how you would cope.

You are on your way to the South of France. You stop the car to ask the way. Your teacher will play the part of a passer-by and will start the conversation.
(a)   Ask if there is a petrol station nearby.
(b)   Ask if it's far.
(c)   Say thank you very much and goodbye.

NEA, May 1989

(a)   If you forget the word for *petrol station* (**station-service**), you can cope by saying what you want to do (*buy petrol*).
(b)   You have already used **près d'ici** in (a), so you cannot ask the same question. Use **à quelle distance?** or **c'est loin?**
(c)   Do not forget to say *very much* or *goodbye*. Often the last bit of a role-play is the least well done, because you are relieved about getting the hard bit over, or because you are already thinking about the next role-play. Do not rush too much.

Now work out how you would cope with these two roles. The first one is recorded on tape (S14). How well do you think the candidate gets the messages across?

You are travelling through France by car with your parents. It's getting late and you want to get to Avignon by nightfall but you are lost. You stop in a village to ask directions from a passer-by.
1.   Ask if it is far to Avignon.
2.   Find out where the road to Avignon is.
3.   Ask if there is a motorway.
4.   Say that you would like to arrive in Avignon today.
5.   Find out if there is a hotel in the village.

MEG, May 1988

You are in France with your parents travelling by car towards Nice. You need petrol so you stop at a service station. Your parents do not speak French, so you must speak to the attendant.
    The role of the attendant will be played by the examiner.
1.   Buy 30 litres of 4-star petrol.
2.   Say you would like 2 litres of oil.
3.   Ask how much you have to pay
4.   Ask if there are any toilets.
5.   Find out if this is the road to Nice.

MEG, May 1988

We will end with one role-play on each of the topics of travelling by coach and travelling by train. Prepare these and make sure you have something to say for each task. How can you get round *a long journey*? (Remember that **journée** means *day*, NOT *journey*.)

You are on holiday in France and you want to take a coach journey from the town in which you are staying to Dijon. You have just arrived at the coach station and you are making enquiries at the information desk.
    The role of the information clerk will be played by the examiner.
1.   Find out if there is a coach to Dijon.
2.   Ask if it is a long journey.
3.   Find out what time the coach leaves.
4.   Ask where you can buy a newspaper.
5.   Find out if there is a cafe nearby.

MEG, Autumn 1988

You are on holiday in France staying in a small town not far from Paris. You decide to go by train to Paris for the day and have just arrived at the station ticket office.

The role of the ticket-office clerk will be played by the examiner.

1.   Ask for a return ticket to Paris.
2.   Find out how much it costs.
3.   Ask when the train leaves.
4.   Find out which platform it leaves from.
5.   Ask if it is a fast train.

MEG, May 1988

Higher Level Role-plays

As usual, you are expected to react to what the examiner says, give further details, make choices etc., so the better prepared you are, the better your performance will be. Look at this example. You have quite a lot to prepare here. Think about it first and then look at the notes below.

You are on a cycling holiday in France and you have travelled to Tours by the 14.15 train from Paris. On arriving, you go to collect your bicycle from the luggage office.

The role of the attendant will be played by the examiner.

1.   Say that you have come for your bicycle.
2.   Say that you have your ticket and give your name.
3.   Describe the bicycle.
4.   Say which train you travelled by.
5.   Ask at what time you should call back.

MEG, Autumn 1988

1.   You can solve this one by saying **je voudrais mon vélo, s'il vous plaît,** rather than try to sort out the verb.
2.   **Voici mon billet.** (The word **ticket** is not used for train travel.)
3.   This is a common task for Higher Level.
4.   Remember 24-hour clock time.
5.   Do not worry too much about *call back*. Probably the examiner is going to say something after Task 4 which will include it. You should be all right just by saying **à quelle heure?**

Here is another example of a problem-solving role-play with the essential information part. The tasks involve a phone conversation, so remember you will need to say **allô** the first time you speak. It may be one of the points being tested. This role-play is recorded for you on the cassette (S15).

TECHNIQUE TIP

> When asked to describe something, mention *colour* (two colours where possible) and *size* if appropriate (**petit** or **grand** will usually be enough). Do NOT get technical. The best colours to use are **bleu, jaune, rouge, noir,** because the pronunciation never changes.

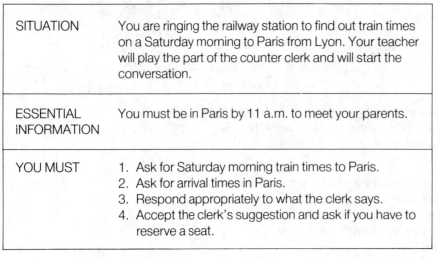

SITUATION	You are ringing the railway station to find out train times on a Saturday morning to Paris from Lyon. Your teacher will play the part of the counter clerk and will start the conversation.
ESSENTIAL INFORMATION	You must be in Paris by 11 a.m. to meet your parents.
YOU MUST	1. Ask for Saturday morning train times to Paris. 2. Ask for arrival times in Paris. 3. Respond appropriately to what the clerk says. 4. Accept the clerk's suggestion and ask if you have to reserve a seat.

NEA, May 1989

Lastly, here is an example of the narrative type of role-play which one exam board (MEG) uses. It is well worth while practising this type of role-play even if your exam board is different, because in the *conversation* part of the Oral for all boards the topic of travel and holidays comes up, and at Higher Level especially you are expected to be able to talk about past trips to France (or anywhere else). It helps a great deal with Writing, too. We have not included a speaking grid for these last four topics but you should certainly make some notes, as part of your Oral preparation, about last year's holiday, and what you did last Easter, as well as holiday plans for the coming summer. Give yourself a few minutes to prepare this task, remembering the technique tips from Unit 4. If you can, record your version on to a blank cassette.

One candidate's answer is on the Speaking Tape (S16): Listen to how she copes.

SPEAKING : CANDIDATE AS NARRATOR   *(20 marks)*

HIGHER LEVEL   PART 2

CANDIDATE'S SHEET

The plan printed below gives an outline of a trip to France last summer.

Tell the Examiner about the journey and what happened on it. You need not mention every detail of the outline on the page and you can, for example, decide whether it was you who made the trip or someone you know.

Be prepared to respond to any questions or observations the Examiner might make.

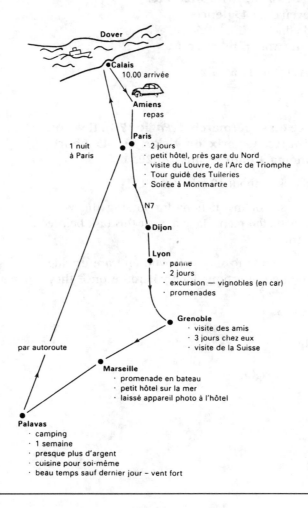

Basic Writing

There are not all that many tasks you could be set purely on the topic of travel and holidays. Most would involve writing about what you did on holiday (e.g. topics such as free time, shopping, food and drink), rather than how you got there. As you cover more topics you should find this kind of task fairly straightforward, and we'll look at some examples later on. Here, first of all, are two more restricted tasks.

It is your French pen-friend's first day at your house. You are at school but you are going to meet her afterwards in town. You leave a note telling her how to get to town from your house by bus. Tell her:
1.   The bus stop is opposite the supermarket.
2.   She should take the number 17 (NOT the 17B)
3.   The bus comes every 10 minutes.
4.   The fare is 45p.
5.   She should get off outside the cinema.
6.   You will meet her at 4.20.

Do you remember how to cope with words you don't know? There is usually a way round. Let's look at some examples.
1.   *bus stop:* You could write **prends le bus.**
       opposite: You cannot write **près de** – she might get the bus going the wrong way! You could say **de l'autre côté,** but if you know that, you probably know **en face de** anyway. You could use **à gauche** and **à droite** to solve this, e.g. **le supermarché est à droite – tu prends l'autobus à gauche.**
2.   Write the figure as a figure. If you cannot remember **pas** for *not* you could put **le 17B est différent.**
3.   *Every 10 minutes:* **Il y a un bus à 3h, 3h10, 3h20, etc.**
4.   *Fare:* Write **le ticket,** or even **c'est 45 pence.**
5.   *Outside:* **au cinéma** will do fine.
6.   For any meeting, just use the word **rendez-vous.**

Here is a more straightforward version of this task.

> **Christine**
> **Pour aller en ville.**
> **Prends le bus 17 en face du supermarché. (***Pas* **le 17B). Il y a un bus toutes les 10 minutes. Le prix du ticket est 45 pence. Descends devant le cinéma. Rendez-vous à 4h20.**

You should be able to do such a task in about 10 minutes.

Another possibility would be a set of instructions for finding the way, possibly linked to a town plan or sketch map. Have a go at this task before checking with the version underneath.

Your pen-friend and family are coming to stay with you and are driving from Dover. You send them written directions for their route once they leave the motorway. Tell them:
1.   Leave the motorway at Exit 18.
2.   Don't go through the town.
3.   Turn left at first traffic light.
4.   Cross the bridge.
5.   Your street is the second on the right.

Write your answer here:

Here is a possible correct version. (Of course, there are other possibilities.)

1. **Quittez l'autoroute à la sortie 18.**
2. **Ne traversez pas la ville.**
3. **Tournez à gauche au premier feu (rouge).**
4. **Traversez le pont.**
5. **Notre rue est la deuxième à droite.**

Now here are the recent exam tasks we promised earlier. The first one is a postcard, with a completed postcard in French as stimulus. Remember, you can use any words from the postcard which fit in with the task. Allow yourself 10 minutes for this task. (Answers p 180)

M

---

4.   You received the following postcard last winter from your French pen-friend.

> Le 2 février
>
> Je suis en vacances de neige avec ma classe du collège. Il fait beau et il y a beaucoup de soleil. On a des cours de ski tous les après-midi, c'est fatigant ! Le soir il y a des boums. C'est fantastique !
>
> Amitiés
> Chantal

Write a postcard of 25–30 words **in French**, saying:

(1) you are in Paris on a school trip.

(2) it is very cold.

(3) you go on outings every day.

(4) what you like about Paris.

(5) what you don't like about the trip.

N Now, a note. Think about this one. Is there anything the note does not say which you must include? (Which hotel?) Also, what will you do about 2 p.m.? Again, give yourself 10 minutes for this one.

On holiday in France, you decide to call on your French friend when passing through the town where he/she lives. Unfortunately there is nobody at home, but your parents say that you can stay in the area for a day or two, so you leave a note telling your friend the following information.
(i)   You are on holiday in France.
(ii)   You arrived here at 2 p.m.
(iii) You are staying at a hotel in town.
(iv)   Suggest having dinner together this evening.
(v)   Ask your friend to phone you at the hotel.

MEG, May 1989

The last task is a letter. You can afford to spend just over 15 minutes on it. When you have done it, it would be worth showing this one to a teacher if you can. You see that three or four topics are involved, so this would be a good test of your progress. Remember to do the tasks in order, so that you do not miss anything out.

O

---

2   Your French pen-friend, Emmanuelle, has sent you this letter.

Le 7 mai

Salut !

J'ai bien reçu ta carte postale. Avec le soleil, je commence à penser aux grandes vacances. Mais toi, pour combien de temps es-tu en vacances cet été ?

Je vais partir en Italie avec mes parents, pour deux semaines. Et toi, qu'est-ce que tu vas faire pendant l'été ?

J'espère qu'il va faire chaud. Quel temps fait-il en Angleterre, l'été ? Je voudrais aller à la plage tous les jours, pour me baigner et faire du sport. Et puis, le soir, je pense que je vais aller voir mes amis au café. Et toi, qu'est-ce.que tu fais le soir pendant les vacances ?

Dis-moi, qu'est-ce que tu penses faire en Septembre, après tes vacances?

Je t'embrasse

Emmanuelle.

Write a letter **in French,** in reply, telling her:

— how long you are on holiday for during the summer;
— what you are going to do this Summer;
— what the weather is like in England in Summer;
— how you spend your evenings when you are on holiday;
— what you are thinking of doing in September, after the holidays.

Put down **all** the information you are asked to give. The number of words is not important.

....
....
....
....
....
....
....
....
....
....
....
....
....
....
....
....
....
....

GOING ABROAD – SOMEWHERE TO STAY

The words you need

un hôtel hotel	**l'étoile** star
l'ascenseur lift	**l'escalier** stairs
la chambre bedroom	**la douche** shower
le cabinet de toilette washing facilities (wash-basin) in room	
la pension complète full board	**la clef** key
la demi-pension half board	**complet** fully booked
la réception reception	**le repas** meal
réserver to book	**la réservation** reservation
servir to serve	**le reçu** receipt
les bagages luggage	**la valise** suitcase
le camping (municipal) (municipal) camp-site	
le terrain (de camping) (camp-)site	
faire du camping to go camping	**le bloc sanitaire** toilet & washrooms
la caravane caravan	**les draps** sheets
l'eau (non) potable (non) drinking water	
l'emplacement site (for tent/caravan)	
l'électricité electricity	**électrique** electric
la poubelle waste-bin	**le supplément** extra payment
la tente tent	**la salle de jeux** games room
se plaindre to complain	**il ne marche pas** it doesn't work
propre clean	**sale** dirty
cassé broken	**à emporter** take-away
	le gardien warden
l'Auberge de Jeunesse Youth Hostel	
le gîte holiday cottage	

What you need to be able to do.

– Understand people talking or writing about holiday accommodation, hotels, camp-sites, hostels, gîtes.
– Make bookings for accommodation both orally and in writing.

This topic seems more restricted than those we have studied so far, but tasks on it come up very often in exams, and of course it is very useful if ever you go to France on holiday.

Listening

Basic Level

Room numbers and prices will come up quite often, and so will facilities at camp-sites, opening and closing dates, etc. You should find most of this straightforward if your numbers are securely learned – and they ought to be by now. Here is a typical example of what you can expect.

While driving through France on a camping holiday with your family, you hear on the radio an advert for a new camp-site which sounds interesting. Listen to the recording and write down the required details.

1. When is the camp-site open? (2)
2. How many places are there altogether? (1)
3. List 3 of the facilities available on the camp-site. (3)
4. How much would it cost per day for a family of four? (2)

This should be fairly easy, but have you read the questions carefully? There could be problems which are not obvious. For example, Question 1 says *When is the camp-site open?* NOT *When does it open?* So you will want *open from . . . to. . . .*

Question 2. The word *altogether* suggests that you may hear different numbers as well as a total. (You should not be expected to add up – this is not an arithmetic exam – but you might be thrown by hearing all these numbers.)

Question 3. You know there will be more than 3 facilities mentioned, but notice the little word *on the camp-site*.

Question 4. There are 2 marks so there must be at least 2 facts.

 Now listen to the recording (L33 on cassette) and write your answers below before checking with the notes on the answers (p. 180).

1.

2.

3. (a)

   (b)

   (c)

4.

Answers: 1. *Easter Monday/to end of September* = 2 marks. (Monday by itself would not mean anything, and the only 'special' Monday is Easter Monday. *Until September* would not be clear enough.)
2. 160 (do not bother to write down the other numbers as well) = 1 mark.
3. Any 3 of games room/swimming pool/(free) hot showers/restaurant/ caravan hire – 3 marks
4. = 89 francs/if two children under seven = 2 marks. (Children become adults very early on French camp-sites.)

6 out of 8 is a fair score for this task, which is quite a long one for Basic Level, and should have warmed you up nicely for these 3 GCSE tasks, one on each of hotel, camp-site and gîte. Work through these (L34–36 on cassette) and check your answers on p. 180.

A   When you arrive in France you go to your holiday gîte (cottage) in a village in the Vendée. You find the owner waiting to greet you.

(a)   What **two** things does she say to you?

Answer 1 _____

   2 _____

(b)   What does she say about the keys?

Answer 1 _____

2 _____

(c)   What two activities does she then mention?

Answer 1 _____

2 _____

NEA, May 1989

B Questions 15, 16 and 17—*You have arrived at a camp site and asked if there is a site free, and what facilities there are.*

15.   Where is the vacant site?   *(2 marks)*

....

....

16.   What facility is available for children?   *(1 mark)*

....

17.   Where is the beach?   *(1 mark)*

....

C Questions 22, 23, 24, 25 and 26—*You are at the reception desk of a French hotel and overhear the following conversation between a man who has just arrived and the receptionist.*

22.   Why can't the man have two rooms on the same floor?   *(1 mark)*

....

23.   Which is his son's room number?   *(1 mark)*

....

24.   Where is the luggage?   *(1 mark)*

....

25.   When is the family going to have dinner?   *(1 mark)*

....

26.   What is the man requested to do before dinner?   *(1 mark)*

....

SEG, Summer 1988

Higher Level

So far at GCSE there have been very few examples of Higher Listening tasks on this topic. You could expect such things as people complaining about facilities or discussing which hotel or camp-site to stay at from a list, interviews with young people about why they like camping, etc.

The following task deals with the topic of Youth Hostels and is a quite demanding one. Look carefully at the questions before you attempt this task. Remember your technique.

TECHNIQUE TIP

Underline the -s of plural words in questions, for example in Questions 27 and 31.

The answers are on p. 180. More than 3 marks out of 6 and you can feel pleased with yourself. (L37 on cassette)

D   MEG Higher Listening, November 1988.

Exercise 4: Questions 27–32

You will hear a conversation recorded in the tourist office in Rennes. A girl is making enquiries about the local youth hostel.

Look at questions 27–32.

Now listen to the conversation, which you will hear twice, and then answer the questions in English.

27   For which months of the year is the hostel open?

. . . . [1]

28   What does the tourist office clerk offer to do for the girl?

. . . . [1]

29   What does the clerk say about the youth hostel card?

. . . . [1]

30   How much does the youth hostel card cost for people over 18 years of age?

. . . . [1]

31   In what parts of the world does she think the International Youth Hostel card is valid?

. . . . [1]

32   What exactly would you be required to pay 51 francs for at the Youth Hostel?

. . . . [1]

[6]

Reading

Basic Level

These tasks will consist mainly of signs and adverts for hotels, camp-sites, etc., and should not be too difficult if you read carefully and keep relying on common sense for such things as prices, opening dates and so on. You may also get extracts from letters offering accommodation.

Look at this extract from a brochure about the Youth Hostel in Caen. In this case the task is a simple yes/no one. Ring YES or NO as appropriate.

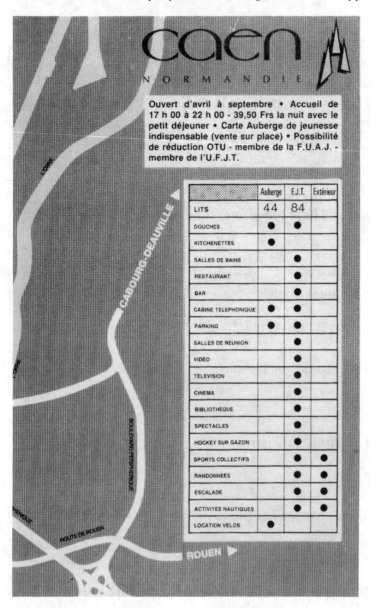

(a)	Open in summer	YES/NO
(b)	Office open in morning	YES/NO
(c)	Breakfast available	YES/NO
(d)	Under 40 francs per night	YES/NO
(e)	Membership card needed	YES/NO

Assuming you know the meaning of **indispensable,** you should get all 5 marks here, unless you forgot that **39,50FR** means **39 francs 50 centimes** (the comma is the same as a decimal point).
Answers: 1. Yes; 2. No; 3. Yes; 4. Yes; 5. Yes.

The next task is from a camp-site brochure. There are 3 marks for it. Be careful not to miss out the first detail. Do the task first and then check below to see whether you got it all.

CAMPING REINE MATHILDE***ᴺᴺ

ETREHAM - 14400 BAYEUX
TÉL. 31 21 76 55
R.C. en cours

SUR PLACE

Restaurant - Petit déjeuner - Bar - Glaces - Gaufres - Crêpes - Beignets - Pâtisserie

Télévision - Bibliothèque - Tournoi de boules - Ping Pong - Portique adultes et enfants - Toboggan

En saison : boulangerie - Alimentation tous les matins sur le terrain.

Where and when can you buy bread and groceries at this camp-site? (3)

Answer:

Notes:

Two of the details are easy. *Every morning* (not *every day*, which you could write if you were careless), *on the camp-site* (it seems obvious but you must put it in – it's probably a van which comes every morning). The third detail comes first: *in the season*. You will find lots of references to *the season* in Reading tasks on this topic. You may have missed it out because your eye went straight to the key words **boulangerie - alimentation.**

Here is a longer example dealing with hotel reservations, which you can make through many tourist offices in France. You need to look carefully at the small print here. It is quite tricky for Basic Level, but it follows on conveniently from what you have just been doing.

Study the following extract carefully and answer the questions about hotel reservations in Paris.

PARIS

ACCUEIL DE PARIS / ILE DE FRANCE
**Départements de Paris / Seine-et-Marne / Yvelines / Essonne
Hauts-de-Seine / Seine-Saint-Denis / Val-de-Marne / Val-d'Oise**

OFFICE DE TOURISME DE PARIS
127, avenue des Champs-Élysées, 75008 PARIS
☎ 47.23.61.72 / ⊺ₓ 611 984

Heures d'ouverture :
Saison : Pâques au 31 Octobre
9 h-20 h tous les jours
Hors saison : 9 h-20 h / 9 h-18 h le Dimanche

AUTRES BUREAUX :
assurant exclusivement les réservations hôtelières à Paris et en Ile-de-France
(fermés le dimanche - sauf les bureaux Gare du Nord et Tour Eiffel ouverts en saison).

GARE DU NORD ☎ **45.26.94.82**
Saison : 8 h-22 h / 13 h-20 h le Dimanche
Hors saison : 8 h-20 h

GARE D'AUSTERLITZ ☎ **45.84.91.70**
Saison : 8 h-22 h / Hors saison : 8 h-15 h

GARE DE L'EST ☎ **46.07.17.73**
Saison : 8 h-22 h / Hors saison : 8 h-20 h

GARE DE LYON ☎ **43.43.33.24**
Saison : 8 h-22 h / Hors saison : 8 h-20 h

TOUR EIFFEL ☎ **45.51.22.15**
Ouvert de Mai à Septembre, tous les jours : 11 h-18 h

ACCUEIL / INFORMATION / PROMOTION / CONGRÈS

PARIS SÉLECTION LOISIRS 24 H SUR 24

**Information en français : 47.20.94.94
English Information : 47.20.88.98
Auskünfte auf Deutsch : 47.20.57.58**

1. I want to reserve a hotel room at the Office de Tourisme in the Champs Elysées. Is it open all year? (1)
2. Where else could I reserve a room on a Sunday in August? (2)

Answers: 1. *Yes.* (You can work out that **hors saison** must mean *out of season*.)
2. *The Gare du Nord and the Eiffel Tower.*

Here are some GCSE questions for you to try. (Answers on pp. 180–181.)

E MEG Basic Reading, June 1988.

---

3 You are looking for overnight accommodation. In the front window of one hotel you see the sign:

L'HÔTEL EST COMPLET

What does this mean? .... [1]

F SEG, May 1989.

---

10.   *This is an advertisement for a hotel, which you have found in a town guide.*

(a) What is the cost of the dearest room without meals?   (*1 mark*)

(b) When is it closed?   (*1 mark*)

(c) Why is it suitable for children?   (*1 mark*)

HOTEL CENTRAL

1, rue Dr. Veyrat.

MONTMELIAN 73800

Tel: 84.07.24.

Prix:

Chambre: Pension:

90f a 160f.   200f a 260f

Ouvert toute l'année sauf octobre.

Jeux pour enfants.

Vue sur les Alpes.

G NISEC, Summer 1988.

---

3. You have received some information about hotels in Saint-Brieuc, where you hope to spend a few days. Read the information and then answer the questions.

Hôtel **"KER-IZEL"** **NN

SANS RESTAURANT – GARAGE

20, rue du Gouët (centre ville)

SAINT-BRIEUC – Tél. 33.46.29   (**lignes groupées**)

LE SAINT-JOUAN Hôtel Bar

Ouvert tous les jours – Parking – Chambres TV couleurs

R. Renault – 38, rue Th.-Ribot – ST-BRIEUC – Tél. 94.43.71

HOTEL D'ARMOR *Chiens acceptés*
CONFORT
Chambre avec cabinet de toilette ou salle de bains
51, rue de la Gare – SAINT-BRIEUC – Tél. 94.02.60

(*a*) Which hotel would allow you to bring a dog?

Answer: .... **(1)**

(*b*) What number would you ring if you wanted to book a room in a hotel in the middle of town?

Answer: .... **(1)**

(*c*) What are you told about the rooms in the Hotel d'Armor?

Answer: .... **(3)**

(*d*) Apart from the fact that it has a garage, what are you told about the Hotel Ker-Izel?

Answer: .... **(1)**

(*e*) When is the Saint-Jouan open?

Answer: .... **(2)**

H SEG, June 1988.

8. *You have written to a hotel in France to reserve two twin-bedded rooms for the period 2nd July to 18th July. This is part of the reply from the hotel.*

Give *full* details of the type of rooms you are being offered and the facilities they contain. *(4 marks)*

> Nous ne pouvons malheureusement pas vous offrir deux chambres
> à lits jumeaux pour la période du 2 au 18 juillet que vous
> désirez.
>
> Cependant, nous pouvons vous proposer pour ces dates une chambre
> à deux lits et une chambre à grand lit. Toutes deux sont équipées de douche et de W.C.

I MEG, June 1988.

Study this leaflet for a campsite. A friend would like your help in deciding whether it will suit his requirements. Answer his questions as fully as possible in English.

CAMPING - CARAVANING
DU BLANC PIGNON
LA CALOTERIE
62170 Montreuil-sur-mer Tél: 21.06.03.64

Au pied des remparts, de la Citadelle de Montreuil-sur-Mer

OUVERT TOUTE L'ANNÉE

TENTES • CARAVANES • MOBIL-HOMES
Forfait à l'année - Week-ends

LOCATION DE CARAVANES

Calme - Promenades
Pêche - Cadre riant

Jeux pour enfants

EAU • LAVABOS • ÉVIERS
DOUCHES CHAUDES GRATUITES

Magasin d'Alimentation à proximité

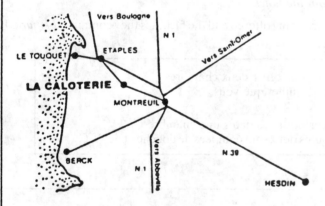

- A 2 kms, Montreuil-sur-Mer :
  Ville historique et commerciale, piscine chauffée, tennis...
- La mer à 12 kms : Le Touquet, Berck, Stella-Plage, Merlimont...

Imprimer 90 Taucourt 22.29.90.79

---

17 When is the site open? ....

....

....

.... [1]

18 What special facilities are there for children? ....

....

....

.... [1]

19 What **two** things does it say about the showers?

   (i) .... [1]

   (ii) .... [1]

20 What opportunities are there for swimming in the area?

   (i) .... [1]

   (ii) .... [1]

21 What **two** other activities are possible?

   (i) .... [1]

   (ii) .... [1]

22 What can be rented on the site? ....

....

.... [1]

23 What sort of shop is nearby?

....

.... [1]

Higher Level

Here, you may well have a lot of small print to read – or rather skim through while you look for appropriate headings. We shall look at two examples. The first one is quite short.

AUBERGE DE JEUNESSE DE BEAUGENCY

Route du Châteaudun
45190 BEAUGENCY
Tél. 38 44 61 31

- **PRÉSENTATION :** Cité médiévale qui conserve l'empreinte d'un passé riche en histoire (donjon féodal du XIème siècle, églises romanes des XI, XIIème siècles, pont médiéval, château restauré du XVème, Hôtel de Ville pure Renaissance), Beaugency est né de la rencontre de la Loire et des régions complémentaires qui l'encadrent : Beauce et Sologne. Située au cœur de ce Val de Loire royal, la ville peut être le point de départ d'une découverte fertile.
- **MOYEN D'ACCÈS A L'AUBERGE :**
Par le train : Gare de Beaugency (ligne directe Paris/Tours/Bordeaux).
Par la route : Paris 145 km par RN 20 et autoroute Paris / Tours / Orléans 25 km - Blois 35 km. Services de car avec Orléans, Blois.
- **DISTRACTIONS ET SPORTS :** Pêche, tennis, équitation (10 km), natation, magnifique stade municipal dans un parc au bord de la Loire.
L'Auberge de Jeunesse offre 80 places. Camping possible. Elle dispose de 100 vélos et d'un matériel de projection. Elle propose diverses activités : cyclotourisme, tennis, équitation, canoë-kayak, randonnée...

You are planning a youth hostelling trip to France and want to visit the Loire valley. Beaugency looks interesting and you decide to stay there for a couple of nights during your trip. Answer the following questions from the brochure above.

1. What kind of town is Beaugency likely to be? (1)
2. You haven't got a car, so how could you get there? (2)
3. If the Youth Hostel was full, what could you do about accommodation? (1)
4. Why might the Youth Hostel be a good base to tour from? (1)

Notes:

1. *Old, historic, mediaeval* or similar words. There are all sorts of clues to this, and you should recognise the words **médiéval, passé, histoire, château.**
2. *By train* is obvious. Did you spot and remember the word **car** = *coach*? *By train/or coach* = 2 marks.
3. *You could camp* = 1 mark.
4. This is an inferential question. The **Auberge** has 100 bikes and presumably hires them out (otherwise why mention them?). There is also the word **cyclotourisme,** so *you can hire bikes* = 1 mark. However, there is another possibility which is less easy to find and relies on good knowledge of vocabulary. The last sentence of the first paragraph tells you that Beaugency is *situated in the heart of the Loire valley*. This is just as good an answer, and if you spotted it, well done!

The second task relates to a very large and popular camp-site on the Mediterranean coast.

You have just arrived at the camp-site with your family and are given a fact sheet about the site. You have to help your family understand it.

BIENVENUE A LA CARABASSE ★★★★
WELCOME TO LA CARABASSE ★★★★

Le CAMPOTEL est ouvert de 8 heures à 22 heures.

La circulation des véhicules n'est plus autorisée au delà de 22 heures. Rentrées tardives : les voitures doivent stationner au **parking extérieur.**

BUREAU D'ACCUEIL : 8 h / 22 h. A votre disposition pour tous renseignements Information touristique.

Courrier : Arrivée : distribution dans casiers alphabétiques le matin. Départ : boîte postale à l'extérieur de la réception.
A timbrer : à la réception uniquement de 17 heures à 18 heures par machine à affranchir.

Téléphone : 5 cabines **à monnayeur :** 2 sur le parking extérieur - 3 à l'entrée du Campotel.

Les appels personnels ne peuvent être transmis - sauf les urgences. Les messages sont notés et classés dans le casier alphabétique à la réception où vous devez les retirer.

Départs : Il est souhaitable que le paiement intervienne la veille du départ.

Ouverture de la caisse : 9 h 30 à 12 h et 17 h 30 à 20 h. Les chèques sont acceptés à partir de 300 francs.

Location de voitures
Location de compartiments réfrigérés   } à la réception, aux heures de la caisse
Location de coffres individuels
Vente de Billets AQUALAND

MACHINES A LAVER : Jetons vendus à la réception.

CABINET MÉDICAL : Le médecin assure une permanence le matin de 9 h 30 à 10 heures, et le soir de 18 h 30 à 19 heures.
URGENCE et DIMANCHE, demande de visite à la réception.

BANQUE - CHANGE : SOCIÉTÉ MARSEILLAISE DE CRÉDIT. Ouvert tous les jours sauf DIMANCHE (horaires affichés à la Banque).

SUPERMARCHÉ - BOUTIQUE : Ouverts tous les jours (horaires aux boutiques).

RESTAURANT - BAR - PIZZERIA : de 11 heures à 23 heures.

PLATS A EMPORTER - ROTISSERIE - FAST FOOD - BAR - GLACES : en permanence de 9 h 30 à 23 h.

PISCINE : Badge obligatoire.

TENNIS : 8 h / 22 h. Inscription à la réception - Règlement à l'inscription.

MINI GOLF : S'adresser à la réception.

RANCH : Ouvert en permanence. S'adresser directement au ranch.

ANIMATION : Programme annoncé par affiches. Rendez-vous et INFORMATIONS chaque jour à 12 heures au POINT FIXE ANIMATION.
Un pot d'accueil est offert aux nouveaux chaque jour.

T.V. - PING PONG : Libre accès aux Salles.

PLAGE DE LA CARABASSE : Accès à pied par le fond du camp (traverser la FORET).
Accès automobile par 1ère route à gauche après la Carabasse sur la route de Farinette Plage (Parking).

Club de plage : S'adresser directement à la plage.

URGENCE : A la réception jusqu'à 22 heures. Aux gardes la NUIT - jusqu'à 23 h 30 (réception et mini golf).
La nuit : le premier 1/4 h de chaque heure à la réception ou boîte à messages à la réception.

BONNES VACANCES......

Answer the following questions and then check your answers below. Allow yourself 10 minutes for this task.

1. When does the camp-site close for the night? (1)
2. What do we do if we get back from a drive after that time? (1)
3. Could we receive phone calls at the site? (1)
4. When do they ask us to pay the bill? (2)
5. Is there a doctor permanently on site? (1)
6. How can we find out when the bank is open? (1)
7. What do we do if we want to play tennis? (1)
8. How do we get to the beach? (4)
9. What do we do if there is an emergency after midnight? (3)

Answers:

1. *10 p.m.*
2. *Park outside camp-site.*
3. *Only emergency calls/urgent calls.*
4. *The day before we leave/between 9.30 and 12 or 5.30 and 8.00.*
5. *No.* (Only half an hour in morning and evening.)
6. *Times displayed outside bank.*
7. *Go to reception/enrol at reception.*
8. *On foot/through forest/by car/first left on road to Farinette.*
9. *Go to reception/first quarter of every hour/or leave message.*

A slightly more difficult task is one where you have to decide whether the information is there or not, as well as whether it is true or false. In the following task, you have to decide what counts as *nearby*, and you have to use logic for the question about hot water. (Answers p. 181.)

J NEA Higher Reading, June 1988.

9   You are looking for a suitable camp site to stay a few days. Look through this camp site leaflet which you have obtained from the local tourist office.

PLEYBEN
Camping municipal

PONT COBLANT XX
29190 PLEYBEN

ACCES

PN 12 MORLAIX
N 785 MORLAIX - QUIMPER
Carte Michelin N° 58
Gares S.N.C.F. Châteaulin (10 km)
       routière Châteaulin
Aéroport à Pluguffan

EQUIPEMENTS 80 EMPLACEMENTS

Eau froide
2 douches
12 lavabos
4 éviers
4 lavoirs
8 W.C.
Prise de courant
pour caravanes
Aire de jeux

Snack/restaurant à 100 m
Dépôt de butane   ''
Bar/buvette   ''
Dépôt de glace   ''
Cabine téléphonique à 2 km
Petits magasins à 1 km

CAMPING OUVERT DE PAQUES A FIN SEPTEMBRE

TARIFS

Campeur adulte : 7,20   Emplacement tente : 2,35   Emplacement caravane.: 2,80
Enfant - 7 ans : 2,10   Automobile : 2,10   Branchement électrique :6,00
Véhicule 2 roues : 125 cm3 et + : 1,30   Garage mort : 6,30

You have drawn up a checklist of things you consider important. Tick the appropriate column of your checklist based on the information given in the leaflet.

	YES	NO	INFORMATION NOT GIVEN
Hot water available?			
Swimming pool available?			
Telephone on site?			
Games area?			
Place to eat nearby?			
Grocery shop nearby?			
Bottles of gas available?			

And finally, here is another grid-filling exercise. This time you have to match details to resorts. (Answers p. 181.)

K   LEAG Higher Reading, May 1989.

---

3.   You are staying with a French family who have three children aged 7, 11 and 16. They are planning a holiday and ask you to help them by looking through this leaflet.

BALÉARES Hôtels en EXCLUSIVITÉ

SAVALON Hôtel 1 étoile, classification locale.

GRATUIT
1 ⁄4 de vin et 1 ⁄4 d'eau minérale par repas

PORTALS NOUS
Tél.: 19 (34.71) 67.50.25/26

SITUATION:
Entre ILLETAS et PALMA NOVA, PORTALS NOUS est une petite station idéale pour les vacances familiales. Bordée par une superbe pinède, elle offre de nombreuses possibilités de promenades. Au cœur de la pinède cet hôtel comporte 4 étages (sans as-censeur). Sa situation offre une vue exceptionnelle sur la baie de PALMA. La mer se trouve à 500 m et un service local d'autobus (arrêt à 200 m) dessert PALMA NOVA (5 km) et PALMA (12 km).

A VOTRE DISPOSITION:
Salon avec télévision. Bar. Piscine dé-couverte. Solarium.
Animaux non acceptés.

RESTAURATION:
Le restaurant donne sur la piscine. Menu avec 2 plats au choix.

LOGEMENT:
57 chambres avec salle de bains et téléphone. Possibilité de 3' lit. Courant 110 volts.

ANIMATION ET SPORTS:
Un programme quotidien d'animation diurne et nocturne est assuré par notre animateur. Il vous proposera di-vers jeux, tournois, concours, activités sportives et soirées dansantes ou spectacle.
Avec participation: tennis, mini-golf, pétanque, bicyclette (location du matériel sur place).

Garderie gratuite
Voyage Conseil
Enfants de 5 a 12 ans

ANFORA Hôtel 2 étoiles, classification locale.

Calle San Antonio de la Playa 41
CAN PASTILLA
Tél.: 19 (34.71) 26.16.62

SITUATION:
CAN PASTILLA est une petite station touristique agréable et animée, située à 10 km de PALMA, près de PLAYA DE PALMA.
Proche du petit port et face à la plage (route à traverser), l'hôtel Anfora

GRATUIT
1 ⁄4 de vin et 1 ⁄4 d'eau minérale par repas

comporte 4 étages desservis par un ascenseur.
Bonnes communications pour PALMA ou EL ARENAL (arrêt d'autobus à 50 mètres).

A VOTRE DISPOSITION:
Salon avec télévision, vidéo, bar. Pas de piscine.
Animaux non acc

RESTAURATION:
Formule buffet à tous les repas.

LOGEMENT:
61 chambres avec salle de bains, té-léphone, balcon, chauffage. Possibilité de 3' lit.
Courant 220 volts.

ANIMATION:
Notre animateur vous proposera un programme quotidien d'animation (jeux, concours, soirées, etc.).
Avec participation (à proximité): tennis, mini-golf.

PAX Hôtel 3 étoiles, classification locale.

Garderie gratuite
Voyage Conseil
Enfants de 5 a 12 ans

Avenida
Notario Alemany
MAGALUF
Tél.: 19 (34.71) 68.03.12/16

SITUATION:
A 14 km, à l'ouest de PALMA, MA-GALUF est une station moderne et bien équipée, notamment pour la pra-tique d'activités sportives. L'hôtel Pax, à environ 200 m du centre et de la plage, un peu en hauteur au milieu des pins, est un immeuble de 8 étages desservis par 2 ascenseurs.
Arrêt d'autobus pour PALMA à 300 m.

A VOTRE DISPOSITION:
Salons, télévision, vidéo, bibliothèque, bar, cafétéria et bar hawaïen, salle de jeux, piscine, solarium.
Animaux non acceptés.

RESTAURATION:
Service buffet à tous les repas.

LOGEMENT:
166 chambres avec salle de bains, té-léphone, terrasse, chauffage. Possibi-lité de 3' lit: quelques chambres qua-druples.
Courant 220 volts.

ANIMATION ET SPORTS:
Nos animateurs vous proposeront un programme quotidien d'animation (jeux, concours, soirées, etc.).
Tennis, mini-golf, pétanque, billard (location du matériel sur place).
Avec participation (à proximité): équitation.

POUR LES ENFANTS:
Sur demande: repas spéciaux (à régler sur place).

You make a list of the various points they consider important. The list is given below. Check off the three hotels against the list, putting ticks where appropriate. Do **not** tick all the boxes.

(a)

	Savalon	Anfora	Pax
(i) heating			
(ii) special provision for children			
(iii) games room			
(iv) swimming-pool			
(v) lift			

(9 marks)

(b) You know that your neighbours, who also have young children, are looking for a holiday hotel. They like lively modern places with plenty of sports facilities. Which of these hotels would you recommend to them?

....

(1 mark)

Speaking

Basic Level

Role-plays on this topic are very common. Here are three for you to look at and prepare, with a few notes on each to help you.

(a) You are on a camping holiday in France with some friends. You arrive at the camp-site which you wrote to before leaving home in order to make a reservation.
    The part of the camp-site owner is played by the examiner.
    1.   Say you have made a reservation.
    2.   Say there are four of you.
    3.   Tell the owner you would like to stay for 5 nights.
    4.   Ask if there are any showers.
    5.   Find out if you must pay for the showers.

MEG, Autumn 1988

Notes:
1.   You can leave out the word *made*.
4.   Make sure your voice goes up at the end of the sentence.
5.   You could use the word **gratuit** here.

(b) You are on holiday in France with a friend. You arrive at the Youth Hostel in Arles where you hope to spend a few days.
    The role of the warden will be played by the examiner.
    1.   Ask if there are any places left.
    2.   Say you would like to stay for three nights.
    3.   Say you would like a sleeping bag.
    4.   Ask where the kitchen is.
    5.   Find out when the hostel closes.

MEG, May 1988

Notes:
1.   Leave out the word *left*.
3.   If the examiner does not give you the word for *sleeping bag* and you don't know it, say, **je voudrais quelque chose pour dormir.** The warden would know that you do not mean a sleeping pill!
5.   If you cannot remember the word for *hostel* use **vous fermez.**

(c) You are on holiday in France with your family and you have just arrived at the hotel in which you had reserved some rooms by letter before leaving England.

The role of the hotel receptionist will be played by the examiner.

1. Say you have reserved two rooms.
2. Ask if breakfast is included in the price.
3. Find out what time breakfast is served.
4. Say you would like to have dinner as well.
5. Ask where the dining room is.

MEG, May 1988

Notes:

2. If you forget **compris,** say **pour le petit déjeuner aussi?**
3. You could use **manger** if you do not know *served*. Say **on mange.**
4. If you forget *dinner*, you could use **manger** again, with **le soir.**

Higher Level

This is where you are going to have to complain, ask for changes, etc. Such tasks are popular with examiners and are good practice for real life too, so make the most of them. Look at this recent GCSE example. How would you cope?

Candidate's Rôle-Play Instructions

You arrive at an hôtel in France and find that your letter of reservation has not been received. The examiner will play the part of the receptionist.

1. Explain that you have booked a room and give your name.

2. Express surprise and ask whether your letter has been received.

3. Say when you wrote the letter.

4/5. Say whom you think you wrote to and state the type of room you asked for.

6. Accept the room offered and say how long you will be staying.

7. Enquire whether it is possible to have breakfast in your room.

LEAG, June 1988

You see that in this case you have to invent details for Nos 3, 4, 5 and 6 as well as expressing surprise in No. 2.

Notes:

1. You should be able to do this by now!
2. **C'est bizarre,** or **oh là là!**
3. If you cannot remember **il y a** = *ago*, give a date about a month ago.
4. Always go for the boss, **le directeur.** Do not forget to include saying the bit about *I think that* . . . . There will be a mark for this. The best way to say it is **je crois.**
5. Give two details if possible, e.g. **pour une personne, avec douche.**
6. You can usually get away with **ça va** for accepting anything. Don't forget to say how long for.
7. Use **je peux,** and raise your voice at the end.

Here is a similar one for you to work through and prepare for yourself.

TECHNIQUE TIP

Oh là là, if said convincingly, can express all sorts of emotions!

Candidate's Rôle-Play Instructions

You are on a motoring holiday with your family and have arrived at a small hôtel. You have made no bookings and must explain your requirements to the receptionist. The examiner will play the part of the receptionist.

1.   Greet him/her and explain that you have not reserved.

2/3.   Say that you need a double room for your parents and answer the receptionist's question.

4.   Ask for a room/rooms for your brother and yourself.

5/6.   Find out when the restaurant is open and then say when you would like dinner that evening.

7.   Explain your plans for the following morning.

LEAG, June 1988

Finally, we have recorded another role-play where you have to communicate essential information. Listen to the way the candidate copes with this situation. (S17 on cassette)

SITUATION	You have arrived at a camp-site where you have a reservation. Your teacher will play the part of the site manager and will start the conversation.
ESSENTIAL INFORMATION	You have arranged to stay for 1 week and in your letter you asked for a site near the games area.
YOU MUST	1. Give your name and say you have booked. 2. Say you wrote two months ago. 3. Respond appropriately to the manager's question. 4. Ask what can be done.

NEA, May 1989

Basic Writing

Some GCSE boards include writing a letter asking for accommodation, which is quite a useful exercise. One board gives you an outline and expects you to fill in words. Here is an example. You will see that each word or phrase gets 1 mark. This task is easy if you know the vocabulary and don't rush it. Notice that for No. 5 you have to write the month; **septembre** is the easiest. Note also that **lundi** is the easiest day to write correctly. **Tennis** is an easy sport for No. 7. The message is: do not try to be ambitious. Play safe.

---

2. **You want to make a reservation at a French campsite for yourself and your family. Your French teacher has given you an outline letter with spaces. Using the information given underneath each space, write in French, a suitable word or phrase in each of the numbered spaces provided, so that the letter makes sense.**

(10 marks)

Monsieur/Madame,

Je voudrais réserver un emplacement pour ....
                                                    (1)   vehicle

et .... pour ....
    (2)   type of camping accommodation   *(3)   length of stay*

à partir de ...., le ....
            (4)   day of arrival   *(5)   date of arrival (month to be written*
                                                              as a word)

Nous sommes .... et ....
                (6)   number of adults   *and number of children*

J'aimerais savoir si on peut jouer ....
                                    (7)   a sport

au camping, et s'il y a ....et
                        (8) and (9)   two facilities

....
(9)

Voulez-vous aussi envoyer ....
                            (10)   a leaflet

Veuillez agréer, Monsieur/Madame, l'expression de mes sentiments distingués.

(Signature)...

LEAG Basic Writing, May 1989

Possible completion:
(1) **une voiture;** (2) **une caravane;** (3) **5 jours;** (4) **lundi;** (5) **2 septem-bre;** (6) **2 adultes et 2 enfants;** (7) **au tennis;** (8) **des douches;** (9) **un supermarché;** (10) **une brochure.**

Don't forget the signature!

Now practise this one for yourself. Get it checked if possible. (Specimen answers p. 181)

L   LEAG, June 1988.

2.   You plan to go youth hostelling in France with some friends. Your French teacher has given you the outline of a letter to a youth hostel. The letter contains several numbered spaces. Using the list **below** the letter, write out **in French** the words with which you would fill the spaces if you wrote this letter.

............(1)............

Monsieur/Madame,

Je voudrais réserver ....(2)............ pour la nuit du ....(3)............ Nous

serons ....(4)............ J'aimerais savoir s'il y a ....(5)............ Est-ce qu'on

peut prendre ....(6)............ et louer ....(7)............ à l'auberge?

Est-ce que l'auberge se trouve près ....(8)............ et est-ce qu'il y a

............(9)............?

J'aimerais aussi savoir quels sont les ....(10)............

Veuillez agréer, Monsieur/Madame, l'expression de mes sentiments distingués.

....

(signature)

Answers to be written below:

(1) today's date...

(2) number of beds...

(3) date you wish to stay..

(4) number of boys and girls..

(5) washing facilities (e.g. showers)..

(6) meal(s) provided...

(7) hire bedding (e.g. sheets)..

(8) what is it near?..

(9) sports facilities (e.g. swimming pool)..

(10) prices...

Having had this practice you should now be able to cope with a full letter. Remember always to use a formal beginning and ending like the ones in the two examples above. Formal letters are easier than informal ones really; all you have to do is to learn a few phrases and then slot into them what you want to ask for.

Learn this list of useful phrases, but remember you cannot use them in letters to friends, which should *always* be informal.

Je vous écris pour vous demander   *I am writing to ask*
                                       you (for)
Pouvez-vous me dire s'il y a   *Can you tell me if there is/are*
Pouvez-vous m'envoyer   *Can you send me*
Je voudrais savoir   *I would like to know*
A partir du 10   *From the 10th*
Jusqu'au 17   *Until the 17th*
Est-ce qu'on peut   *Is it possible to*

With these phrases to help you, you should be able to cope with this GCSE question. It would certainly be worth showing it to a teacher for his or her opinion. Allow yourself 15 minutes for this task. Don't forget the beginning, including the date, or the ending, and do the tasks in order. (Specimen answer p. 181)

M   SEG, June 1988.

---

2.   Write a letter in French, of 70/80 words, to the Syndicat d'Initiative at Dinard, including the points below:

(a)   Give the dates when you will be at Dinard with your family.

(b)   Say you would like some information about the town.

(c)   Ask for a town plan and some brochures.

(d)   Ask if you can also have a list of comfortable hotels which are near the sea and which are not expensive.

(e)   Find out if there are some beaches where you can swim, and if there is a swimming pool.

Le
**Syndicat
d'Initiative**
de
D I N A R D

2, boulevard **FÉART**
TÉL. (99) 46.94.12

est à votre
disposition
pour tous
Renseignements

8

FOOD AND DRINK

What you need to be able to do.

- Understand people talking about buying, selling and consuming food and drink.
- Understand menus, shopping lists, adverts etc.
- Buy food and drink in shops, cafés and restaurants.
- Write on the topic of food and drink.
- Know about French eating and drinking habits.

The words you need

les fruits fruit
l'ananas pineapple
la cerise cherry
la fraise strawberry
le melon melon
la pêche peach
la pomme apple

la banane banana
le citron lemon
la framboise raspberry
l'orange orange
la poire pear
le raisin grapes

les légumes vegetables
l'ail garlic
la carotte carrot

le chou cabbage
les haricots verts French beans
les petits pois peas

la salade lettuce

les asperges asparagus
le champignon mushroom
le chou-fleur cauliflower
l'oignon onion
la pomme de terre potato
la tomate tomato

la viande meat
l'agneau lamb
le boeuf beef
le lapin rabbit
le porc pork
le rôti roast meat
saignant rare (steak)
à point medium rare
bien cuit well done

le bifteck steak
le jambon ham
le mouton mutton
le poulet chicken
le steak steak
le veau veal

le poisson fish
les fruits de mer sea-food
les provisions provisions
le fromage cheese
un oeuf egg
une omelette omelette
le saucisson salami
le pain bread
la confiture jam
la farine flour
le poivre pepper
le riz rice
l'huile oil
le vinaigre vinegar

la truite trout
la sardine sardine

le beurre butter
le yaourt yoghurt
le pâté pâté
la baguette French loaf
le biscuit biscuit
le croissant croissant
les pâtes pasta
le sel salt
le sucre sugar
la moutarde mustard
le miel honey

la boisson drink
l'apéritif aperitif
la pression draught beer
le café-crème coffee with milk
le chocolat (chaud) (hot) chocolate
le Coca (cola) Coke

le jus de fruit fruit juice
la limonade lemonade
le vin wine

la bière beer
le café coffee
le cidre cider
l'eau (minérale) (mineral) water
le lait milk
l'Orangina Orangina
une orange pressée orange juice (freshly squeezed)

le repas meal
le petit déjeuner breakfast
le goûter tea (afternoon snack)

le déjeuner lunch
le dîner supper/tea/evening meal

le restaurant restaurant
le self (-service) self-service restaurant

l'addition bill	**le service** service	**l'assiette** plate	**le bol** bowl
la serveuse waitress	**les hors d'oeuvre**	**le couvert** place-setting	**le couteau** knife
	hors d'oeuvre	**la cuiller (à thé)**	**la fourchette** fork
le garçon waiter	**une entrée** starter	(tea)spoon	
	le plat principal	**la nappe** tablecloth	**la soucoupe** saucer
	main course	**la tasse** cup	**le verre** glass
		la carafe jug	
le dessert dessert			
les crudités salads	**les frites** chips	**bon appétit** enjoy your meal	
le potage soup	**la soupe** soup	**à ta santé**	
le gâteau gâteau	**la glace** ice-cream	good health, cheers	
le parfum flavour	**vanille** vanilla	**à votre santé**	
noisette hazelnut	**une portion** a helping	**un pique-nique** picnic	
une tranche slice	**un morceau** a little		
le plat du jour dish of the day			
le menu menu	**la carte** menu		
un sandwich sandwich	**les chips** crisps		
la crêpe pancake	**le hamburger** hamburger		
la saucisse sausage			

Although this unit is a fairly straightforward one, you can see that there is a lot of vocabulary to remember, though you probably already know most of it. It is worth trying to group the words together and learn a group at a time. Some people go to France just for the food, either on mammoth shopping trips in hypermarkets or to have a few really good meals, so the better you can cope with this topic, the more you'll get out of any future trip to France.

Listening

Basic Level

If you think back to Unit 5, we said we would leave shopping for food until now. In this topic area, therefore, you can expect shopping situations as well as restaurant and café ones. You can expect supermarket or hypermarket announcements as well, if they are straightforward. You need to remember some basic facts about food shops in France: for example, you can buy fruit and vegetables at a grocer's; for ham and pork you go to a **charcuterie,** which some examiners call a *pork butcher's* and others a *delicatessen*. You can buy prepared salads and cold snacks here, too.

Here is a straightforward shopping situation where you have to note down four items – remember your note-taking technique, it will help you to keep up. The first time you hear it you could concentrate on items, the second time on amounts, but make sure you listen to the total price each time.

A   You have gone shopping with your pen-friend's father for a few items one Sunday morning. What four items does he buy and what is the total price?

ITEM	QUANTITY
1.	
2.	
3.	
4.	
TOTAL PRICE	

(9 marks)

 With such a task, once you recognise the items you know what kind of quantity is likely, and this helps. Don't forget that you can use short forms for kilo (kg) and grammes (gr). Listen to this one (L38 on cassette), before you check with the answers on p. 181. Set yourself a high target on this task – 8 marks out of 9.

Answers: 1 kilo/tomatoes/6/eggs/1 packet/flour/250 gr/butter/Total price 26F40.

How well did you do? If you did not pick up the *eggs*, for example (notice how the word is pronounced in the plural – no *f* sound), go back and listen again. You will see that you recognise it now that you know the answer, but, more important, you are much more likely to remember it *next* time you hear the word.

Now try your hand at a similar recent exam task. This time, different shops are involved. The last question involves a different topic which you have already covered. (L39 on cassette. Answers on p. 181)

B You are going camping for a few days with a French family. Before setting off on the trip you go shopping for food and some items of camping equipment with your friend's sister.

15. Your friend's sister is asking for some things at the grocer's shop. Name *three* things she asks for.

....

....

....

16. Next, you go to the delicatessen. What does your friend's sister ask for?

....

17. What does she finally buy?

....

18. Now you need to go to a shop which sells camping equipment. Name *two* things she wants to buy there.

....

....

LEAG, June 1988

Restaurant and café tasks at Basic Level usually consist of recognising simple food and drink items. This recent one used the announcement technique. Notice that for the second mark, you had to get both types of meat. (L40 on cassette. Answers on p. 181)

C You go into a large store to do some shopping. At what time do they start serving lunch? (1)

A further announcement in the store gives details of today's menus in the restaurant. What choice of meats is there?
(i) .... (ii) .... (1)

MEG, November 1988

An alternative technique is to use a menu for you to look at. At Basic Level this is very likely to be in English, which is a better test of vocabulary. On the task below you have 16 items to skim through. As you look at this task, you could give yourself a quick vocabulary check. How many of these items could you *say* in French? Of course, *recognising* the vocabulary is much easier than *producing* it. For instance, you will not have to worry about *grated*. If you hear **carottes,** that must be it. The other thing about choosing from a menu is that people sometimes change their minds, or find out that a certain dish is finished and have to choose something else. You need to be careful not to write down or tick too early, in case you have to alter your answer.

Now do the task and check answers on p. 181. Be careful not to get the customers confused. (L41 on cassette)

TECHNIQUE TIP

> Always *cross out* anything you do not want to be marked. Do not just write the correct answer above the error. Examiners will mark what is written *on* the line if there are two choices, so always leave one clear answer. With ticks, do not just put a cross through a tick when you change your mind. Blot it out completely.

D   MEG Basic Listening, November 1988.

You are training to be a waiter/waitress in an English restaurant which specialises in French cooking and attracts French tourists in England. One day a French man and his wife visit the restaurant. The head waiter takes their order in French whilst you tick the items they order on the check list below.

Look at the check list below.

Now listen carefully to the customers' orders and tick what they order in the correct column. Customer one is the man, and customer two is the lady. **Each customer orders FOUR items.**

You will hear the conversation twice.

		FIRST CUSTOMER	SECOND CUSTOMER
Starters:	Onion Soup		
	Tomato Salad		
	Grated Carrot		
	Sardines		
Main course:	Chicken		
	Duck		
	Steak		
	Pork		
Vegetables:	Peas		
	Beans		
	Mushrooms		
	Potatoes		
Drinks:	Beer		
	Red Wine		
	White Wine		
	Mineral Water		

Finally for this level, here is a café situation which has a slightly unexpected last part. See how you cope with this one. (Answers on p. 181. L42 on cassette)

E You are on a day-trip to France.
You get off the boat and head for the nearest café. The waiter comes across.

(a)   What does he ask you?

Answer: .... (1)

(b)   You order two coffees.
What does he ask you next?

Answer: .... (1)

(c)   You ask to pay.
What does he tell you?

Answer: .... (1)

NEA Basic Listening, June 1988

Higher Level

There have not been many exam tasks on this topic at Higher Level as yet. One possibility would be understanding complaints in a restaurant. This could be done as a series of short recordings, which makes it more difficult. You have to listen out for clues and key words as well as remembering what people are likely to complain about. Here are three such complaints. (L43 on cassette)

The restaurant you are in with your friend's family is having a bad day. You can hear quite a few people complaining. Jot down what you think is wrong in each case.

1.   The first customer is complaining about . . . (1)

2.   The second customer doesn't like . . . (1)

3.   The third customer is complaining about . . . (1)

This is quite a testing item. You need to give more than one word for your answers. Detail is important.

Notes:
1.   It is easy to pick up *steak*. But at Higher Level this will not be enough. Common sense tells you that the complaint is going to be about steak being underdone or overdone. But which? You need to listen carefully for what goes with **demandé.** In this case **bien cuit** does, so the answer is **saignant.** *The customer is complaining about the steak being underdone/not cooked enough* = 1 mark.
2.   In this case **15 minutes** is a strong clue. The best answer would be *the slow service.* You would get a mark for *having to wait 15 minutes for his soup,* but probably not for just *having to wait.*
3.   Here you have to spot the word **aussi** to realise that there are two grounds for complaint. *A dirty plate* is not sufficient. You need to recognise **mon verre;** (**verre** can be a difficult word in French as there are several words which sound the same). You should write either *a dirty plate and glass* or *dirty crockery* for 1 mark.

Remember that at Higher Level you often have to put two and two together to get 1 mark. You need to use a similar technique in this recent exam task set in a large store. The second part is slightly unexpected for a shopping situation, but you should have enough vocabulary to cope with it by now. (Answers p. 181. L44 on cassette)

F NEA Higher Listening, June 1988.

---

1   You are shopping in a department store. You hear three announcements. For each
     announcement, to which part of the store are customers referred and for what particular reason?

	PART OF STORE	PARTICULAR REASON
(a)		
(b)		
(c)		

(6)

Reading

Basic Level

Tasks will include shop labels and adverts, menus, etc. Usually these are
some of the easiest questions on the exam paper, if you are careful. These
were the first two questions on a recent paper and should give you three
marks.

NEA, November 1988.

---

1   While walking through a **market** you note some of the prices of vegetables. You see these signs.

PETITS
-POIS
6·70 F
½ kilo

POMMES
DE TERRE
4 F 30
le kilo

HARICOTS
VERTS
8 F 30 le kilo

CHOU-
FLEUR
5 F 00
le kilo

How much would you pay for a kilo of beans? .... *(1)*

2   You are in a **café** looking at the list of ice-creams on the menu. You want a pineapple ice for
     yourself and a strawberry ice for your friend. Put a tick by **each** of the **two** flavours on the list.

Glaces

Abricot	
Ananas	
Banane	
Chocolat	
Citron	
Fraise	
Framboise	
Vanille	

(2)

Answers: 1. *8F30;*   2. **ananas, fraise.**

Just as simple is this recipe extract, provided you read the setting carefully.

---

2.   *Your mother has bought some escalopes of veal in a market in France, and you have found a recipe in a French cook-book. This is the list of ingredients. You have already bought flour, cream and a lemon.*

What **three** other ingredients do you need?   *(2 marks)*

Escalopes à la crème

Ingrédients pour 4 personnes :
4 escalopes
3 dl de crème,
30 g de farine,
50 g de beurre,
1 citron,
sel, poivre.

Préparation : 15 mn
Cuisson : 10 mn

SEG, June 1988

Answers: Butter, salt and pepper.

Sometimes a word is based on another one which you know. Look at this restaurant sign.

MOULIN DE MAINTENAY
CRÊPERIE BRETONNE

2   What sort of restaurant is this? ....,
.... [1]

MEG, June 1988

The key word is obviously **crêperie.** It is safer to write *pancakes* as your answer in this case, and not **crêpes**. Not all British people know what **crêpes** are.

Here are two slightly longer tasks. The first one is based on a Canadian restaurant advert.

1.   What is the Saturday Special at this restaurant?

_____ (3)

2.   When is it available?

_____ (1)

Notes:

For Question 1 you need to include *tea* or *coffee* to get all three marks, as well as soup, roast beef and dessert/sweet/pudding.

    Question 2 looks a bit strange until you notice the top line of the advert. The answer is *in March*.

Look at this advert, which is a good example of the point we have just been making. When could you get a meal in this restaurant? (2 marks)

TECHNIQUE TIP

Treat adverts differently from other reading texts. You can find information spread all over the advert, sometimes even written sideways, diagonally, etc.

Answer
Did you get both points? *From 12 noon to midnight/except on Sundays.*

The second longer task we mentioned is designed to remind you not to take notice of illustrations unless you can see the same items mentioned in the text. Study this advert for Willy's Burger, which sounds like an interesting place to eat in. (Answers p. 181)

G

1.   Apart from burgers, name *three* things you could buy to eat there. (3)

2.   Give *four* reasons why young people might want to eat there. (4)

Higher Level

Tasks on this topic are likely to be quite long and complicated. Recipes, for instance, can be used at this level, and if you can cook you have a much better chance of doing well on them! In this example there are illustrations, but they are not much help with the details. Have a go at this task, allowing yourself 8–10 minutes maximum, then look at the notes below.

1.   While camping in France, you have bought a packet of instant potatoes. Read the instructions, and then answer the questions.

mousline®
au lait

MODE D'EMPLOI
Pour 1 sachet (4 personnes)

Cette purée contient déjà du lait,
vous pouvez donc la préparer
simplement à l'eau en respectant
la quantité de liquide totale.
Si vous aimez
une purée encore plus onctueuse
suivez le mode d'emploi.

(a)   How much milk should you put in the saucepan?

Answer . . . . (1)

(b)   In addition to the liquid, what else should you put in the saucepan, and how much?

Answer . . . .

. . . . (2)

(c)   After bringing the liquid to the boil, what should you do with it?

Answer . . . .

. . . . (2)

1 Mettre dans une casserole 1/2 litre d'eau
+ 1/4 de litre de lait
+ 1 cuillerée à café de sel.
Porter à ébullition.
VOIR CONSEIL MOUSLINE

2 Verser ce liquide dans le plat de service et ajouter un bon morceau de beurre.

3 Dès que le beurre est fondu, verser le contenu du sachet et remuer **très brièvement** de façon à bien recouvrir tous les flocons avec le liquide.

4 Laisser reposer quelques instants (environ 2 minutes) pour que votre purée retrouve sa consistance habituelle.

5 Un tour de cuillère pour la mettre en forme et votre purée est prête.

Proportions pour 2 personnes
Flocons : 1 verre - Lait : 1/2 verre
Eau : 1 verre - Sel : 1/2 cuillerée à café.

(*d*) After adding the contents of the packet to the liquid, what TWO things should you then do?

Answer ....

....

....   (3)

(*e*) If you only want to make 2 portions, how much water would you use?

Answer ....   (1)

NISEC Higher Reading, June 1988

Notes:

(a) *¼ litre*. (It could not be *1–4 litres*.)

(b) *Salt/one teaspoon*. (They will accept *coffee spoon*, but if you put in coffee as an ingredient you'll end up with some very strange mashed potatoes!)

(c) *Pour into serving dish or bowl/Add (knob of) butter*. Once you have worked out the French you could check with the illustration to see that it tallies, but do not work the other way round.

(d) *Stir/briefly*. (This detail is in bold print and is therefore obviously very important.) *Let it stand for 2 minutes or so.*

(e) *One glass*.

If you got 6 out of 9, you are doing quite well (especially if cooking is a mystery to you).

To end with, here is one of the longest tasks you could expect to get at Higher Level. Technique is very important in this kind of task, because at first sight it looks very difficult. You can allow 15 minutes on this one, but not much more.

A few notes first, then work through it and find out how you did by checking with the answers on p. 181. Half marks on this would mean that you are coping with Higher Level. Better than half marks means that you are doing well.

TECHNIQUE TIP

Watch timing very carefully with long questions. It is very easy to lose track of time if you get bogged down.

Notes:

Make sure you read the questions before starting the text. You will get a lot of help with understanding the text if you do.

Be sure you understand what the questions mean. Underline key words. Do not get confused between *employer* and *employee*.

Look at the layout of the text. The direct speech is set out differently. This is a help, and so is the paragraphing.

Remember to underline important parts of the text.

In question (e) you will see that it says, *Put a tick in the box in your answer book.* Just put a tick next to the ones you think are correct.

Once you have finished, read over all your answers to check that they make sense as a whole. For example, your answer to (f) should support the rest of the article.

H LEAG, June 1988.

---

5. You are glancing through a magazine called *QUE CHOISIR?* which is like the English magazine *WHICH?*. You come across this article about Fast Food Restaurants:

L'envers du décor ne vaut pas toujours l'endroit !

Que se passe-t-il dans les cuisines d'un fast-food? Pour le savoir, nous avons interrogé quatre employés, tous syndiqués, qui désirent garder l'anonymat. Deux d'entre eux, qui travaillent dans une toute petite chaîne vendant des hamburgers, racontent : *« les conditions d'hygiène sont très mauvaises. Par exemple, nous utilisons le même seau pour rincer le chiffon qui sert à nettoyer le sol et pour laver la salade. Parfois, quand nous sommes en train de laver par terre dans la salle et que l'on a rapidement besoin de nous dans la cuisine, on y va sans même avoir le temps de se laver les mains. »*

« L'huile de friture n'est changée qu'une fois par semaine, et parfois seulement toutes les deux ou trois semaines. Les distributeurs de boissons ne sont jamais nettoyés, sauf quand il leur arrive de tomber en panne. »

« Vers onze heures du matin, on commence à préparer une grande quantité de hamburgers pour faire face à l'affluence du déjeuner, qui dure de midi à deux heures et demie. Certains hamburgers sont donc vendus trois heures et demie après leur préparation et même plus car, s'il en reste, on les garde et on les vend petit à petit dans l'après-midi. En été, quand la clientèle est surtout composée de gens de passage que l'on ne voit qu'une fois, le patron en profite pour faire des économies et achète des produits de moins bonne qualité ».

Bien sûr, cette situation, que l'on rencontre surtout chez certains « petits », n'est pas généralisable à l'ensemble de la profession. Bien au contraire, puisque les deux personnes travaillant dans les « grands » ont mentionné les bonnes conditions d'hy-

giène qui régissent leur travail, conditions cependant parfois prises en défaut (cf qualité des milk shakes).

Par contre, le point commun entre les employés des fast-foods, qu'ils soient grands ou petits, connus ou non, ce sont leurs difficiles conditions de travail : 20 minutes ou une demi-heure seulement pour manger, obligation de consommer les produits du fast-food avec interdiction d'apporter sa propre nourriture, impossibilité de se reposer, de quitter sa caisse, même cinq minutes, s'il y a du monde, etc., le tout avec le sourire et pour des salaires très faibles. D'où un roulement important, possible grâce à l'inépuisable source que constituent les étudiants, français ou étrangers.

Au royaume du fast-food, si le client est roi, les employés sont des sujets bien mal traités.

(a) On what evidence is this article based?

(b) The two employees working in the chain of hamburger restaurants refer to poor conditions of hygiene: explain in detail any **two** of the examples they use to illustrate this.

(c) Why are some hamburgers sold several hours after they have been prepared?

(d) The article refers to the management cutting costs in the summer:

(i)   Why is this thought by the management to be an acceptable practice in the summer?

(ii) How is this cost-cutting achieved?

(e) Examine the section of the article that deals with the complaints made by employees about their working conditions. The list below contains **four** of the complaints they make. Show which these are by putting a tick in the box in your answer book:

(i)   They get no more than half-an-hour for their own meal.

(ii) They have to wear a uniform at work.

(iii) They are not allowed to bring their own food to work to eat.

(iv) They have to work late at night.

(v)   They are always likely to be made redundant.

(vi) They cannot stand the constant smell of fried food.

(vii) They cannot be away from their post for five minutes during working hours.

(viii)They are very poorly paid.

(f) What does the writer conclude about the employers' attitude towards customers and staff in Fast Food Restaurants?

Speaking

Basic Level

Role-plays set in cafés, restaurants and food shops are very common tasks and you should be able to cope without any difficulty if you know the basic vocabulary. Paying is straightforward, too. Remember that the service-charge problem is likely to crop up in café roles, and also asking where the toilets are. Here is a typical café role-play of *five* tasks for you to prepare.

You are sitting in a French café with your friend when the waiter comes across.
1. Order a fruit juice and a black coffee.
2. Say what flavour juice you want.
3. Ask if they do sandwiches.
4. Order a cheese sandwich for your friend.
5. Pay the bill and ask for some change for the phone.

This is quite a lot to do in this task. Here are a few notes to help you.
1.   You must say *fruit* juice, not, for example, orange juice, because of task 2.
2.   Orange is easiest (**jus d'orange**). Don't mix it up with **Orangina** (fizzy orange).
3.   **Vous avez** will be fine.
4.   You must include *for my friend*. The best way to do this is **pour monsieur** or **pour mademoiselle**.
5.   To pay, say **voilà**. If you cannot remember *change* (**la monnaie**), you could ask for *some 1 franc coins* (**des pièces d'un franc**).

 Now here are three recent exam roles for you to prepare and practise with a friend, if possible. We have recorded the third one on the cassette (S18).

You have gone to Boulogne on a day-trip with your mother and your brother. You want to have lunch in a restaurant. You find one and go in. As you are the only one who can speak French, you must order the meal.

The role of the waiter or waitress will be played by the examiner.
1. Ask for the 60-franc menu.
2. Choose soup for you all.
3. Then order the steak with any vegetable you like.
4. Say you would like a bottle of red wine.
5. Ask for some water as well.

MEG, May 1988

You are at a restaurant with your brother. Your teacher will play the part of the waiter and will start the conversation.
(a) Say you want the chicken and a cheese omelette.
(b) Ask for chips and green beans.
(c) Ask for an orange juice and a beer.

NEA, May 1989

You are on holiday in France and you want to buy some food and drink for a picnic. You find a small grocery open.
The role of the grocer will be played by the examiner.
1. Ask for 200 grams of ham.
2. Find out if the grocer sells bread.
3. Buy a small amount of Bonbel cheese.
4. Ask for a bottle of apple juice.
5. Ask how much you have to pay.

MEG, May 1988

Higher Level

Role-play tasks at this level are very unlikely to come up. The only real possibility is a restaurant scene with a problem or complaint. Here is a typical example of what you might get.

SITUATION	You are in a restaurant in France with your friend. You have both decided to have the 60-franc set menu (service is included). Your friend doesn't eat meat. Your teacher will play the part of the waiter or waitress and will start the conversation.
ESSENTIAL INFORMATION	You can't afford to spend more than 60 francs each for your meal.
YOU MUST	1. Say you have enjoyed your first course. 2. Order a steak for yourself and grilled sardines for your friend. 3. Respond appropriately to what the waiter says. 4. Check what the total price will be.

This looks very difficult when you first see it. You need to keep a cool head (**pas de panique!**). By now you have enough French and enough knowledge of technique to be able to cope. Do things in order.
1. Check the situation carefully. Key fact: *your friend doesn't eat meat*. This must come in what *you* have to say, otherwise, why is it written there? Remember that the waiter cannot know this unless you tell him/her.
2. Look at the essential information. Again, you have to use this in some way, and *not* at the beginning of the role-play.
3. Look at the tasks. The first one looks tricky. *But*, remember you say this *in answer to* the waiter's first speech, so obviously he/she is going to ask you: *'Did you enjoy the snails?'* or whatever you are supposed to have had. But remember also that **oui** will not be a sufficient answer – you need to express enjoyment. Task 2 is straightforward, even the word *grilled*. Task 3 is going to be about your friend's choice – it looks as though the sardines are going to be 'off'. It looks, too, as though you

could be offered something more expensive, or another meat dish. You have to listen carefully to what the waiter says. Key words will be **supplément, plus cher**, etc., or some other meat, so you must react accordingly. It may be that you are left to suggest an alternative, in which case **une omelette** is usually a safe bet! What you do *not* do is start complicating things unnecessarily. If the waiter offers you, eventually, a trout for the same price, accept it like a shot. Task 4 is OK provided you make sure you are asking a question.

Here is an example of how this role could develop.

You say	*The waiter says*
	Alors, c'était bien, les crudités?
1. **Oui, c'était délicieux, merci.**	
	Bien, qu'est-ce que vous prenez comme plat principal?
2. **Alors, pour moi un steak et pour mademoiselle les sardines grillées.**	
	Je regrette, il n'y a plus de sardines. Je vous apporte deux steaks?
3. **Non merci, mon amie ne mange pas de viande. Vous avez un autre poisson?**	
	Il y a une truite, mais avec supplément de 10 francs. Dans le menu il y a une omelette au fromage.
4. **D'accord, un steak et une omelette. C'est 60 francs par personne, c'est ça?**	
	Oui, mademoiselle, c'est ça.

Conversation

Food and drink is a topic which could come up, and it would be a good idea to prepare some material – perhaps using a grid form – on what you eat for various meals, likes and dislikes, whether (and what) you can cook, and what you think about French food if you've been to France. Remember, for most people it is worth writing this material down and learning it.

Basic Writing

All you are likely to get at this level is a shopping list, which is a five-minute task and would be the first question on a Basic Writing paper. It may seem obvious, but where there is a choice pick items you are sure of, not the ones you like most, and do not write down English or even French brand names. The task below should be a certain 10 marks for you if you know the vocabulary.

---

1   You are camping near a small town in France with your parents. The French family in the next tent are about to go to the shops and offer to do some shopping for you. You make out in French a list of 5 items:

> Bread
>
> Fruit (say which)
>
> Cakes
>
> Meat (say which)
>
> Stamps

You add against each item the shop where you would expect them to get it. There are no supermarkets in the town.

MEG Basic Writing, June 1988

Here is a possible answer:

2 baguettes	**boulangerie**
1 kilo d'oranges	**épicerie**
4 gâteaux	**pâtisserie**
4 steaks	**boucherie**
6 timbres (à 2 francs)	**tabac**

You are expected to choose five different shops. It would not matter if you missed out the price of the stamps, or put **poste** instead of **tabac**.

PROBLEMS AND SERVICES

What you need to be able to do.

- Understand people talking and writing about health, lost property, accidents, bank, post office, cleaners etc.
- Perform speaking and writing tasks related to these topics.

The words you need

le corps body		**j'ai mal à . . .**
		my . . . is hurting
la tête head		**les cheveux** hair
un oeil eye		**les yeux** eyes
une oreille ear		**le nez** nose
le pied foot		**le bras** arm
le ventre stomach		**l'estomac** stomach
la bouche mouth		**la dent** tooth
la gorge throat		**le coeur** heart
la main hand		**le doigt** finger
le dos back		
le genou knee		**la jambe** leg

le médecin doctor   **le médicament** medicine
le pharmacien chemist   **la pharmacie** chemist's shop

se faire mal to hurt oneself
malade ill   **aller mieux** to be better
se brûler to burn oneself
se casser (le bras) to break (one's arm)
un hôpital hospital   **le coup de soleil** sunburn
une ambulance ambulance   **le choc** shock

le rhume cold   **l'aspirine** aspirin
la pilule pill   **la pastille** lozenge
le comprimé tablet   **le coton hydrophile** cotton wool

le pansement dressing   **la piqûre** injection/sting
le sirop cough medicine
la crème cream   **le sparadrap** sticking plaster

la fièvre fever   **la grippe** flu
grave serious   **le mal de mer** seasickness
blessé hurt, wounded   **mort** dead
se reposer to rest   **souffrir** to suffer
vomir to be sick   **fatigué** tired
avoir faim to be hungry
avoir soif to be thirsty
avoir chaud to be hot
avoir froid to be cold

un accident accident   **marcher** to walk
une assurance insurance   **s'arrêter** to stop
au secours! help!   **avoir peur** to be frightened

freiner to brake   **glisser** to slide
heurter to collide with
gravement seriously   **un incendie** fire
le pompier fireman   **le trottoir** pavement
mouillé wet   **le passant** passer-by
le piéton pedestrian   **le témoin** witness
trop vite too fast   **rouler** to drive, to go (car)

les Postes, Télécommunications et Télédiffusion (PTT) the French post office and telephone service
le bureau de poste post office   **la poste** post office
la boîte aux lettres letter-box
la carte postale post-card   **le colis** parcel
le courrier post, letters   **le facteur** postman
la lettre letter   **le guichet** PO counter
le jeton token (for machine)
le paquet package   **le timbre** stamp
téléphoner to phone   **composer un numéro** to dial a number

décrocher   to remove the receiver
raccrocher   to hang up   **en PCV**
                                                reversed charge call
la tonalité   ringing tone

la banque   bank   **l'argent**   money
la monnaie   change, coins   **la caisse**   cash-desk
le billet (de 20 francs)   (20 franc) note
le bureau de change money exchange office
la carte de crédit   **la pièce (d'un franc)**
                 credit card   1 franc coin
changer   to change   **le chèque de voyage**
                                                traveller's cheque
la livre sterling   **signer**   to sign
                 pound sterling

le bureau des objets trouvés   lost-property office
perdre   to lose   **voler**   to steal
le voleur   thief   **le vol**   theft

cambrioler   to burgle
l'appareil-photo   camera
la description   description
marquer   to mark
dedans   inside
le parapluie   umbrella
le portefeuille   wallet
le sac à dos   rucksack
trouver   to find

réparer   to repair
le nettoyage à sec   dry cleaning
la laverie automatique   launderette
la machine à laver   washing machine
être/tomber en panne   to break down
se plaindre   to complain
rembourser   to give your money back

chercher   to look for
la caméra   ciné-camera
laisser   to leave
neuf (neuve)   brand-new
oublier   to forget
le passeport   passport
le porte-monnaie   purse
le sac à main   handbag

nettoyer   to clean

You will have noticed that there is quite a lot of vocabulary for this chapter, which brings together some of the more difficult topic areas. Much of this material is used only in Higher Level tasks, but we hope you will be attempting at least Listening and Reading at Higher Level – especially after doing this practice!

Listening

Basic Level

You are likely to get simple post-office situations, or situations where people talk about feeling unwell. Most other areas are for Higher Level only. A typical task would be one where you have to understand a chemist's instructions. (L45 on cassette)

You have had a stomach upset while staying in France, and you take a prescription to the chemist's. Can you understand what she tells you about the medicine?
(a)   What exactly is she giving you? (1)
(b)   When do you have to take the medicine? (2)
(c)   What is the last thing she tells you? (1)

Notes
Did you check carefully for wording of questions and for marks available? If so, you will have noticed the key word *exactly* in Question 1, and the fact that there are 2 marks for Question 2. That, plus your expectations from the situation, should help to give you at least 3 out of 4 on this task.

Answers
(a)   *30 pills.* (Must have number to get the mark.)
(b)   *3 times per day/after meals.*
(c)   *Finish the box.*

Sometimes tasks will cover more than one topic, as we have already seen. In this recent one, an accident was used as the key item in such a task. Do this one and check your answers with p. 181. (L46 on cassette)

A   MEG Basic Listening, May 1989.

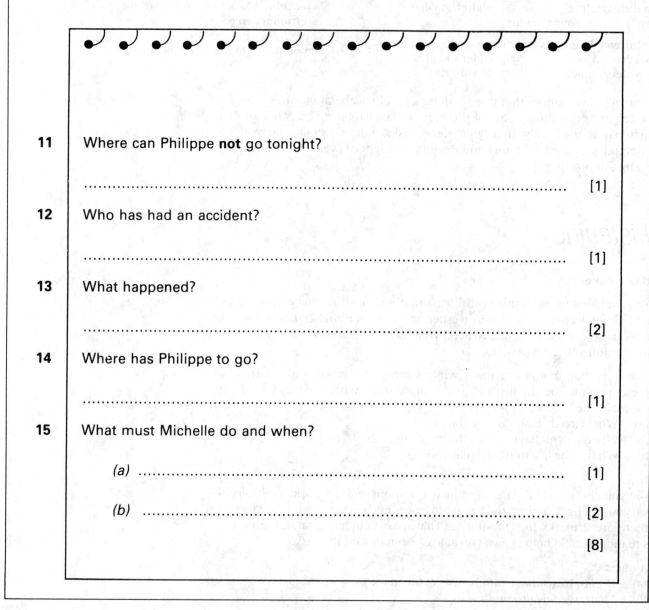

Exercise 1 Questions 11–15

You are staying with a French family. One afternoon the telephone rings and you take a message from Philippe to give to Michelle.

Look at questions 11–15 below.

Now listen to Philippe and make a note of the information in **English**. You will hear the message **twice**.

11 | Where can Philippe **not** go tonight?

.... [1]

12 | Who has had an accident?

.... [1]

13 | What happened?

.... [2]

14 | Where has Philippe to go?

.... [1]

15 | What must Michelle do and when?

(a) .... [1]

(b) .... [2]

[8]

Higher Level

Here you *can* expect to be tested, as the tasks could include radio broadcasts and telephone messages as well as ordinary conversations. This recent task included two of these types. Read the setting carefully before you attempt the questions. Also, look carefully at Question (a). It is a double-barrelled question with an extra question word tacked on at the end. (L47 on cassette. Answers on p. 181)

TECHNIQUE TIP

Always read to the very end of the question. In reading English we generally have a very good idea before the end of the sentence what is being said, and we tend to skip the last few words, or pay less attention to them.

B   While you are in Poitiers, you decide one evening to ring up a friend who is working for a year in a boarding-school in Bordeaux. When you get through, you hear the following:

Question 7

What are you advised to do and when?

....

....

(2 marks)

You decide to try again the next day, and this time you go to a post-office. While you are queueing up, as you are a little anxious, you listen carefully to the conversation of the man in front of you with the woman at the counter.

After listening to the conversation answer Questions 8 and 9.

Question 8

What type of call is he trying to make?

....

(1 mark)

Question 9

Explain why he suddenly starts shouting angrily.

....

(2 marks)

LEAG, June 1989

Accidents, and people's reactions to them, are very common tasks at Higher
Level. Here is another recent exam one for you to try. 3 marks out of 5 on
this is quite a good score. (L48 on cassette. Answers on p. 182))

C   Your pen-friend's father has been involved in an accident. He comes home and explains to the
family what happened.

Answer the questions below to show that you have understood the events.

(a)   Who was to blame for the accident?

Answer: _____ (1)

(b)   Give *two* reasons why it happened.

Answer 1 _____

2 _____ (2)

(c)   What damage was done to the car?

Answer _____ (1)

(d)   Apart from the damage to the car, what problem faces your friend's father?

Answer _____ (1)

NEA, November 1988

And as the very last Listening exercise for you to do, here is one, also from a
recent exam, about a missing car. We wouldn't want you to get the idea that
life in France is all about things going wrong – far from it. Also, we hope that
with the better technique and increased confidence you ought to have in
your ability to understand spoken French by now, you'll be keener to visit
France and perhaps more interested in taking your French further.

This task (L49 on cassette) offers you no less than 18 marks if you can
cope with it. See how you do and check with the answers on p. 182.

D   NISEC Higher Listening, May 1988.

---

5.   Your French penpal's father has just discovered his car is missing from outside their apartment. This
is what your friend's parents have to say about the matter.

(a)   Why was the father so surprised to find his car missing?

....

.... **(4)**

(b)   Why is the mother not surprised?

....

.... **(4)**

(c)   What had the father left in the car?

....

.... **(4)**

(d)   What does the mother advise him to do immediately?

.... **(2)**

(e)   What makes the father feel optimistic about getting his car back?

.... **(4)**

READING

Basic Level

Again, you won't find many tasks at Basic Level on this topic. Notices outside banks, in post offices, simple instructions on medicine, etc. are the most likely tasks.

You have been prescribed some cough medicine while on a skiing holiday in France. The instructions are written on the label.

> **POSOLOGIE: Une cuillerée à soupe toutes les quatre heures diluée dans l'eau chaude.**

When and how do you have to take this medicine? (3)

How many marks would you get out of 3 for the following answer: *1 spoonful every 4 hours in water*?

   This gets only 1 mark. You probably realised that there are two key details missing – a *tablespoon* (you might be given the mark for *a soup spoon*), *in hot water*.

The next task is based on a booklet you pick up in a tourist office in France.

E   What does this booklet give advice on? (2)

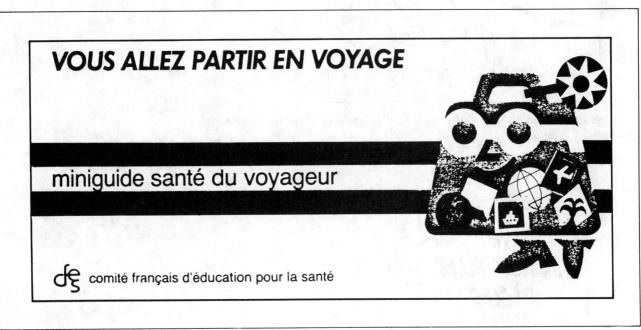

(Answer p. 182)

The following advert is on a leaflet you are given as you are walking through the town of Dax. What is it advertising? (2)

(Answer p. 182)

F

Another leaflet you pick up at the tourist office looks interesting. Whom do
you think it is aimed at? (1)

(Answer p. 182)

G

Higher Level

Tasks here are likely to be about problems, so there is a wide range of possibilities available, and careful reading and common sense will be very important. Look at this extract from a leaflet about safety at the sea-side.

It contains a list of useful pieces of advice for safe bathing.

Give three of the pieces of advice mentioned. (3)

In this kind of text there will usually be some long words you may not have seen before and don't need to worry about. It's more important to make sure you understand the rest of the text, in which there will be words which look like English words **(zone, respectez, signalisation, difficulté, alertez)**; words based on other words which you should recognise **(éloignez, progressivement)**; and words you can guess in the context **(flottants, ramener)**. Remember always that what you write must make sense. It must be sensible advice. There are six different pieces of advice. Score 1 mark for any you got.

Answers:
1. Choose an area which is guarded and obey the signals.
2. Don't go too far out if you are alone.
3. Go into the water gradually. (You may be interested to know that **hydrocution** means losing consciousness through sudden immersion in cold water!)
4. Don't go after toys or beach equipment if they float away.
5. Parents, keep a close eye on your children. (NOT *don't leave your children*. Remember, read to the end of the sentence.)
6. If someone looks as if they are in trouble, inform the lifeguard.

Here is a similar task for you to try.

While looking through some French magazines for young people, you come across this article on what to do in case of accidents. Answer these questions on the passage. (Answers p. 182)

H

1. The first thing it tells you is what not to do. What shouldn't you do?

   .... (1)

2. How should you cope if you are alone?

   ....

   .... (4)

3. If your little sister is hurt through your fault, what should you do?

   .... (1)

Finally, here is an example of more personal problems. Allow yourself 7–8 minutes for this task and then check how well you did with the answers on p. 182. This is quite a testing piece. 6 marks out of 11 is a satisfactory mark, but see if you can get more than that.

I   MEG Higher Reading 1, November 1988.

Read this letter that appeared in a magazine for young people, then answer the questions in English.

S.O.S. ACNE

Tout le monde sait qu'un adolescent est souvent couvert d'horribles boutons qui défigurent. Mais, dans mon cas, c'est atroce. Je n'ai plus une seule partie du visage en bon état. Quant à mon dos, n'en parlons pas. Je suis désespérée. Je ne sais plus que faire. Après avoir vu sept médecins, et avoir suivi une bonne dizaine de traitements, j'en suis toujours au même point. Je n'ose même plus sortir dans la rue en dehors de mes heures de cours. Et à 15 ans, c'est vraiment grave pour le moral.

Je sais que je ne suis pas seule dans mon cas, mais je n'ai jamais vu quelqu'un d'aussi abîmé, ravagé que moi. Alors, je me permets de vous lancer un S.O.S. que, peut-être, d'autres n'ont pas osé envoyer. Je demande aux lecteurs qui sont passés par là et qui en sont sortis de me dire quelle porte ils ont empruntée. Au point où j'en suis moralement et physiquement, j'accepterai n'importe quoi, du remède de grand-mère aux traitements les plus médicaux.

Séverine

7   How does Séverine describe the condition of her face?

....

.... [2]

8   What steps has she already taken in an attempt to put matters right?

....

.... [2]

9   What is she now afraid to do?

....

.... [2]

10   To whom does she make an appeal at the end of her letter?

....

.... [2]

11   What does she ask them for?

....

.... [2]

12   Which of the following best describes Séverine's state of mind as she wrote this letter?

   A   level-headed
   B   angry
   C   desperate
   D   anxious   [1]

                                                                                   [11]

Speaking

Basic Level

Role-plays at Basic Level will be based on bank and post-office situations, and simple tasks relating to health. Look at this post-office situation. How would you cope with this task?

You have gone to the local post office to buy stamps.
1.   Ask for 4 stamps for postcards.
2.   Say the cards are for Great Britain.
3.   Offer a 50-franc note in payment.
4.   Ask for some 5-franc coins in your change.
5.   Find out where the post-box is.

Notes:
1.   This is straightforward.
2.   If you don't know *Great Britain*, use **Angleterre**.
3.   **Voilà** is not enough here. You need to say **cinquante francs** as well.
4.   You do not need to say *in my change*. But make sure you say *some* **(des pièces de 5 francs).**
5.   If you forget **boîte aux lettres,** you can cope with **où est-ce que je peux mettre (or poster) les cartes?**

Now work out how you would do the following task set in a **Bureau de Change.**

You are trying to change money in a Bureau de Change.
1.   Say you want to change some English traveller's cheques.
2.   Say you want to change £20.
3.   Offer your passport as identification.

Finally, here is a task set in your French pen-friend's house for you to look at.

You wake up in your French pen-friend's house feeling unwell.
1.   Tell your pen-friend's mother you don't feel well.
2.   Say you have a headache and stomach-ache.
3.   Ask if you can stay in bed for the morning.
4.   Say you would like only a drink of water.
5.   Say there is no need to call the doctor.

Higher Level

This is an area on which you are quite likely to be tested in the Oral exam. Complaints and problems are not all that difficult to deal with, provided, as always, you know the vocabulary or can see a way around it. We will look at some examples in a moment. One thing you often have to do in such role-plays is *express your annoyance,* or *express your dissatisfaction.* Don't be tempted to do this by just raising your voice (or thumping the table!). A very useful phrase indeed is **Ça ne va pas!** = *It's not on!; It just won't do!* (just as the best way to say *That's better* is **Ça va mieux**). A less emphatic way would be **Ce n'est pas bien.** Here is a recent task with a vocabulary problem. How would you get around the word *noisy* if you didn't know it? (*noise* = **bruit;** *noisy* = **bruyant**)

You have just spent your first night at a camp-site in France where you have booked in for a week. Unfortunately your pitch is not far from the games room and you find it rather noisy. You go to reception to ask whether you may move. The role of the receptionist/warden will be played by the examiner.
1.   Ask if you can change your pitch.
2.   Explain that it is too noisy.
3.   Say that you could not sleep last night.
4.   Choose which pitch you would prefer.
5.   Ask if you may stay there for a week.

MEG, May 1988

The solution, if you can't think of a word for *noisy*, is to think yourself into the situation. Ask yourself what might be making the noise and say that, for example, **il y a beaucoup de musique le soir** or **les gens dans la tente à côté parlent beaucoup la nuit.**

Look at this next task. Anybody getting this in the Oral would think himself/herself very unlucky, but it is all clearly covered by the syllabus, and if you have learned your vocabulary it would really show on this task.

During a holiday in France you fall from your bicycle and badly graze your knee. You go to a chemist's shop for some ointment and advice. The role of the chemist will be played by the examiner.
1.   Say that you have hurt your knee.
2.   Explain how it happened.
3.   Ask for some antiseptic cream.
4.   Say which one you want.
5.   Ask if you should put on a plaster.

MEG, May 1988

Notes
1.   *Knee?* If you don't know it, say **au milieu de la jambe.**
3.   *Antiseptic* is the kind of word which is likely to exist in French as well. As a *general* rule, the longer the word, the more likely it is to exist in both languages.
      Cream? If you don't know it, say **un produit.**

5. *A plaster?* Difficult, this one. **Quelque chose** would be better than nothing.

Here are a couple more roles for you to think about and prepare. The second one is recorded on the cassette (S19).

You go into a bank in France to change £50 either in traveller's cheques or in cash. The role of the bank clerk will be played by the examiner.
1. Say that you want to change some money.
2. Say that you have your passport.
3. Ask whether there is a commission.
4. Ask what the value of the pound is.
5. Decide what you want to change and how much.

MEG, May 1988

SITUATION	You are in a large shop. An umbrella you have bought is faulty. Your teacher will play the part of the shop assistant and will start the conversation.
ESSENTIAL INFORMATION	You bought it yesterday and it must be replaced as it is a present.
YOU MUST	1. Say you want to complain. 2. Say the umbrella is already broken. 3. Respond *fully* to the shop assistant's question. 4. Show annoyance and ask to see the manager.

NEA, May 1989

Finally for this unit, here is another example of the role-play with outline in French, where you have to tell a story. This time there are no pictures or diagrams to help – you have to understand quite a lot of French, too. In this case it's very important to choose the details you are sure you understand. Watch, too, that you understand who did what. The notes don't always make this clear and you are expected to work it out for yourself. As a general rule, remember that where there is a verb mentioned you will use the Perfect Tense **(passé composé),** and where there is *not* a verb specified, you can usually get away with using **avais (avait)** or **étais (était)** – but you need to know which one is correct. This kind of role is very like a Writing exercise. You'll find it will help you in your writing of accounts, etc. if you practise this kind of role. If possible, do a written version and get it checked.

HIGHER PART 2

The notes below give an outline of a set of circumstances which arose last Easter.

You are staying for ten days with your exchange partner in France but you almost had to cancel your visit because your mother developed 'flu and the household was thrown into chaos. You tell your friend what happened.
The role of the friend will be played by the examiner.
You need not mention every detail contained in the notes, but you should try to include at least **one** of the items in each group.

lundi – arrivée à la maison
– Maman endormie dans un fauteuil
– forte grippe
– préparer le dîner

---

mardi	– Papa au travail de bonne heure
	– Maman accident dans l'escalier
	– téléphoner au médecin
	– garder le lit plusieurs jours
	– rater la matinée au collège
mercredi	– maison en désordre
	– Papa jour de congé
	– examen à préparer pour vendredi
	– téléphoner à grand-mère, absente
jeudi	– Maman toujours besoin de repos
	– voisine très gentille
vendredi	– examen, très fatigué
	– préparer le départ
	– faire les valises
	– l'arrivée de grand-mère

MEG Higher Speaking 2, May 1988

Basic Writing

The only task you are likely to get is a lost-property exercise. Suppose you have lost your wallet or purse and are asked to describe it and mention four things which were in it. This is how you could do such a task.

> **Mon porte-monnaie.**
> **Description: petit, rouge et noir.**
> **Contenu:** 1. **20 livres en argent anglais.**
> 2. **Des timbres français.**
> 3. **Une photo de ma famille.**
> 4. **Les clefs de ma maison et ma valise.**

This is about 30 words long, which would be fine for a first task on a Basic Writing paper. Before we go on to the Higher Writing chapter, try this similar task, set in a recent exam, and get it checked over, if possible. We have given a specimen answer on p. 182.

J   LEAG Basic Writing, June 1988.

1. You have travelled to France by plane with your family. At the French airport one piece of your luggage cannot be found.

An airport official gives you this form about the lost luggage and its contents.

Fill in the form **in French**, after filling in your name and first name.

Nom ....

Prénom ....

Objet perdu ....

Description (i) ....

(ii) ....

et couleur ....

Contenu (i) ....

(ii) ....

(iii) ....

(iv) ....

(v) ....

(vi) ....

HIGHER WRITING

You have arrived at the last chapter. Well done! But if you followed the advice given at the beginning of this book you will not have left all this chapter till the very end. If you are aiming at Higher Writing, and aiming at a grade A or B, the best plan is to spread these tasks out so that you do perhaps 1 or 2 a week. In any case, all the French you have covered in this book will help you with the Higher Writing tasks.

Why a special chapter on Higher Writing tasks?

This book has so far been organised around some of the topics which form the basis of the GCSE French syllabuses. We have already had examples where topics overlap. For example, you may find that the topic *Food and Drink* overlaps with the *Shopping* topic. However, it helps to plan your revision around the topics so that you know you are covering the ground required by the syllabus. When we consider Higher Writing, it is not so easy to divide up the tasks according to separate topics, which is why we have given Higher Writing a chapter of its own. You will see that any of the topics you have covered might crop up in a Higher Writing task, so all the vocabulary you have learned will help you and can be used again.

What sorts of tasks are set for Higher Writing?

Remember that all aspects of the GCSE French exam are intended to be *communicative*. That means that in Writing, just as in Speaking, you will be asked to carry out real-life tasks which involve communicating information to a French person. What sort of real-life situations are there where you might be asked to write in French? The most obvious one is a letter, and letters might be formal or informal. A *formal* letter is the sort you might write when booking a hotel room, or writing to a **Syndicat d'Initiative** to ask for information. An *informal* letter is the sort you would write to your pen-friend. We have already seen that both sorts of letter can come up at Basic Level.

Other sorts of writing task are:
- a report on something you have observed (for example, a report to the police on an accident you have seen);
- a short article for a school magazine;
- a diary of activities during a holiday, and so on.

Examples of these and other Writing tasks are given later in this chapter.

What are examiners looking for in Higher Writing tasks?

If you are aiming for a high grade in the GCSE, Higher Writing tasks are the place where you can improve your score. Different exam boards have slightly different approaches to marking the work, but the main features are those following.

Content

You will see that all the tasks are quite specific about the items of information that you are asked to communicate. It is important that you should read the task carefully and make sure that you carry out each of the things it asks you to do. Also, although the task may not state this, you will be expected to give further details, or expand in some way on the tasks. If you don't do this you are unlikely to get more than half marks for content.

Appropriateness

This is a long word, but all it means is that you should use vocabulary and expressions which relate to the task. For instance, if you were writing about what you ate in France, you would score well if you mentioned some typical French dishes; or if you were writing a story, it would help if you used different verbs rather than **je suis allé** all the time. It helps, too, if your sentences follow on well from each other.

Quality of language

What you write is then assessed for its accuracy. Remember that marking at GCSE is *positive*. This means that you do not have mistakes underlined and marks taken off every time you make a slip. You are *awarded* marks for getting things right, and the more you can get right, the better your mark.

Now here is some more information about tackling Higher Writing tasks, and some examples taken from exam papers.

1. Letters
Letter writing is an important skill and you must know the usual ways of beginning and ending letters in French.

1.1 *Informal letters*

Begin: **Cher Michel; Chère Anne-Marie.**
End: **Avec mon amical souvenir;**
        Ton ami . . .;
        A bientôt, j'espère, amicalement . . .;
        Amitiés;
        Avec mes amitiés;
        Je t'embrasse (affectueusement);
        Réponds-moi vite!

As you will see in the next example, the stimulus for the letter you must write is often given by a letter from a French friend. Of course, this is a great help in giving you a framework for things you might say in your letter. What kind of things will you be expected to do in replying to such a letter? Accepting or rejecting invitations are very common tasks; so are commenting on news, expressing pleasure or sorrow, as well as asking and answering questions. Here are some useful phrases which will help in such situations.

Accepting an invitation: **Merci pour ta gentille invitation de . . .** (say what it was, for example **venir pour Noël**), **c'est très sympa.**

Turning down an invitation: **Merci pour ta gentille invitation de . . .** (as before). **Je regrette beaucoup mais je ne peux pas venir, parce que . . .** (give reason, for example **je dois travailler pour mes examens).**

Expressing pleasure at news: **J'ai été très content(e) de savoir que . . .** (repeat news, for example **ta soeur va se marier**).

Expressing sorrow at news: **J'ai été désolé de savoir que . . .** (e.g. **tu ne pourras pas venir en Angleterre cet été**).

Learn these, and if you get the chance to use them, take it! The most important thing to remember about writing in French is to use as much pre-learned material as you can. Avoid making up sentences in English and then translating them. Use French you are pretty sure is correct.

In the letter which follows, your friend tells you his family is going to the Pyrenees and asks the question: **Est-ce que tu pourrais nous y accompagner?** You might reply to this: **Merci beaucoup pour ta gentille invitation de t'accompagner dans les Pyrénées. C'est très sympa. Je voudrais beaucoup y aller avec vous.** He then says in his letter: **Demande tout de suite la permission à tes parents,** so you might write: **J'ai tout de suite demandé la permission à mes parents.**

Now try the task, then read the further notes which
follow on p. 157.

Example

2   You receive a letter from your French friend, part of which appears below.

> ..... et nous comptons partir dans les Pyrénées
> à Noël pour faire du ski. Nous avons pensé à
> toi. Est-ce que tu pourrais nous y accompagner?
> Si cela te plaît, demande tout de suite la
> permission à tes parents, puis écris-nous et
> dis-nous quand tu seras libre.
>
> Est-ce que tu as déjà fait des sports d'hiver?
> As-tu fait du ski? Tu as des skis à toi? Si non,
> cela ne fait rien.
>
> As-tu beaucoup de vêtements chauds? Si tu
> as des questions, pose-les.
>
> Je joins des photos que nous avons prises
> l'an dernier.

You ask your parents and they approve, subject to cost, so you write an immediate
reply to your friend giving all the information asked for in this letter and asking questions
about:

(i)   cost
(ii)   accommodation
(iii) length of stay

Earlier the point was made that you are always given quite clear information about the tasks you must fulfil to score marks for the content of your letter. Here you have three tasks stated, and you must also respond to the information asked for in the letter. You might begin by writing a short key sentence for each task, to remind yourself of important vocabulary and to make sure you miss nothing out. For example:

(i) Cost: **Combien est-ce que le séjour coûtera?**
     OR: **Quel sera le prix du séjour/des vacances?**

(ii) Accommodation: **Où est-ce que nous allons dormir?**
      OR: **Est-ce que nous serons dans un hôtel?**

(iii) Length of stay: **Combien de temps est-ce que nous allons passer dans les Pyrénées?**
       OR: **Les vacances vont durer combien de temps?**

In addition, here are some possible replies to the questions asked by your friend.

(iv) When will you be free?:
      Je serai libre à partir du 18 décembre;
      OR:
      Les vacances commenceront le 18 décembre.

(v) Have you already done winter sports/skiing?:
     C'est la première fois que je suis allé aux sports d'hiver (mais ça m'intéresse beaucoup).
     OR: **J'ai déjà fait du ski une fois avec l'école, et j'ai beaucoup aimé.**

(vi) Have you got your own skis?:
      Malheureusement je n'ai pas de skis, mais on pourra en louer sur place, sans doute.

(vii) Have you got plenty of warm clothes?:
       Pour les vêtements chauds, pas de problème! J'ai beaucoup de pulls et un anorak.

(viii) Finally, you will need to thank him for the photos he has sent you.

So your whole letter might look like this.

Cher Michel,
Merci beaucoup pour ta lettre. J'ai tout de suite demandé à mes parents la permission d'aller avec vous dans les Pyrénées. Il sont tout à fait d'accord, mais ils voudraient savoir quel sera le prix du séjour. Aussi, où est-ce que nous allons dormir? Ils demandent aussi combien de temps vont durer les vacances. Pour moi, c'est la première fois que je vais faire du ski. Malheureusement, je n'ai pas de skis, mais on pourra en louer sur place sans doute. Pour les vêtements chauds, pas de problème. J'ai beaucoup de pulls et un anorak.

Je te remercie des photos que tu as envoyées, et j'attends ta prochaine lettre avec impatience.
Amitiés

This is just over the 100 words required for the task.

Below is another example of an informal letter. In this exam you are told that the number of words is not important, but, in general, aim to write between 100 and 150 words for a task of this kind. It is important to remember that in addition to completing the tasks as laid out in the question, you must give extra detail if you are to get full marks for content. Here are some ways in which you might do this.

(i) Identify what you are talking about. Instead of just saying **je suis allé au cinéma,** say, **je suis allé dans un cinéma qui s'appelle le** *Rex.*

(ii) Give a reason why you did something. **Je suis allé au cinéma pour voir le nouveau film** *Batman* **avec mes amis.**

(iii) Give an opinion about what you did. **Je suis allé au cinéma avec mes amis. J'ai trouvé le film formidable.**

(iv) Say what you did next. **Je suis allé au cinéma . . . et ensuite on a mangé une pizza dans un restaurant italien.**

Now underline or highlight the questions asked by Annie in her letter and think how to respond to other things she says. For example, express an interest in what she says she did on her birthday. **(Ça m'a beaucoup intéressé de savoir comment tu as fêté ton anniversaire.)** (Model answer p. 182)

A NEA, May 1989.

---

1 Your French pen-friend has sent you this letter.

Lille, le 2 mai

Salut!

Je te remercie pour ta carte d'anniversaire. Pour fêter mes 16 ans, mes amis et moi sommes allés manger un hamburger car nous n'avions pas assez d'argent pour aller au restaurant. Vas-tu quelquefois au restaurant ou au fast food?

Raconte-moi comment cela se passe. Tu sais, ici, les fast foods ne sont pas encore très populaires. Est-ce la même chose en Angleterre? Mes amis et moi, nous avons bien mangé mais c'était très différent de ce que ma mère prépare chez nous. Que manges-tu, toi, à la maison?

L'été prochain, j'aimerais bien travailler dans un fast food car l'ambiance a l'air bonne et en plus je voudrais m'acheter un vélomoteur. J'aurai donc besoin d'argent de poche! Est-il facile de trouver du travail à 16 ans en Angleterre?

Je pense que si on travaille tous les deux cette année, on pourrait passer de bonnes vacances en Espagne l'année prochaine, si on a assez d'argent!

Si ça t'intéresse, dis-le-moi. Bon, je dois te quitter car ma mère m'attend pour faire les courses.

A bientôt,

Annie

With reference to your own **experiences** and **opinions**, write a reply **in French**, telling her about eating out in Britain, meals in your home and part-time jobs. Don't forget to respond to Annie's suggestion for next year's holiday and give reasons for your decision.

Put down **all** the information you are asked to give. The number of words is not important.

1.2   Formal letters

Chapter 7 introduced some ideas about writing formal letters. Here are a few more tips.

Formal letters in French often do not start **Cher. . . .** The French equivalent of *Dear Sir* or *Dear Madam* is usually simply **Monsieur** or **Madame.** Such letters end more formally than in English. Most formal English letters end *yours faithfully*. There are a number of possibilities in French, for example:

Je vous prie d'agréer, Monsieur, mes respectueuses salutations.

Je vous prie de croire, chère Madame, en mes sentiments les meilleurs.

It is worth noting that for exams, the beginnings and ends of letters do not count as part of the total number of words you may be asked to write, although they do score marks if you get them right.

Some more fixed expressions you might like to remember for formal letters are:

J'ai bien reçu votre lettre du 2 novembre dernier et je vous en remercie.

Je vous accuse bonne réception de votre lettre du 27 août.

Example

> *Write about* **100** *words in French on* **one** *of the following topics:*   [20 marks]
>
> **Either**
>
> **1**   You are helping your parents who intend to go to France for their holidays. They will be taking their car and crossing to Dieppe and would like to spend their first night in France in this hotel as they do not wish to drive too far on the first day.
>   Write a letter to the owner of the hotel in Veulettes, giving all the necessary details:
>
> (i)   Date, length of stay, number of people, beds, rooms required.
> (ii)   estimated time of arrival.
> (iii) Ask for the time of the evening meal and charges.
> (iv)   Your parents want you to ask especially for a quiet room with a view of the sea.
> (v)   They also want you to find out about car-parking arrangements.

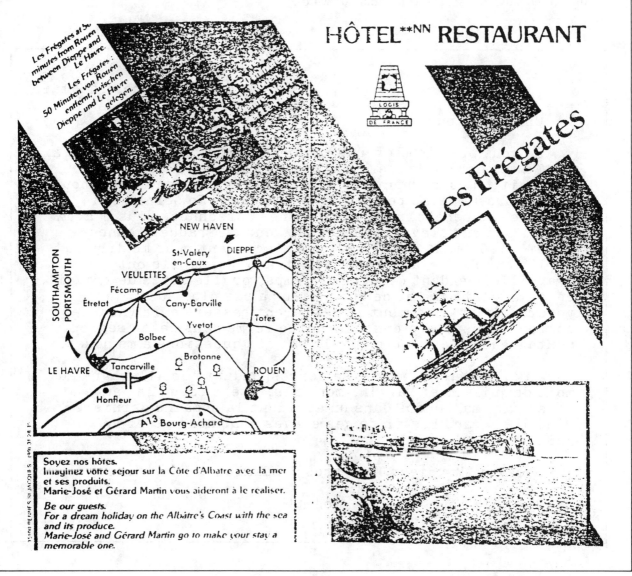

Here again you notice that the tasks required are clearly stated. So you need to find a way to start and finish the letter, and then put it together carefully, following the sequence of tasks.

Here are some suggestions.

Monsieur,
Je vous écris pour réserver une chambre pour deux personnes, pour une nuit, le 4 août.
Monsieur et Madame Jones arriveront vers six heures du soir et voudraient dîner à l'hôtel. Veuillez m'indiquer à quelle heure vous servez le

repas du soir, et quel est le prix du repas et de la chambre.

Monsieur et Madame Jones voudraient surtout une chambre calme avec vue sur la mer. Ils arriveront en voiture et voudraient bien savoir quelles sont les facilités pour garer leur voiture.

Je vous serais reconnaissant de bien vouloir me confirmer par écrit cette réservation et me donner les renseignements que je vous ai demandés.

Je vous prie de croire, Monsieur, en mes sentiments les meilleurs.

Here is another example of a formal letter for you to try. This is quite a long task, and you need to think and plan it carefully. How many tasks can you see? There are at least 6 tasks which you are told to do in the first paragraph. However, in addition you should note that the invitation to ask questions is one you are expected to pick up. Is there anything in the last paragraph which you should also deal with in your letter? Look carefully before you start writing. Allow yourself 45 minutes for this task. We have done a specimen answer for you on p. 182.

B   NISEC Higher Writing, June 1988.

1. A French teacher in your school has written to a French friend hoping to arrange summer work for you and another pupil. Below is the reply which the teacher passes on to you. Write a letter in French to the French lady. You should write about 200 words.

Aigueblanche, le 2 mai.

Cher Monsieur,

Je vous prie de m'excuser pour ma négligence à répondre si tard à vos deux lettres. Je vous réponds quant à la proposition concernant vos élèves qui souhaitent venir nous aider dans la ferme pendant l'été de 1988. Je serai bien heureuse de recevoir ces deux jeunes personnes. Vous m'avez dit qu'ils ont travaillé tous les deux en France l'année dernière. Il faut que les élèves m'écrivent pour me dire ce qu'ils ont fait exactement, c'est-à-dire, où ils ont travaillé, pendant combien de temps, quelle sorte de travail, ce qu'ils ont aimé et ce qui ne leur a pas plu. Aussi je voudrais savoir comment ils espèrent passer leurs vacances cette année s'ils viennent à notre ferme dans cette région montagneuse. Peut-être qu'ils ont des questions à me poser.

Ma fille Marie va chez sa correspondante en Allemagne au mois de juillet et Martin, mon fils, s'est cassé la jambe et s'est fait mal au dos dans un accident la semaine dernière. Donc j'ai grand besoin de ces élèves pour nous aider en juillet.

Recevez, Monsieur, mes très cordiales salutations.

Josette.

2. Reports

Reports are another sort of rather formal writing which you may be asked to do. Here are two examples for you to try.

During a visit to Paris you have lost something valuable on the Métro. When you go to the lost property office you are given a form on which you have to write a report about the loss. Write this report and include the following points:

– when and where you were travelling on the Métro

- *full* details and description of what was lost
- when the loss was noticed
- what you did next and why
- give details of how and where you can be contacted in the next few days

LEAG Higher Writing, June 1988

You can see in this example that the use of the tenses is important. For example, you might begin this report in the Imperfect:

Le 6 juillet j'étais à Paris et je voyageais dans le Métro entre le Louvre et la Place de la Concorde.

To describe the moment when you noticed you had lost something, you will need to use the Perfect:

Je suis arrivé à Concorde et je suis sorti du Métro. C'est alors que j'ai remarqué que je n'avais plus mon portefeuille.

The description of the wallet (or whatever you decide you have lost) will be Imperfect again:

C'était un portefeuille en cuir noir.

To say what you did next will require the Perfect:

J'ai immédiatement cherché le bureau des objets trouvés pour faire une déclaration sur cette perte.

To say where you can be contacted in the next few days, you will need to use the Future:

Je serai à Paris encore trois jours, et pendant ce temps je logerai à l'Hôtel Esméralda, rue de St Jean le Pauvre. Vous pourrez me contacter par téléphone.

Now try this example. (Specimen answer pp. 182–3)

C   LEAG Higher Writing, May 1989.

---

1.   Your class is compiling a dossier to send to your French Exchange school. You are asked to write a report in French on your experience of doing a job – during the holidays, or as a regular part-time employment, or to help somebody.

Write the report in about 100 words, including some of the following points:

— What kind of job it was.

— How you heard about it.

— What you had to do.

— When you worked.

— Whether you were paid.

— What you liked or disliked about the job.

— Anything else of interest about the job.   *(40 marks)*

---

3.   Articles

You may sometimes be asked to write an article for the school magazine of your French pen-friend. This sort of writing is more informal because, when writing, you must try to imagine your 'audience'. The audience for a school magazine article will be people of your age and interests, and they will want something which will interest them and make them want to read on. Here is an example. (Specimen answer p. 183)

D

You have been asked to write an article *in French*, as part of a package of material to be sent to your twinned school in France. Your article is to describe life at home. Mention your daily routine (times, meals, evenings and weekends) and talk about what you do to help at home. Say which are the best and the worst days of the week for you, and why. You have been asked to write about 100 words. There is no need to count the number of words.

(NEA Higher Writing, June 1988, Question 2)

Notice how the work you have done on Speaking skills can also help you in your Writing. All that you have learned to *talk* about in your daily routine could help you here to *write* about it. Just writing down times and days might not be very interesting. Think of ways in which you could add some variety to your French by using exclamations, such as: **quelle horreur!; c'est affreux!** and so on. Or you might express an opinion, for example: **Tous les jours il y a un cours de maths. Je n'aime pas ça!; Le mercredi après-midi il y a du sport. J'aime beaucoup ça!.**

Sometimes the article you are asked to write may have some stimulus to help you, such as photos or, as in the following example, a brochure.

The wording of this task gives you some clue to another aspect of Higher Writing. For the highest mark on content you need to be able to express your attitudes and opinions in French, not just give a factual account. So you will want to say things like:

L'activité que j'ai préférée . . .
Personnellement, je n'aime pas beaucoup les jeux d'équipe, mais tout de même . . .
J'ai surtout aimé . . . (Model answer p. 183)

E

2   You have just returned from a school visit to an Outdoor Pursuits Centre in Scotland. Your French teacher asks you to write an account of the visit to send to your twinned school in France.

OUTDOOR ADVENTURE

ACTIVITIES AVAILABLE

SWIMMING
SAILING
WIND-SURFING
WALKING
CYCLING
RIDING
TEAM GAMES

FUN IN THE EVENINGS

DISCOS
FILMS
T.V. ROOM
GAMES ROOM
MUSIC NIGHT

ACCOMMODATION

8—10 BED DORMITORIES.
FULLY EQUIPPED LARGE DINING ROOM.
MODERN TOILETS & SHOWERS.
CENTRAL HEATING.

Using the information from the centre's brochure, write an article **in French,** saying who took part in the trip and what the centre was like. Then write about the best day of the holiday and say what you did on the last evening. Make sure that you include your opinions and impressions of the holiday.

Put down **all** the information you have been asked to give. The number of words is not important.

NEA Higher Writing, May 1989

4. Storytelling

Some exams set various tasks which aim to get you to tell a story (usually a not very interesting one!) in French. Sometimes you are given a situation to write about, as in the following example, for which you are asked to write about 150 words. (Model answer p. 183)

F

> **2   The people in the house opposite were abroad on holiday and their house was empty. One day you were in the garden and noticed a strange man and woman trying to get into the house. Half an hour later they came out carrying large suitcases and walked off down the street. At this stage you decided it was time to phone the police.**
>
> **Write the full story of this incident including the eventual outcome as part of a letter to your French correspondent.**

MEG Higher Writing 2, November 1988

If you like writing stories in English, you will probably like to use your imagination in a task of this kind. Unlike some of the other tasks you have tried, there is no control on what you put into this story, as long as you know the French for what you want to say.

Another type of storytelling task set by some exam boards is the picture story. Here is an example.

You have received the following drawings from your French pal who is a good artist. They relate to an incident during the summer holidays in France last year. Your French teacher has suggested that you write an article in French of about 200 words for the school magazine, based on the drawings.

Although this task takes the form of an article, it is really just a story, but you are given more guidance on what you should write than in the earlier example. Because you are told that this relates to incidents last year, you should write the story in the past tense. When writing picture stories of this kind, you might start by writing one or two French sentences for each picture, just to make sure that you have got the sequence of action and the vocabulary. Look at the pictures on the following page and then at the suggested sentences.

NISEC Higher Writing, June 1988

For the six pictures you might write:

(i)   **On faisait du camping. On jouait au football.**

(ii) **Une vache est arrivée. Elle a détruit nos tentes. Nous sommes partis à toute vitesse.**

(iii) **Nous avons trouvé l'auberge de jeunesse.**

(iv) **Nous avons préparé notre repas du soir.**

(v)   **Il pleuvait. Nous avons fait de l'autostop.**

(vi) **Nous sommes arrivés tout mouillés à la maison. Nous nous sommes assis devant le feu.**

This gives you the basic facts, but it is flat and boring to read. How can you liven it up?

(a)   Add words of time to show *when* things were happening.
      L'année dernière pendant les grandes vacances on faisait du camping. *Un soir* on jouait au football. *Soudain* une vache est arrivée . . . *le lendemain* il pleuvait . . . etc.

(b)   Add adjectives and adverbs to *describe* things, and say how things were happening.

Une vache *furieuse* est arrivée... nous avons *très vite* trouvé une auberge de jeunesse... nous nous sommes assis *très fatigués* devant le feu.

(c)   Add exclamations to give variety to your style.

Soudain, *quelle horreur*, une vache furieuse est arrivée... Le lendemain, *quel désastre*, il pleuvait.

Try some of these techniques with another example.

G   You recently went to a party at a friend's house while her parents were out for the evening. During the party some gatecrashers arrived. The events of the evening are illustrated below. You are now writing to your French pen-friend and decide to describe the evening. Basing your account on the pictures below, write a description of the evening in about 100 words. You are not required to write any other part of the letter.

LEAG Higher Writing, June 1989

In the Reference Section (p. 183) you will find a possible answer to this question – although, of course, there are many ways in which the story could be written.

This last Unit on Higher Writing has covered some of the most difficult of the tasks you will meet at GCSE. What we hope is clear, however, is that after the techniques you have learned in this book, and the help you have been given with handling the topics, even these Higher Writing tasks begin to look quite manageable.

It only remains for us to wish you the very best of luck in your exam, and even before you get that far you deserve congratulations for the hard work you have put into preparing yourself with the help of this book.

11

REFERENCE SECTION

Notes on pronunciation

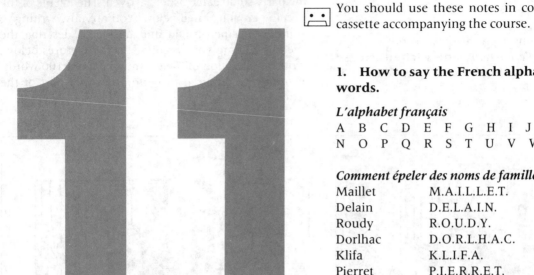

You should use these notes in conjunction with the cassette accompanying the course.

1. How to say the French alphabet and spell words.

L'alphabet français

A B C D E F G H I J K L M
N O P Q R S T U V W X Y Z

Comment épeler des noms de famille

Maillet	M.A.I.L.L.E.T.
Delain	D.E.L.A.I.N.
Roudy	R.O.U.D.Y.
Dorlhac	D.O.R.L.H.A.C.
Klifa	K.L.I.F.A.
Pierret	P.I.E.R.R.E.T.
Weiss	W.E.I.S.S.
Schreiner	S.C.H.R.E.I.N.E.R.
Jolibois	J.O.L.I.B.O.I.S.
Lagorce	L.A.G.O.R.C.E.

2. Spelling

The spelling of French, like the spelling of English, has not changed significantly over the centuries, while pronunciation has altered in many ways. The written form of the language therefore looks very different from the spoken form, and each sound can be spelt in a number of ways. In the table below, each sound is given its approximate value compared with English, and a summary of the different ways in which it might be written. Listen to the tape to hear the exact way in which the sound is pronounced.

3. Vowels

Approximate sound	Written form in French	Examples
like *a* in *made*	1. **é, ée, és, ées**	**été, poupées, écrire**
	2. **ez**	**allez, chez**
	3. **er** (final)	**aller, plancher**
		(an exception is **cher,** pronounced like *share*)
	4. **ied, ieds**	**pied, assieds-toi**
	5. **ef**	**clef**
	6. **et, es**	**les, mes, des, et**
like *e* in *bed*	1. **è, ê**	**père, tête**
	2. **ai, ei**	**palais, reine**
like *e* in *perhaps* but even shorter	1. **e** in monosyllables	**le, te, de, se**
	2. **e** in unstressed position	**boulevard, avenue**
like *a* in *rack*	1. **a**	**cheval, ami**
	2. **emm**	**femme**
like *a* in *father*	1. **â**	**château, âge**
	2. **as**	**pas, gras**
	3. **ase**	**phrase**
	4. **able**	**aimable**
like *o* in *hope*	1. **o** when final (consonant not pronounced)	**dos, trop**
	2. **au, eau, aux**	**autre, auto, beau**
	3. **ô**	**côté**
	4. **o** followed by **se, sse, tion**	**chose, grosse, émotion**
like *o* in *lot*	**o** followed by a pronounced consonant	**robe, comme, bonne**
like *oo* in *pool*	**ou**	**chou, vous, toujours**
like *ee* in *keen*	**i, î**	**fini, dîner**

There are some vowels which exist in French but not in English.

u: Put your lips into position to pronounce *oo* in English *pool*. Now keep your lips in that position and try to pronounce the sound of English *ee* in *peel*. You will produce a sound which must not be allowed to slip into the *oo* of *pool*. Practise with **sur, vue, plus, tu.**

eu: When followed by **r,** this sound is a little like *ur* in English *murder*. Try with **soeur, peur.** When not followed by **r,** the sound is similar, but much shorter. Try with **feu, peu, deux.**

4. Nasal Vowels

Vowels are produced by a passage of air through the mouth. If some of the air comes through the nose as well, these are called nasal vowels, and they give French some of its characteristic sounds. In written French the nasal sound is always shown by an **m** or **n** after the vowel. This **n** or **m** is not pronounced itself, but just shows that the vowel is nasal. Listen to the tape to get the right pronunciation.

Written Form	Examples
in, im, aim, ain, ein	**fin, important, faim, main, sain, frein**
un, um	**un, lundi, parfum**
on, om	**bon, ombre**
an, am, en, em	**quand, camp** (note there is no difference in the pronunciation of these two words), **lent, client, emballage**

5. Semi-Vowels

Approximate sound	Written forms in French	Examples
like *y* in *yes*	1. **i** or **y** before a vowel	**piano; pierre; yeux**
	2. **-ill-** in the body of a word	**briller; travailler**
	3. **il** or **ille** at the end of a word.	**fille; feuille; gentil**
	(There are a small number of exceptions where the final **lle** is pronounced: for example, **mille, ville.**)	
like *w* in *wait*	1. **ou** before a vowel	**oui**
	2. **oi, oy** (pronounced *wa*)	**oiseau; voilà; trois**
	3. **oin** is the same sound as **oi**, but nasalised	**coin**

6.   Consonants

The main characteristic to note is that French consonants are not pronounced with such an escape of breath as English ones. The *p* in English *pair* is pronounced with a puff of breath which does not occur in the French equivalent **paire.** French consonants are therefore more tense and precise in their pronunciation. In the list that follows, no further explanation is given for the consonants that are most like English (**b, d, f, m, n, p, t, v**), but remember that the sounds are not exactly as in English and you should listen to and copy the French voices on the tape.

Another important point to notice is what happens to final consonants. We said earlier that French spelling has not changed significantly over the centuries, whereas pronunciation has altered. One important difference between written and spoken French is that final consonants are hardly ever pronounced (for example **dos, pied, main**). But the final consonant is sounded if the word ends with **e**. This explains the difference in pronouncing masculine and feminine forms of some adjectives, for example **vert, verte; grand, grande; petit, petite.**

The following list draws attention to some consonants which might provide problems either because of their pronunciation or because of the difference between their written and spoken forms.

Approximate sound	Written form in French	Examples
like *c* in *cat*	1. **c** before **a, o, u**	**Cannes; école**
	2. **k** (rare in French)	**képi**
	3. **qu**	**que; quand**
like *g* in *gate*	**g** before **a, o, u**	**gare**
like *s* in *pleasure*	1. **g** before **e, i**	**gentil; plage**
	2. **j**	**je; jour**
like *s* in *save*	1. **s** (initial and after nasal **n**)	**santé; service; danser**
	2. **c** before **e, i**	**ciel; ici**
	3. **ç**	**français**
	4. **ss**	**poisson**
	5. **sc**	**scène**
	6. **ti** (in words ending **tion**)	**émotion**
like *z* in *zoo*	1. **z**	**gazon**
	2. **s** when between two vowels	**chaise; chose**
like *sh* in *shine*	**ch**	**cher**
like *ni* in *onion*	**gn**	**gagner**

Among the other letters you will notice that:

h is silent **(homme)**;

th is pronounced like **t (thé)**;

x is like *gs* before a vowel **(examen)** and like *ks* before a consonant **(excuser)**;

w occurs only in words of foreign origin and is pronounced like **v (wagon)**. But notice that **weekend** is pronounced as in English;

l and **r** offer particular difficulties.

> **l** is a very different sound from the English, as you can see if you compare English *bell* and French **belle**. In English the *l* sound is pronounced with the tongue turned up and touching the ridge behind your teeth. In French the tongue is placed further forward, so that it is touching the point at which the front teeth meet the gums. Examples: **belle; long; allemand.**
>
> Note also that **l** is one of the consonants that is nearly always pronounced when it is final (for example **cheval**). Note, however, that the final **l** is *not* pronounced in the word **gentil.** For the pronunciation of the group of letters **ill,** see the section on semi-vowels.
>
> **r** is perhaps the most difficult French sound for foreigners to imitate. It is pronounced well back in the throat. The best way to explain it is to say that it is rather like the action of gargling! Examples: **jardin; grand; crier.**

7. Liaison

As we stated above, final consonants are generally silent in French. But when the following word begins with a vowel or with a silent **h,** the final consonant is usually pronounced together with the vowel starting the following word, for example **les enfants; très important; un petit homme,** etc. This process is called liaison. Note that there are no breaks of any kind between words linked in this way. Each of the groups of words above sounds like a single word when it is spoken.

Although liaison is essential in the examples given, there are many cases where the rule is not so clear-cut, and might depend on the person speaking. For example, you might hear someone say **je veux aller** whereas someone else might say **je veux/aller.** This is a question of listening to the tape and to French people speaking, so that you pick up the regular patterns. Watch out for familiar words like **deux, trois** which might sound different because of liaison, for example **deux heures; trois heures.**

8. Stress and Intonation

English places a heavy stress on one syllable in a word, for example *magnificent*. This has the effect of causing unstressed vowels to lose some of their quality. French is different and has a very even stress applied to each syllable, so that each vowel retains its full value wherever it occurs. The note of the voice is also more regular in French. English intonation tends to go up and down a lot, so that when French is spoken with an English accent, it sounds rather sing-song. The French

voice tends to remain on a fairly even note, rising at pauses, and dropping at the end of the sentence. In questions requiring the answer **oui** or **non**, the voice rises at the end of the sentence. Listen to these examples.

Tu as un frère?

Non, je n'ai pas de frère, mais j'ai une soeur.

Quel âge a-t-elle?

Elle a quatorze ans.

TRANSCRIPT OF LISTENING MATERIAL

Unit 1: Me, my family and other people

(L1) Ma meilleure copine s'appelle Monique. Elle a quatorze ans comme moi, mais elle est beaucoup plus petite. Elle a les cheveux blonds et les yeux verts. Je m'entends très bien avec elle parce qu'elle est fille unique, comme moi.

(L2) Alors, demain à 8h30 on a Mme Lambert. Elle est très grande avec les cheveux gris. Elle est toujours gentille et elle rit souvent. Ensuite à 9h30 il y a maths avec Mlle Richard, qui est petite et mince. Elle est très stricte, surtout avec les garçons. Après la récréation nous avons espagnol avec M. Suarez. Son nom s'écrit S.U.A.R.E.Z. Il a les cheveux noirs et une barbe grise. En général il est très sympa mais quelquefois il est fâché.

(L3) A. Et si je rentre après 11h, oh là là, c'est épouvantable! 'Qu'est-ce que tu as fait? Tu étais avec qui? Tu ne pouvais pas téléphoner?' etc., etc.

B. Oui, d'accord, mais au moins tu peux sortir. Les miens, ils veulent que je reste à la maison à part le samedi soir, et encore je dois rentrer avant 10h30. Tu te rends compte?

Unit 2: Where I live

(L4) Bonjour. Je m'appelle Anne-Marie. J'ai 22 ans. Je vis avec mes parents dans une petite maison à Epinal, une assez petite ville près de la frontière allemande.

(L5) Bienvenue chez nous, Michel. Voilà l'appartement. Il n'est pas très grand, tu sais. Il y a seulement deux chambres, plus la cuisine, la salle de bains et WC et une petite salle de séjour, 5 pièces en tout. Alors, tu vois, ta chambre est à gauche, en face de la salle de bains. Regarde, il y a une vue magnifique sur les Alpes, et on peut même voir la Suisse quand il fait très beau.

(L6) – Ecoute Marie-Dominique. Je viens de ta chambre. Voilà trois jours que tu ne l'as pas rangée.
– Bon, d'accord, Maman. Je vais le faire après le déjeuner.
– Ah non! Tu vas le faire tout de suite.
– Mais c'est très injuste! Jean-Michel ne fait jamais rien à la maison.
– Ça, ce n'est pas vrai. Ton frère a fait la vaisselle ce matin.

(L7) (MEG 2, May 88, Questions 7–14)
Interviewer: Cet appartement a quelque chose de très reposant, parce qu'on y est bien, et surtout,

surtout il y a plein, plein de plantes vertes, partout.

Artiste: Oui, oui, c'est Simone. Elle a les doigts verts d'abord, et puis adore les plantes, ainsi que moi, d'ailleurs. Alors, évidemment, la pièce dans laquelle nous étions, vous l'avez vue, celle qui était sur les bords de la Seine . . . on a une vue d'ailleurs superbe sur Notre Dame et le Pont St Michel.

Interviewer: Vous voyez cela de vos fenêtres.

Artiste: On a une vue admirable là. Nous sommes là depuis trente ans, vous savez. Et quand nous sommes arrivés dans cet appartement, ce quartier était quelque chose de délicieux, parce que . . . il avait un parfum de province. La rue Dauphine était une rue extraordinaire, où il y avait de petits commerces, des merceries, de petits épiciers. C'était le calme admirable. C'est devenu un peu Pigalle, maintenant. La rue Dauphine, c'est extrêmement bruyant, c'est extrêmement vivant, ça a beaucoup changé, mais la beauté du lieu, elle, est restée.

Interviewer: C'est un luxe d'avoir une vue comme vous l'avez.

Artiste: C'est admirable, c'est très beau. C'est une chose qu'on apprécie énormément. Vivre dans un cadre comme ça, c'est vraiment beaucoup de chance.

Interviewer: Il vous appartient?

Artiste: Non, il ne m'appartient pas. J'aurais pu l'acheter il y a vingt-cinq ans. C'est comme un regret. Il était à vendre, très bon marché, mais à l'époque nous étions en train de construire une petite maison à la campagne, et il n'était pas question en même temps d'acheter ici.

Interviewer: C'était l'un ou l'autre.

Artiste: C'était l'un ou l'autre. On a laissé passer cet appartement à acheter, mais par contre on a eu la chance aussi d'avoir un endroit à la campagne qui est un endroit de rêve. Une véritable maison de rêve.

Unit 3: School, work and future career

(L8) **Comptez de 1 à 100, de 100 à 1000.**

(L9) (a) **une heure cinq;** (b) **deux heures dix;** (c) **trois heures vingt;** (d) **quatre heures vingt-cinq;** (e) **cinq heures et quart;** (f) **six heures trente;** (g) **neuf heures trente-cinq;** (h) **neuf heures moins vingt;** (i) **dix heures et demie;** (j) **midi moins le quart/minuit moins le quart;** (k) **neuf heures dix;** (l) **huit heures cinquante;** (m) **deux heures et demie;** (n) **six heures cinq;** (o) **onze heures quinze;** (p) **trois heures quarante;** (q) **dix heures cinquante-cinq;** (r) **cinq heures et demie;** (s) **quatre heures et quart;** (t) **une heure vingt-cinq.**

(L10) **Alors, demain, c'est mardi, on commence à neuf heures avec un cours de maths. Tout de suite après il y a deux heures de français, c'est très ennuyeux. A midi on va à la cantine et ensuite on est libre jusqu'à 2 heures. L'après-midi, on a une heure de sciences, suivie d'une heure d'allemand, et on finit à 4 heures, heureusement!**

(L11) (MEG BL, June 88, Section 3, Exercise 1, Questions 22–26)

Vincent: **Salut Christian, qu'as-tu fait ce matin?**

Christian: **J'ai travaillé sur un devoir de mathématiques, en fait. C'était un peu difficile. Et Vincent, qu'est-ce que tu fais cet après-midi?**

Vincent: **Cet après-midi, j'aurai un cours d'allemand, suivi d'un cours de sciences naturelles puis de physique.**

Françoise: **Et Christel, quelles sont tes matières préférées à l'école?**

Christel: **Oh je crois que ce sont les maths ou encore la physique. Les matières scientifiques sont pour moi les meilleures.**

Christian: **Philippe, tu penses qu'on a trop de travail?**

Philippe: **En ce moment, oui, énormément. On a beaucoup trop de devoirs.**

Christel: **Et toi, Françoise, qu'en penses-tu?**

Françoise: **Oui, je pense aussi que nos journées sont trop longues, et que le soir on travaille de trop.**

(L12) (LEAG HL, June 88, Questions 1–10)
PART 1
Questions 1 and 2:
Je suis interne dans un lycée à Poitiers. Je prépare mon Bac. Après, à l'université, je voudrais faire des études de médecine. J'aime bien toutes les matières que j'étudie, surtout la biologie. Mais malheureusement je ne suis pas très fort en maths.

Questions 3, 4 and 5
Il faut dire que la vie comme interne ne me plaît pas du tout. On ne nous permet pas de sortir de l'établissement, et il n'y a même pas de téléphone pour les élèves. Le soir on est cinquante à étudier dans une grande salle. Moi, dans ces conditions-là, je n'arrive pas à me concentrer. Je n'en peux plus, j'ai envie de tout laisser tomber.

PART 2
Questions 6 and 7
Bonsoir, chers auditeurs et auditrices. Aujourd'hui nous consacrons notre émission aux jobs d'été – ces petits emplois d'un mois ou deux, qui permettent aux étudiants, aux lycéens et aux jeunes chômeurs de gagner un peu d'argent. Mais attention! Certains employeurs ont nettement tendance à exploiter leurs jeunes employés.

Questions 8, 9 and 10
Prenons le cas de Michèle . . .
Je travaillais douze à quatorze heures par jour depuis le premier juillet dans un hôtel-restaurant. A la fin du mois je me suis aperçue que mon salaire ne comprenait pas les heures supplémentaires que j'avais faites. J'en ai parlé au patron, mais comme je n'obtenais aucune satisfaction, je lui ai dit que je ne resterais pas une seconde de plus.

Unit 4: Free time

(L13)   **Voici les prévisions de la météo pour ce weekend. Samedi, en Normandie, il fera beau temps avec une température maximale de 21 degrés. Il pleuvra par contre en Bretagne. Dimanche en Normandie il y aura du vent et en Bretagne le temps sera couvert avec du brouillard sur la côte.**

(L14)   (SEG, November 88, Questions 23–26)
– **Salut, Pierre.**
– **Salut, Jean-Paul.**
– **Tu viens à la discothèque chez André, vendredi soir?**
– **Je sais pas. A quelle heure ça commence?**
– **Vers neuf heures. Je pourrais passer te chercher.**
– **Mais comment? C'est assez loin, ça.**
– **Pas de problème. J'ai mon permis de conduire depuis une semaine. On y va en voiture?**
– **Ah bon! A vendredi, alors.**

(L15)   (NEA HL3, June 88)
Ce soir sur TF1 à 18h30 notre feuilleton pour toute la famille *Dynastie*.

(L16)   (MEG HL1 May 88, Questions 1–7)
Vous êtes ici dans le Musée de la Poste et des Techniques de Communication à Caen. Ce musée, situé dans un immeuble du 16e siècle, a été ouvert en 1986. Il y a six salles d'exposition, où vous pouvez voir toute l'histoire de la Poste, depuis la poste aux chevaux jusqu'au téléphone par satellite. Vous pouvez voir, bien sûr, des timbres, et surtout des timbres français, mais nous faisons aussi des expositions de timbres thématiques sur un sujet déterminé. Ainsi, nous avons une exposition sur les transports, et l'on peut voir des timbres de tous les pays du monde y compris, bien sûr, des timbres anglais. Et en même temps nous proposons au visiteur de voir un certain nombre de films sur l'ensemble de l'activité de la Poste et des Télécommunications. En hiver, les heures d'ouverture sont du mardi au samedi, de 13h à 17h30. En été, du 1er juin au 30 septembre, le musée est ouvert de 10h à 18h, tous les jours sauf le mardi. Le tarif d'entrée est de 8 francs par personne. Nous faisons demi-tarif pour les scolaires et les groupes, donc ce tarif est de 4 francs.

Unit 5: Shopping and money

(L17)   **Un franc, deux francs, trois francs, quatre francs, cin(q) francs, si(x) francs, sept francs, hui(t) francs, neuf francs, di(x) francs.**

(L18)   (MEG BL, May 89, Question 1)
Cela fait 9F50.

(L19)   (MEG BL, May 89, Question 10)
Vous avez de la monnaie?

(L20)   **Mais il est très joli ce collier, vous ne trouvez pas? Il est espagnol, en plastique et je peux vous le montrer en cinq couleurs différentes. Il est en solde à 75 francs seulement.**

(L21)   (NEA BL, June 88, Question 14)
(a)   **Aujourd'hui promotion spéciale sur les disques. Deux disques pour le prix d'un.**
(b)   **Au rayon pharmacie achetez le dentifrice Pepsodent, le meilleur pour vos dents.**
(c)   **Au rayon primeurs achetez nos belles tomates à dix francs le kilo. C'est donné, mesdames.**

(L22)   (LEAG HL, June 88, Questions 11–17)
Questions 11–13
Vendeuse: **Vous désirez, monsieur?**
Ami: **J'aimerais voir la chemise bleue que vous avez en vitrine.**
Vendeuse: **Oui monsieur, vous avez les deux modèles – avec poches et sans poches.**
Ami: **Euh . . . Je préfère celle sans poches.**
Vendeuse: **Quelle taille? Ce sera du 38 pour vous, je pense.**
Ami: **Euh . . . C'est que c'est pour mon frère, alors . . . Je ne suis pas tout à fait sûr. Quand j'emprunte ses chemises, elles sont toujours un peu trop grandes pour moi.**
Vendeuse: **La taille 40, alors?**
Ami: **Oui, d'accord.**

Questions 14–17
Vendeuse: **Je regrette, je n'ai pas de taille 40 en bleu – je l'ai en blanc, en beige, ou rayée bleu et blanc.**
Ami: **Je ne sais pas . . . Je peux voir la chemise beige?**
Vendeuse: **Voilà monsieur. C'est en coton pur, alors à F94, ce n'est pas cher.**
Ami: **Non, c'est vrai. A ce prix-là je pourrais même acheter autre chose – une cravate peut-être?**
Vendeuse: **Oui, bien sûr, monsieur, sur le tourniquet là-bas.**
Ami: **Bon, je prends cette cravate marron. Ça ira bien avec la chemise beige. Pouvez-vous me faire un paquet, s'il vous plaît? C'est pour un cadeau.**
Vendeuse: **Certainement, monsieur. Ça vous fait F145 en tout. Voulez-vous passer à la caisse?**

(L23)   (NEA HL, June 88, Question 6)
F1: Et qu'est-ce que tu penses de ce Thomson avec lecteur de cassettes, maman?
F2: Ah mais, c'est celui qu'il a déjà. L'autre, regarde, regarde l'autre, l'autre n'est pas mal.
F1: Ah oui, il y a un crayon optique.
F2: Puis, dis donc, il est bon marché.
F1: Mm, mm.
F2: Ah, 'y a pas de moniteur, oh bah non, oh bah non.
F1: Ah non, moi, j'veux pouvoir regarder la télévision.
F2: Oh, puis moi aussi. Ils nous ont fait trop voir comme ça avec euh, avec celui qu'il a. Dis, et celui-là, là-bas? Lecteur disc... de disquettes, moniteur (mm, mm) et le prix n'est pas mal.
F1: Celui-ci aussi a un lecteur de disquettes et un moniteur.
F2: Oh, formidable.
F1: Oh, oui, mais regarde le prix, c'est beaucoup trop cher.
F2: Oh non, non, non, non, non, bah non, n'en parlons plus. Bon, écoute, Celui-ci, celui-ci je crois que c'est le mieux, tu crois pas?
F1: Hm, hm, à peu près quatre mille cinq cents francs, ça va.

Unit 6: Going abroad – Travel

(L24)   Pour l'autoroute? Eh bien, c'est très simple. Vous allez traverser le pont, puis, au deuxième feu, vous tournez à droite, et vous arrivez à l'autoroute.

(L25)   (NEA, November 88)
(a)   Vos passeports, s'il vous plaît.
(b)   Combien de temps allez-vous rester en France?

(L26)   (MEG, November 88, Questions 35–40)
Voici des détails sur les trains desservant Rouen aujourd'hui. Pendant la matinée il y a quatre trains qui font le trajet Dieppe–Rouen. Le premier part à huit heures quinze (8h15) et arrive à Rouen à neuf heures cinquante (9h50). Ce train part du quai Numéro 1. Le prix du trajet Dieppe –Rouen est de soixante-quinze (75) francs en première classe et quarante (40) francs en deuxième classe. Les autres trains qui partent eux aussi du quai Numéro un sont à neuf heures dix (9h10), à onze heures cinq (11h05) et à onze heures cinquante-cinq (11h55). Tous ces trains ont un service de wagon-restaurant. Renseignez-vous davantage au Bureau de Renseignements à la Gare Principale ou à la Gare Maritime.

(L27)   20h43;   17h19;   21h50;   15h06;   18h32.

(L28)   (NEA BL, May 89, Question 5)
(a)   Euh, oui, alors écoutez, nous avons quelque chose d'intéressant, eh, il y a le Musée de la Nature sur la Route Nationale 960 à la sortie de la ville.
(b)   Il y a beaucoup d'animaux à voir là et c'est très intéressant. Alors, euh, l'entrée c'est 22F par personne.

(L29)   (NISEC, Summer 88)
1.   Le vol de 17h30 pour Londres aura du retard à cause du brouillard. Nous espérons partir dans une demi-heure.
2.   S'il vous plaît, puisque le vol a été retardé ... est-ce que vous pourriez vous occuper de mes bagages un petit moment? Je voudrais acheter quelques journaux avant le vol. Est-ce que ça vous dérangerait de me les garder?
3.   *Passenger A:* C'est vraiment ennuyeux. J'ai des amis anglais qui m'attendent à Londres et ils viennent d'assez loin: en plus ils ont retenu des places de théâtre pour ce soir. J'ai l'impression que ça va être juste.
     Passenger B: Pour moi ce qui m'embête, c'est que je dois prendre le train dès mon arrivée à Londres. Si j'arrive pas à avoir la correspondance, je serai obligée de passer la nuit à Londres.

(L30)   (NEA HL, May 89, Questions 1–3)
Question 1
Je ne vais pas exactement à Poitiers mais à huit kilomètres de là dans un petit village ... mais comme c'est sur mon chemin ... allez, montez.

Questions 2 and 3
Moi-même, je faisais de l'autostop quand j'étais plus jeune, mais vous savez, il y a des risques, avec tous ces voyous, ces voleurs sur nos routes. Maintenant je m'arrête rarement ... seulement si j'ai besoin de compagnie. Alors vous voyez, vous avez de la chance ... je suis seul au volant aujourd'hui.

(L31)   (NEA HL, November 88, Question 4)
– Dis donc, eh, chérie, pour, eh, les vacances, eh, pour cet été-là, eh, qu'est-ce qu'on fait? Moi, j'ai envie d'aller en Espagne.
– Eh, bah, non, pas en Espagne, bof, il fait trop chaud, trop chaud en juillet, non. Pourquoi pas Edimbourg? C'est une belle ville, il y a de beaux monuments.
– Baf ... oui, oui, mais enfin, il pleut, il pleut, il pleut tout le temps, il pleut en été, il pleut en hiver, et moi, hein, non, la Côte d'Azur, là, eh, il y a du soleil, on peut se baigner.
– Ah non, pas la Côte d'Azur, il y a trop de monde et trop de circulation, non, pourquoi pas la Suisse? Il y a des lacs, des montagnes, on peut se promener.
– Ah, oui, et la vie est chère, la vie est très chère même en Suisse, hein? Mais j'ai une bonne idée. Ça te dirait d'aller en Italie?

– Ah, l'Italie, ah bah, oui, c'est, c'est pas une mauvaise idée ça – ah oui . . .
– Tu es d'accord?
– Hm, hm, oui, en plus, eh, l'essence n'est pas chère en Italie, eh, em, c'est bien.
– Et puis la cuisine italienne est appétissante.
– Et moi, j'adore, hein?
– Et bon, c'est d'accord pour l'Italie.
– D'accord pour l'Italie, parfait.

(L32)   (MEG HL2, November 88, Questions 27–28)
Sans aucun doute, la journée d'aujourd'hui sera une journée difficile sur les routes de France avec le grand départ d'une grande partie des juilletistes. Alors tout de suite nous retrouvons Alain Mainquet à Rosny-sous-Bois. Quelle est la situation, Alain?
Alain: Eh bien, les embouteillages commencent à se former sur les autoroutes en direction de la province entre Villefranche-sur-Saône et Lyon. Il y a un ralentissement de douze kilomètres. Après Lyon, entre Vienne et Valence, queue de quinze kilomètres. Et dans le sens nord-sud près de Tournon, difficultés sur plus de dix-sept kilomètres à cause d'un accident. Dans la Drôme, sur l'autoroute A7, près de Montélimar dans le sens nord-sud, un ralentissement de quatre kilomètres sur deux voies, suite à la densité de la circulation.

Et puis dans le Vaucluse à Orange un accident entre deux véhicules a fait deux blessés. Une déviation a été mise en place. D'autre part, il est à noter que dans le Vaucluse également, tout près d'Avignon, la visibilité à cause du brouillard est réduite à moins de cinquante mètres. Enfin, les voyageurs qui s'approchent de Marseille sur la A7 devront faire attention aux poids lourds aux environs de la ville, surtout aux heures d'affluence. La police marseillaise conseille à tout automobiliste de ne pas dépasser sans bien regarder dans le rétroviseur. Et maintenant, aux informations.

Unit 7: Going abroad – Somewhere to stay

(L33)   Visitez le nouveau camping des dunes. Ouvert cette année du lundi de Pâques jusqu'à la fin septembre. 160 emplacements en tout, dont 110 pour caravanes et 50 pour tentes. Nous sommes à 50 mètres de la plage, à 200 mètres du grand supermarché. Ici, il y a tout pour les enfants, une salle de jeux, une piscine, etc. Les douches chaudes sont gratuites et vous pouvez manger dans notre restaurant. Vous pouvez même louer une caravane si vous voulez. Pour une famille de 4 personnes, dont 2 enfants de moins de 7 ans, ça ne coûte que 89 francs par jour seulement.

(L34)   (NEA BL, May 89, Question 2)
(a)   Ah, bonjour monsieur-dame, comment allez-vous? J'espère que vous avez fait bon voyage.
(b)   Voici les clefs. Celle-ci est la clef de la maison et celle-là est la clef du garage.
(c)   Vous avez bien de la chance parce qu'il fait beau en ce moment. Vous savez . . . vous pouvez aller à la pêche à la rivière, ou bien louer des bateaux.

(L35)   (SEG, Summer 88)
Mais oui, bien sûr. Il y a un emplacement libre, près des douches, sous les arbres. Nous avons un petit restaurant, et pour les enfants, une piscine. La plage est à deux cents mètres d'ici. Voulez-vous me suivre, et je vous montrerai l'emplacement.

(L36)   (SEG, Summer 88)
– Bonjour, madame. Avez-vous une chambre à deux lits pour ma femme et moi, avec salle de bains, et une autre à un lit avec douche, pour mon fils.
– Certainement, monsieur. Mais comme nous avons beaucoup de monde ce soir, les chambres ne seront pas au même étage.
– Ça ne fait rien, madame.
– Alors, pour vous, ce sera la chambre vingt et un. Et pour votre fils, ce sera la chambre quarante-cinq. Vous restez pour combien de temps?
– Pour trois jours. Vous avez un ascenseur?
– Oui, monsieur. Où sont vos bagages?
– Je les ai laissés dans la voiture.
– Voici vos clefs. Vous allez dîner chez nous?
– Mais oui. Un quart d'heure pour faire notre toilette, et nous descendons.
– Le restaurant est juste à côté, à droite, monsieur. Vous remplirez la fiche avant le dîner, n'est-ce pas?

(L37)   (MEG HL1, November 88, Questions 27–32)
Touriste: Bonjour madame, est-ce qu'il y a une Auberge de Jeunesse?
Dame: Oui, il y en a une qui est ouverte toute l'année. C'est pour combien de personnes?
Touriste: Pour moi toute seule.
Dame: Vous toute seule. Oui, d'accord, je vous donnerai l'adresse si vous voulez. Est-ce que vous voulez que je réserve? Est-ce que vous voulez que je téléphone pour vous?
Touriste: Oui, je voudrais bien.
Dame: D'accord, c'est pour combien de nuits?
Touriste: Deux nuits.
Dame: Deux nuits, d'accord. Pas de problème. C'est à quel nom?
Touriste: Le nom, c'est Gabot.
Dame: D'accord. Bon, ben, je vais leur passer un coup de téléphone si vous voulez bien attendre un petit peu.
Touriste: Euh . . . les tarifs?
Dame: Alors, les tarifs . . . attendez . . . je vais les chercher parce que je ne les ai pas en tête. Alors

. . . Auberge de Jeunesse. Est-ce que vous avez une carte d'adhérent d'Auberges de Jeunesse? Vous avez une carte d'Auberges de Jeunesse?
Touriste: Ah, non.
Dame: Alors, il faut la faire sur place, absolument. On ne peut pas coucher à l'Auberge de Jeunesse si on n'a pas sa carte. Donc la carte, ça dépend de votre âge.
Touriste: J'ai 18 ans.
Dame: 18 ans, alors pour les 18 à 26 ans c'est 43 francs. C'est une carte qui est valable toute l'année. Quand on est étranger il y a une carte internationale qui est valable dans tous les pays où il y a des Auberges de Jeunesse – dans toute l'Europe, dans le monde entier, je pense. Alors, pour une personne, les chambres, il y a des chambres à partir de 40 francs. Des lits sans draps. Alors, avec les draps en plus, il faut compter 51 francs. Mai c'est à vous de faire le lit. Si vous voulez avoir une chambre avec le lit fait, les draps, c'est 58 francs maximum. Ça va donc de 40 à 58 francs.
Touriste: Et le petit déjeuner?
Dame: Le petit déjeuner? 9F50.

Unit 8: Food and drink

(L38) – Bonjour, Madame Forrestier.
Bonjour, Monsieur. Vous désirez?
Je voudrais un kilo de tomates, s'il vous plaît, et six oeufs et un paquet de farine.
C'est tout, Monsieur?
Ah non, donnez-moi aussi 250 grammes de beurre, s'il vous plaît.
Voilà, Monsieur. Ça vous fait 26F40 en tout, s'il vous plaît. Merci, Monsieur.

(L39) (LEAG, June 88)
15. Je voudrais une boîte de sardines, un paquet de sucre en poudre, deux cent cinquante grammes de beurre, et . . . un pot de confiture de fraises.
16. Je voudrais du jambon, s'il vous plaît.
17. Vous n'en avez pas? Tant pis, donnez-moi trois cents grammes de pâté s'il vous plaît.
18. Nous avons besoin d'un ouvre-boîtes. Et je voudrais aussi une lampe de poche.

(L40) (MEG BL, November 88, Questions 5 and 6)
5. Messieurs, dames, le déjeuner sera servi à partir de midi moins le quart.
6. Aujourd'hui nous vous proposons steak frites ou côte de porc avec haricots verts.

(L41) (MEG BL, November 88, Section 3, Exercise 1, Questions 27–34)
Garçon: Eh bien, monsieur, vous avez choisi?
Monsieur: Oui, oui – alors, pour commencer je prends une salade de tomates.
Garçon: Bon, et avec cela?

Monsieur: Après, je voudrais une côte de porc avec des pommes de terre.
Garçon: Très bien. Et comme boisson?
Monsieur: Donnez-moi un quart de vin rouge, s'il vous plaît.
Garçon: Avec plaisir, monsieur. Et madame, qu'est-ce que vous désirez pour commencer?
Madame: Je ne veux pas de hors d'oeuvres. Je voudrais un poulet rôti avec des petits pois et des champignons.
Garçon: Et que voudriez-vous boire, madame?
Madame: Voyons, je ne bois pas de vin ni de bière, donc je prendrai une eau minérale, s'il vous plaît.
Garçon: C'est entendu, madame.

(L42) (NEA BL, June 88, Section C, Question 11)
(a) *Garçon:* Et pour monsieur, 'dame, qu'est-ce que ce sera?
(b) *Garçon:* Est-ce que vous voulez également quelque chose à manger?
(c) *Garçon:* Oui, vous allez payer à la caisse.

(L43) 1. Garçon, j'avais demandé mon steak bien cuit. Celui-ci est très saignant.
2. S'il vous plaît monsieur, ça fait 15 minutes que j'attends ma soupe à l'oignon. Qu'est-ce qui se passe?
3. Ecoutez, monsieur, cette assiette est sale, mon verre aussi. Pouvez-vous les changer, s'il vous plaît?

(L44) (NEA HL, June 88, Question 1)
(a) Mesdames, messieurs, n'oubliez pas notre rayon maison et jardin au sous-sol. Offres spéciales – nos frigidaires, nos congélateurs, nos transistors. Achetez aujourd'hui. Les soldes vont finir samedi prochain.
(b) Votre attention s'il vous plaît. Monsieur et Madame Leblanc sont priés de se présenter au bureau de renseignements où leur petite fille, Nathalie, les attend. Elle s'est perdue dans notre magasin.
(c) Mesdames, messieurs, vous avez faim? Vous avez soif? Allez au quatrième étage de notre magasin. Nous vous proposons un menu à 45 francs, vin compris, ainsi qu'un menu spécial pour les enfants, mais seulement avant la rentrée scolaire.

Unit 9: Problems and services

(L45) Alors, voilà, jeune homme. Vous avez là une boîte de 30 pilules. Vous en prenez 2, 3 fois par jour après les repas. Attention, il faut finir toute la boîte, n'est-ce pas?

(L46) (MEG BL, May 89, Exercise 1, Questions 11–15)
Allô, c'est Philippe à l'appareil. Je peux te

demander de passer un message à Michel? Dis-lui que je ne peux pas aller au Club des Jeunes ce soir. Mon père s'est cassé la jambe au travail, et je dois aller le voir à l'hôpital. Demande-lui de me téléphoner demain matin. Merci beaucoup.

(L47)   (LEAG HL, June 89, Questions 7–9)
Question 7
Madame, monsieur, bonjour. Vous êtes en communication avec le répondeur téléphonique du Lycée Montaigne de Bordeaux. Durant les vacances scolaires les bureaux ne sont ouverts au public que de neuf heures à douze heures. Vous voudrez bien rappeler pendant cette période.

Questions 8 and 9
– Oui, monsieur, qu'y a-t-il pour votre service?
– Je voudrais téléphoner à Bordeaux, c'est très urgent.
– Oui, monsieur, c'est quel numéro?
– Le 61–92–03 . . . et je voudrais appeler en PCV.
– Ah, je regrette, monsieur, mais pour Bordeaux il y a des problèmes. Il semble qu'il y ait une panne – je ne sais pas quoi, moi – mais pour l'instant, impossible de communiquer avec Bordeaux.
– Ah, ça alors . . . ah, mais c'est incroyable . . . c'est toujours pareil . . . le moment où on a besoin du téléphone, quelque chose d'urgent . . . le système ne fonctionne plus!

(L48)   (NEA HL, November 88, Question 3)
– Oh, chérie, quelle journée, alors!
– Pourquoi? Qu'est-ce qui t'est arrivé encore?
– Beh, euh, je rentrais du travail, eh, en voiture, eh, je descendais la rue Jeanne d'Arc, et puis il

y a, il y a un vélomoteur qui est sorti de la rue Gros Horloge, il m'a refusé la priorité, euh, eh, il a heurté la voiture.
– Mais tu ne l'as pas vu venir?
– Mais, c'était de sa faute, c'est lui qui est . . . qui a pas regardé, il allait trop vite, il a pas pu s'arrêter à temps.
– Mon Dieu! Et lui, il est blessé?
– Eh non, non ce . . . ce n'est pas grave, il n'est pas blessé lui, eh. Euh, mais, la voiture alors, eh, il a cassé le feu arrière-droit.
– Et le vélomoteur?
– Ah, bah, son vélomoteur, euh, tu sais, hein, il est en mauvais état, euh.
– Et qu'est-ce qui va se passer, alors?
– Bah, je sais pas, parce qu'il y a un autre problème, euh, il n'est pas assuré en plus.

(L49)   (NISEC, Summer 88)
Father: Je ne comprends pas. J'ai bien vérifié toutes les portières tout à l'heure quand je suis rentré. Elles étaient fermées à clef.
Mother: Mais tu sais chéri, on arrive à tout ouvrir aujourd'hui. Est-ce qu'il y avait des choses importantes là-dedans?
Father: Eh ben, oui, comme j'allais sortir tout de suite, j'avais laissé ma serviette avec des documents qui ne m'appartiennent pas. Qu'est-ce que ça va me poser des problèmes!
Mother: Il faut appeler la police tout de suite. On ne sait jamais. Il faut faire vite.
Father: Quand j'y pense, il y avait très peu d'essence dans la voiture, donc ça peut les empêcher d'aller très loin. Donc comme tu dis, il faut contacter tout de suite la police.

13

KEY TO EXERCISES

Unit 1: Me, my family and other people

Listening

A (L1) 1. 14 years old. 2 Blond hair and green eyes. 3. Because she is an only daughter, like the pen-friend.

B (L2)

Teacher	Description	Character
Mme Lambert	(i) very tall (ii) grey hair	
Mlle Richard		(i) very strict (ii) especially with boys
M. Suarez	(i) black hair (ii) grey beard	sometimes gets cross

Reading

C 1. Blue jeans, navy-blue and green jacket, brown shoes.
2. On right arm.

D Any four of the following for a correct answer.
(i) 37 years old. (ii) Born in Paris. (iii) 1m80 tall. (iv) brown eyes. (v) Black hair. (vi) Married. (vii) With 3 children.

E 1. Rather shy/mixed up/full of complexes. 2. Her going out. 3. She doesn't think Frédérique is positive enough.

F (a) Very tense. (b) (i) Mother gets on at her all the time. (ii) Mother always wants to know what she is doing/where she is going/whom she has been out with/why she is back so late/if she has given her address to anyone. (Any one of these will get the mark.)

Unit 2: Where I live

Listening

A (L4) (a) 22 (b) Small house. (c) Quite a small town close to the German frontier.

B (L6) (a) The room has not been tidied/for three days. (b) Says she will do it straight after lunch. (c) No/mother says she must do it straight away. (d) He did the washing up/this morning.

C (L7) 7. (i) View. (ii) Plants. 8. 30 years. 9. It has become very noisy and extremely busy. 10. The beauty of the place. 11. Not having bought the flat. 12. It was very cheap at the time. 13. At the time they were having a little house built in the country, and they could not consider buying the flat as well. 14. They have a dream place in the country.

Reading

D (a) North of Tunis, in the suburbs. (b) 10 minutes. (c) Garden; balcony. (d) References. (e) Every day between 6 p.m. and 8.30 p.m.
(SB = **salle de bains**)

E   No visits on Sundays./Visit between 10 a.m. and 6 p.m.

F   40 minutes from the Gare de Lyon.

G (a) 2 months. (b) The lift is always in working order/the neighbours are nice/and two friends from school live in the block. (c) Share a room/with Richard. (d) There is a radiator close to the bed. (e) Watch TV/and work at his computer. (f) The flat is on the 8th floor/it is very noisy sometimes because they are building a block next door.

Basic Writing

H   One possible answer might be:
Echange de domiciles
Nom: *Smith*
Adresse exacte: *3, Woodburn Close, Bradford, Angleterre.*
Type de domicile: *Maison.*
Nombre de pièces: *5*
Détail des pièces: *2 chambres, salon, cuisine, salle à manger.*
Avez-vous un jardin? *Oui*
Situation du domicile: *Ville*

I Oui, chez nous c'est très calme, parce qu'on habite dans un petit village.

J Nous avons une maison, mais elle est assez petite, deux chambres, un salon et une salle à manger seulement.

K J'ai une grande chambre, avec une fenêtre qui donne sur le jardin. Il y aura certainement de la place pour toi.

L Cher ami,
Je vais te parler de ma maison. C'est une grande maison avec quatre chambres, une salle de bains, un salon, une salle à manger et une cuisine. Ma chambre se trouve en face de la salle de bains, et elle est grande avec un bureau, où je travaille, un lit et une armoire. Derrière la maison se trouve un beau jardin avec beaucoup de fleurs.
Amitiés

M Faire la vaisselle et ranger la cuisine.
Passer l'aspirateur dans le salon.
Mettre la table pour le repas du soir.
Aller chez le boulanger chercher du pain.
Acheter des fruits et des légumes.

Unit 3: School, work and future career

Listening

A (L9) (k) 9.10 (l) 8.50 (m) 2.30 (n) 6.05 (o) 11.15 (p) 3.40 (q) 10.55 (r) 5.30 (s) 4.15 (t) 1.25.

B (L11) (i) Christian – C. (ii) Vincent – F. (iii) Christel – B. (iv) Philippe – E. (v) Françoise – A.

C (L12) 1. Medicine. 2. Maths 3. Can't go out; no telephone for the pupils. 4. He cannot concentrate when there are so many pupils studying in one room. Because it is a boarding school, all the pupils have to do their evening work in the same classroom. 5. He can't stand any more, it makes him want to give up.

D 6. Students, sixth-formers, young unemployed. 7. Some employers have a tendency to exploit the young workers. 8. 12–14 hours per day. 9. Her overtime payment. 10. She did not want to stay a second longer.

Reading

E (a) Working abroad – 2. (b) Working at weekends – 3. (c) Working in a school – 4. (d) Working full-time – 4. (e) Working in the countryside – 1. (f) Working at Easter – 1. (g) Working only with secondary age children – 2. (h) Working which involves sport – 2.

F (a) To discover the history of their country. (b) To learn to speak their language better. (c) To learn to live together.

G (a) A lot of work at school/teachers are strict with pupils. (b) Languages. (c) Backache. (d) Not to do sport/for about two months. (e) He practised/4 times a week. (f) Holidays come to an end/and he has an important exam. (g) Yes. He is keen to work hard and pass his exam.

Basic Writing

H Cher ami,
Merci beaucoup pour ta lettre, et pour l'emploi du temps que tu m'as envoyé. Pour moi l'école commence tous les jours à 9 heures et se termine à 4 heures de l'après-midi. Pour le déjeuner nous avons une heure seulement, et nous mangeons à la cantine de l'école. Moi, j'aime beaucoup les langues, et je fais du français et de l'allemand. Mais je déteste les maths et les sciences. Mon professeur préféré est Monsieur Brown, notre professeur de français. Il est petit et mince avec des cheveux noirs, et il est très enthousiaste. Tous les soirs nous avons au moins 2 heures de devoirs à faire. Mais c'est important, parce que, plus tard, je voudrais devenir interprète.

Et toi, qu'est-ce que tu espères faire dans l'avenir? Réponds-moi vite.
Ton ami

J – Arrivé ici jeudi soir.
– Pour passer une semaine.
– Pour le moment il fait chaud.
– Donc ce matin j'ai nagé dans la mer.
– Ce soir je vais à un concert.

Unit 4: Free time

Listening

A (L14) (a) At André's house. (b) Friday evening. (c) About 9 o'clock. (d) One week.

B (L16) 1. 1986. 2. The whole history of the Post Office. 3. Many French, some from all the countries in the world. 4. Films about Post Office and Telecommunications. 5. Tuesday to Saturday. 6. 1 June–30 September. 7. (i) 8F per person (ii) 4F for school pupils and groups.

Reading

C

	True	False
You can get there by bus	x	
It is open in the afternoons		x
You have to bring roller-skates		x
Girls get in free in the evenings		x
It is open every evening	x	

D (a) Invent a computer game. (b) 30th August. (c) Make of computer used.

E (a) Play in English. (b) Make your own clothes. (c) Babies. (d) First Friday in each month/from 8.30 p.m. It is a club for people who own radio-controlled cars.

F (a) Parents can leave their children there in the morning. They are then taken to school. They are collected from school at 4.30. (b) Children of nursery and primary school age (4–11). (c) Meals; children can stay whole or half day. (d) Games and toys available for children, young people and adults.

G (a) Fine. (b) For a parcel she has been sent. (c) She has been to the swimming-pool and been horse-riding. (d) Play golf. (e) To spend her holidays with Sylvie in Scotland. She hopes to visit some haunted castles and see the Loch Ness monster. (f) On foot. (g) Eaten in a pub. (h) Cold weather. She tells Françoise to bring warm clothes.

Basic Writing

H (a) **Mon amie anglaise Claire a téléphoné.** (b) **Nous allons en ville ensemble regarder des vêtements.** (c) **Je serai de retour à 6 heures du soir.** (d) **Il y a une émission de musique pop anglaise ce soir à la télé. J'aimerais la voir.**

I (a) **Je reste à la maison cette année.** (b) **Je joue au tennis l'après-midi.** (c) **Il pleut aujourd'hui, alors je vais à la bibliothèque.** (d) **Je vais en France faire du ski à Noël.**

Unit 5: Shopping and money

Listening

A (L18) 9F50.

B (L19) Have you got any change?

C (L21) (a) Records. Two for the price of one. (b) Toothpaste. In the chemist's department. Best for your teeth. (c) Tomatoes. 10 francs a kilo.

D (L22) 11. Blue/without pockets/in the window. (Any 2 for the marks) 12. The shirt is for his brother. 13. Because when he borrows his brother's shirts they are a bit too big for him. 14. 94 francs. 15. It is cheap for a pure cotton shirt. 16. To go with the beige shirt he has chosen. 17. Gift-wrap the shirt.

E (L23) (i) It has a monitor. The price is right. (ii) (a) A is the one he has already. (b) B has no monitor. (c) C is too expensive.

Reading

F One pair free for every five pairs bought.

G (a) C. (b) A. (c) E. (d) D.

H (a) Make suggestions. (b) 200 francs of purchase price given back between 13.5 and 17.6 (c) Long sleeves/cashmere effect/100% cotton; costs 90 francs. (d) Writing paper. (e) Lowest prices/guaranteed prices/guaranteed freshness/provide choice. (f) Refund difference in price if you can buy same item cheaper within 30 kilometres within 30 days.

Basic Writing

I Here are some possible answers. (a) **Oui, près de chez moi il y a une boulangerie, une pharmacie et deux épiceries.** (b) **Oui, tous les samedi matins je vais en ville faire des courses dans les supermarchés.** (c) **Je n'achète pas souvent de vêtements, parce que cela coûte trop cher.**

Unit 6: Going abroad – Travel

Listening

A (L25) (a) Your passports please. (b) How long are you going to stay in France?

B (L26) 35. 4 trains. 36. 8.15. 37. Platform 1. 38. 40 Francs 39. 11.55. 40. Restaurant car.

C (L27) (a) 20.43. (b) 17.19. (c) 21.50. (d) 15.06. (e) 18.32.

D (L28) (a) RN960. (b) 1. There are lots of animals. 2. It is very interesting. 3. It costs 22F to go in.

E (L29) 1 (a) Fog. (b) In half an hour. 2 (a) look after his luggage for a moment. (b) Buy newspapers (=2). Buy newspaper (=1). 3 (a) Quite a long way/ from London. (b) Seats/for theatre/that evening. (c) get/a train. (d) She will miss her connection/and have to spend the night in London.

F (L30) 1. 8 km. 2. He doesn't like picking up hitch-hikers because of the dangers. 3. Because he was driving alone and wanted company.

G (L31) (a) Spain   – Too hot.
Edinburgh   – It rains too much.
Côte d'Azur – Too many people and too much traffic.
Switzerland – too expensive.
(b) Italy.
(c) 1. Petrol not dear. 2. Good food.

H (L32) 27. 12 km. 28. Accident. 29. Heavy traffic. 30. Diversion. 31. Less than 50 metres. 32. Heavy lorries. 33. Do not overtake without a good look in the mirror.

I (a) Single. (b) Bus station. (c) Bus or coach/ In front of, or outside the station. (d) **Correspondance.** (e) **Côté de stationnement.** (f) On the pavements. (g) Bikes. (h) Dangerous bend. (i) Have a full night's sleep. Drink plenty of pure water to get rid of poisonous substances. Rest for at least 2 hours, have some light refreshment. Go to bed. (j) 19 – 4; 20 – 3; 21 – 6; 22 – 9; 23 – 1.

J (a) Coach. (b) After an 8 a.m. departure on Friday morning. (c) In the morning a conducted tour on foot of the town centre. Visits to Duomo, Cathedral, Baptistery, Ponte Vecchio. Free in afternoon for individual sightseeing and shopping. (d) Passport or identity card.

K 14. Aged 4 to under 14. 15. Care of the child and entertainment for child during the journey. 16. In railway stations and travel agencies. 17. Friday noon. 18. Reservation of sleeping accommodation. 19. One piece of hand luggage which the child can carry him/herself. Weight not more than 10kg. 20. They should have been date-stamped. 21. If the child has food and drink. 22. 15 minutes before the arrival of the train. 23. They should inform the JVS service at the station of arrival, in plenty of time.

L You may choose any 3 out of the 6 possibilities given below.

Type of traveller	Type of ticket	Reduction
Occasional	5-ticket booklet	25%
Daily travellers to work	Weekly booklet	50%
Frequent travellers	Monthly	50%
Children under 10	Free	Free
Non rush-hour travellers	5-ticket booklet	50%
Groups	Group ticket	50%

Basic Writing

M (1) Je suis à Paris avec mon école. (2) Il fait très froid. (3) On fait des excursions tous les jours. (4) J'aime surtout les grands magasins. (5) Je n'aime pas la circulation à Paris.

N (i) Je suis en vacances en France. (ii) Je suis arrivé ici à 14 heures. (iii) Je passe la nuit dans un hôtel en ville, le Lion d'Or. (iv) Est-ce qu'on peut dîner ensemble ce soir? (iv) Tu peux me téléphoner à l'hôtel?

O Salut,
Merci pour ta lettre. Cet été nous avons six semaines de vacances. Je vais partir en Ecosse avec mes parents pour deux semaines. En Angleterre cet été il a fait très beau. On a de la chance cette année. Le soir, quand je suis en vacances, j'aime sortir pour aller dans les discos. En septembre, après les vacances, je vais retourner à l'école.
Amitiés

Unit 7: Going abroad – Somewhere to stay

Listening

A (L34) (a) 1. Greetings. (How are you?) 2. Hope you had a good journey. (b) 1. There is a key to the house. 2. And a key to the garage. (c) 1. Fishing in the river. 2. Hiring a boat.

B (L35) 15. Near the showers. 16. Swimming pool. 17. 200 metres away.

C (L36) 22. Because the hotel is very full. 23. Room 41. 24. In the car. 25. In quarter of an hour. 26. Fill in the form.

D (L37) 27. All year. 28. Give her the address. (Also, she offers to make a reservation and to telephone for her.) 29. She must get a card on the spot. It is not possible to sleep at a hostel without a card. 30. 43F. 31 Everywhere. 32. If sheets are provided for the bed.

Reading

E Hotel full.

F (a) 160F. (b) October. (c) There are games.

G (a) Hôtel d'Armor. (b) 33.46.29. (c) The rooms have washing facilities (i.e. wash-basins). (d) No restaurant. (e) Every day.

H Bedroom with twin beds/and room with double bed./Both rooms have shower/and WC.

I 17. All year. 18. Games. 19. Hot and free. 20. Heated swimming pool/sea 12km away. 21. Fishing/walks. 22. Caravans. 23. Food shop.

J

	Yes	No	No information
Hot water available		x	
Swimming pool available			x
Telephone on site		x	
Games area	x		
Place to eat nearby	x		
Grocery shop nearby			x
Bottle of gas available	x		

K (a)

		Savalon	Anfora	Pax
(i)	Heating		x	x
(ii)	Special provision children			x
(iii)	Games room			x
(iv)	Swimming pool	x		x
(v)	Lift		x	x

(b) Pax.

Basic Writing

L Here is a possible answer:
1. **le 3 mars 1990.** 2. **quatre lits.** 3. **14 août.** 4. **deux filles et deux garçons.** 5. **des douches.** 6. **le petit déjeuner.** 7. **les draps.** 8. **d'une ville.** 9. **une piscine.** 10. **tarifs.**

M Le Syndicat d'Initiative
   2, boulevard Féart,
   Dinan.

   Monsieur, Je serai à Dinard avec ma famille du 24 juillet au 12 août cette année. Je vous écris pour obtenir des renseignements sur la ville. Pouvez-vous m'envoyer un plan de la ville et des brochures? Est-ce que je peux avoir aussi une liste d'hôtels confortables situés près de la mer et pas trop chers? Est-ce qu'il y a des plages où on peut nager? Je voudrais savoir aussi s'il y a une piscine à Dinard.
   Je vous prie d'accepter, Monsieur, mes sentiments les meilleurs.

Unit 8: Food and drink

Listening

A (L38) Tomatoes/1 kilo; eggs/6; Flour/1 packet; butter/250 g; Total price 26F40.

B (L39) 15. Tin of sardines/packet of sugar/250 grammes of butter/jar of strawberry jam. 16. Some ham. 17. 300 grammes of pâté. 18. Tin opener/pocket lamp or torch.

C (L40 Starting at quarter to noon (11.45). Steak or pork.

D (L41)

		First customer	Second customer
Starters:	Onion soup		
	Tomato salad	x	
	Grated carrot		
	Sardines		
Main Course:	Chicken		x
	Duck		
	Steak		
	Pork	x	
Vegetables:	Peas		x
	Beans		
	Mushrooms		x
	Potatoes	x	
Drinks:	Beer		
	Red wine	x	
	White wine		
	Mineral water		x

E (L42) (a) What would you like? (b) Do you want something to eat as well? (c) Pay at the cash-desk.

F (L44)

Part of store	Particular reason
Basement	Special offers on fridges, freezers, transistors.
Information office	Daughter Nathalie Leblanc lost/has been found.
4th floor	To eat and drink/menu 45F/special kids' menu/till start of term.

Reading

G 1. Chips, salads, desserts, kebabs. 2. Brightly coloured/music/friendly atmosphere/quick/cheap/open until late.

H (a) 4 employees interviewed. (b) Same bucket used to rinse the floor cloth and wash the lettuce. Sometimes when they have been washing the floor they do not have time to wash their hands before going to work in the kitchen. (c) Because a quantity are prepared starting at 11 a.m. and they may not be eaten until the end of the midday rush at 2.30. (d) (i) Because many customers are in transit and will not return. (ii) They buy lower-quality products/ingredients. (e) Correct answers are (i), (iii), (vii), (viii). (f) The customer may be king, but the employees are badly treated subjects.

Unit 9: Problems and services

Listening

A (L46) 11. Youth club. 12. His father. 13. Broke his leg at work. 14. Hospital. 15. (a) Ask Michel to phone. (b) Tomorrow morning.

B (L47) (a) To call back/during office opening hours (9–12). (b) Transferred charge. (c) Because there is a technical problem (breakdown) and it is not possible to get through to Bordeaux.

C (L48) (a) Moped rider.   (b) Moped did not give way. He did not look and was going too fast.   (c) Near-side (right-hand side) rear light broken.   (d) The moped rider was not injured.

D (L49) 5. (a) Checked all doors/when he got home/all locked.   (b) People manage/to open everything/nowadays.   (c) Briefcase/with documents/not belonging to him.   (d) Call police.   (e) Very little/petrol/in car./They can't/get far.

Reading

E Protecting health/while travelling.

F Self service/washing and drying facilities.

G Road-users (drivers).

H 1. Do not get into a dangerous situation.   2. Ring the fire station/the police, the ambulance service./Explain what has happened without panic/Give your own number/and the exact place where the accident has occurred.   3. Describe the accident. Tell your parents as soon as possible.

I 7. She has not got a single part of her face/which is not covered with spots.   8. She has seen 7 doctors/and followed at least ten courses of treatment.   9. She is afraid to set foot in the street/outside school hours.   10. The readers who have had the same problems/and have found a solution.   11. Any remedy, whether an old-fashioned one/or the latest medical treatment.   12. Desperate.

Basic Writing

J Here is one possible answer.

Nom:	*Brown*
Prénom:	*Tracy*
Objet perdu:	*Valise*
Description:	*(i) En cuir (ii) petite*
Couleur:	*Noire*
Contenu:	*(i) 2 chemisiers (ii) un pantalon (iii) deux paires de chaussures (iv) articles de toilette (v) des collants (vi) deux livres.*

Unit 10: Higher Writing

Note that in all the examples of Higher Writing there will be many possible answers. The following answers are given as suggestions and examples.

A Salut,

Je te remercie pour ta lettre. Moi aussi, j'aime aller manger dans des restaurants si j'ai de l'argent, ou des fast food, si j'en ai moins. Chez nous, les fast food sont très populaires parmi les jeunes. On sort pour manger un hamburger ou une pizza, mais en même temps on a le plaisir de retrouver ses amis et de bavarder. Ma mère est aussi comme la tienne; elle fait très bien la cuisine. Je sais qu'en général les Français n'ont pas une bonne opinion de la cuisine anglaise, mais cette réputation n'est pas toujours juste. Maman prépare des repas délicieux.

En principe, il est possible de trouver du travail en Angleterre pendant les vacances. Moi, j'ai travaillé cette année dans un hôtel. On habite près de la mer, comme tu sais, alors il y a beaucoup de travail dans les hôtels et les restaurants pendant la saison. Beaucoup de jeunes Anglais trouvent du travail le weekend, dans des magasins, par exemple. C'est important de pouvoir gagner un peu d'argent pour s'acheter des vêtements ou pour aller en vacances.

En parlant de vacances, ce sera vraiment bien d'aller ensemble en Espagne l'année prochaine. Je n'ai jamais voyagé seule à l'étranger, mais j'ai maintenant 16 ans, comme toi, et je suis sûre que mes parents me laisseraient partir avec toi. Je vais commencer à faire des économies pour ces vacances. Amitiés.

B Here is a possible answer written by a girl on behalf of herself and her friend.

Chère Madame,

Je vous remercie beaucoup de la lettre que vous avez écrite à mon professeur au sujet de la possibilité de travail dans votre ferme. Mon amie et moi, on voudrait beaucoup venir passer temps en France, et nous sommes ravies que vous seriez prête à nous accueillir. Vous avez demandé des renseignements sur notre travail en France l'année dernière. Eh bien, nous étions toutes les deux employées comme femmes de chambre dans un grand hôtel aux environs de Rouen. C'est un travail qui a duré presque tout le mois d'août, c'est-à-dire pendant la saison des vacances. On devait surtout nettoyer les chambres et faire les lits, mais de temps en temps nous avons aussi aidé à servir dans le restaurant. C'est surtout le travail dans le restaurant que nous avons préféré, parce qu'on rencontrait plus de gens. Le travail dans les chambres était assez pénible.

Nous voulons faire autre chose cette année, et l'idée d'aider dans une ferme nous plaît. Dans une région montagneuse, il serait possible pendant notre temps libre de faire des randonnées. Où est-ce que votre ferme est située exactement? Quelle sorte de travail est-ce qu'on pourrait faire? Nous aimons beaucoup toutes les deux travailler avec des animaux. Quelle sorte de bêtes est-ce que vous avez?

Notre professeur va vous écrire, mais il me demande de vous exprimer ses regrets concernant l'accident de votre fils.

Nous vous remercions de votre gentille invitation de venir travailler chez vous, et nous attendons avec impatience votre prochaine lettre.

Je vous prie d'accepter, chère Madame, mes sentiments les meilleurs.

C Je vais vous parler du travail que j'ai fait pendant les vacances de Noël. Je travaillais comme facteur, pendant une période où il y a beaucoup de courrier.

Tout d'abord, j'avais vu une annonce dans le journal qui demandait des candidats pour des postes de facteur.

Il a fallu écrire une lettre à la Poste Centrale, au Service du Personnel, pour donner des détails sur mon âge et mon expérience.

J'ai travaillé pendant la période du 17 au 24 décembre.

Le travail était assez bien payé.

C'était un travail assez intéressant, parce qu'il y avait beaucoup à faire et qu'on n'avait pas le temps de s'ennuyer. Mais je n'aimais pas me lever si tôt le matin.

Ce que j'ai aimé le plus, c'était de parler avec les gens qui recevaient des paquets de Noël.

D   Pendant le trimestre je dois me lever très tôt, parce que j'habite assez loin de l'école et je dois prendre le bus à huit heures. Alors je me lève à sept heures. Quelle horreur! Je préfère le weekend, quand je peux rester plus longtemps au lit. Une fois levé, je fais ma toilette en vitesse, et je descends déjeuner vers 7h30 – mais je ne mange pas beaucoup. Ça ne me dit rien de manger à cette heure du matin, alors je prends juste une petite tasse de café. On a des cours de 9h à 12h, une heure et demie pour déjeuner, puis on rentre à la maison à 4 heures de l'après-midi. C'est le mardi que je déteste, parce que, non seulement la journée est pleine à l'école, mais j'ai toujours beaucoup de devoirs le soir. Après être rentré, je me repose un peu, puis nous mangeons en famille vers six heures du soir quand mon père rentre de son travail. Le weekend, comme j'ai déjà dit, c'est le moment que je préfère. On est plus décontracté, et on peut écouter de la musique, retrouver ses copains – et rester plus longtemps au lit!

E   Pendant quinze jours cet été, j'ai eu la chance de passer du temps dans un Centre en Ecosse, et j'aimerais vous parler un peu de ce séjour. Nous étions 14 élèves de ma classe, et deux professeurs. Comme nous nous intéressons tous à toutes sortes d'activités de plein air, ce Centre était vraiment idéal. C'était un ancien manoir qu'on avait modernisé à l'intérieur en y construisant des dortoirs pour les élèves, des chambres individuelles pour les profs, une magnifique salle de jeux, une grande salle à manger et il y avait même le chauffage central – ce qui est important quand on rentre trempé après une journée en montagne. On avait le choix entre toutes sortes d'activités pendant ces 15 jours, par exemple natation, randonnée pédestre, cyclisme. Il y avait aussi des jeux d'équipe, ce que je n'aime pas personnellement, mais qui étaient quand même assez intéressants. Pour moi, la journée la plus passionnante a été certainement celle de la randonnée en montagne. Il faisait un temps froid mais clair, et il y avait des vues extraordinaires des sommets aux alentours du Centre.

Le dernier soir, on a eu toute une soirée de jeux, suivis d'un disco. C'était vraiment bien pour terminer les vacances les plus actives et les plus intéressantes que j'ai jamais passées.

F   C'était pendant les vacances, et ce jour-là, j'étais assis sur une chaise pliante, dans le jardin, avec un livre. Pour dire la vérité, je m'étais presque endormi, mais tout à coup, je me suis réveillé en sursaut, à cause d'un bruit qui venait de la maison en face de chez nous. C'était surprenant, parce que je savais bien que les gens étaient partis en vacances et que la maison était vide. Un homme et une femme étaient en train d'ouvrir la porte de la maison, et c'était ce bruit-là qui m'avait réveillé. Je ne savais pas quoi faire. Apparemment, l'homme et la femme avaient une clef, ils étaient peut-être des amis de nos voisins, alors? J'ai décidé d'attendre un peu, mais pendant une bonne demi-heure, rien ne bougeait. Et puis, quelle horreur, la porte s'est ouverte lentement, et l'homme et la femme sont ressortis, mais cette fois avec deux grosses valises. Ils ont fermé la porte, regardé autour d'eux, et puis ils sont partis. Pendant un moment je les ai regardés descendre la rue, puis, enfin, je me suis décidé à agir, et j'ai couru téléphoner à la police.

Heureusement, il n'était pas trop tard, et la police est vite arrivée sur la scène, et j'ai vu alors les deux cambrioleurs partir, toujours avec les valises, dans une voiture de la police.

G   (1) La semaine dernière, les parents de mon ami Michel ont annoncé leur intention de sortir pour aller au théâtre, et ils ont donné à Michel la permission d'inviter ses amis à passer la soirée chez lui. Tout a très bien commencé. La mère de Michel avait préparé à manger, et il y avait du Coca cola et de la limonade à boire. Quelques-uns bavardaient, d'autres dansaient ou écoutaient de la musique.

(2) Soudain, il y a eu un grand bruit à la porte, et une bande de jeunes, qu'on ne connaissait pas du tout, est entrée chez Michel. C'étaient des types qui avaient déjà beaucoup bu, et qui avaient certainement entendu la musique en passant devant la maison. En entrant ils ont bousculé des gens, et ils ont pris tout ce qu'ils trouvaient à manger.

(3) Après, ça a été affreux! Il n'y avait pas moyen de les faire sortir. Ils ont cassé les meubles et les disques, ils ont fait du bruit, ils ont tout bu et tout mangé. Plusieurs de nos amis sont partis, et on avait vraiment peur, mais que faire?

(4) Enfin, à minuit cinq, les parents de Michel sont rentrés. Les voyous étaient partis, mais quel désordre! Les disques étaient par terre, et tout était détruit. La soirée avait été un vrai désastre, et il a fallu tout expliquer aux parents pour qu'ils comprennent que nous, on n'était pas responsables.

GRAMMAR REFERENCE SECTION

Grammar Reference Section

Table of Contents

Grammar Summary

This summary does not, of course, claim to be a complete grammar of French. It does, however, cover all the grammar normally required for the GCSE examination. The Table of Contents gives you a general indication of where to find the information you want about verbs, tenses, adjectives and so on. Many of the examples given have been taken from texts in the book. A reference such as (L4) directs you to Listening text number 4 to find the example given. The reference (10D) means that you will find the example in the Key to the Exercises for Chapter 10, Exercise D.

1. Nouns

Definitions

Nouns are the parts of speech which act as *names* for objects, actions, feelings, ideas and animate beings. For example, the following words are all *nouns*: **table** (object), **promenade** (action), **colère** (feeling), **idée** (idea), **cheval** (animate being). There is a special sort of noun called a *proper noun*. These nouns are always written with a capital letter and refer to objects which have their own, individual name, like towns **(Paris)**, countries **(Angleterre)**, people **(Christine).**

Gender

French nouns are classified into two genders, masculine and feminine. As a general rule it can be said that male animals and people are masculine and female animals and people are feminine. English divides words into masculine (males you can refer to as *he*), feminine (females you can refer to as *she*), and neuter (objects you can refer to as *it*). So you can see that all those objects which you call *it* in English must be either masculine or feminine in French. Deciding whether a French word is masculine or feminine can be a problem. Below you are given some rules for recognising gender from the *form* of the word. But the safest way is to make sure that when you learn a word you learn its gender at the same time.

(a) Rules for recognising masculine gender
The following words are masculine.
(i)   Words ending in **-ier, -age, -as, -ement, -ament, -in, -is, -on, -illon, -isme, -oir.** (But note the small group of feminine words ending in **-age: plage, cage, page, image.**)
(ii)   Words ending in **-eau.** (Except **l'eau** = *water*; **la peau** = *skin*)
(iii)   Names of trees (e.g. **le chêne** = *oak*)
(iv)   Names of metals (e.g. **le fer** = *iron*)
(v)   Names of languages (e.g. **le français, le russe**)
(vi)   Names of days, months and seasons (**le lundi** = *Monday*; **le printemps** = *spring*)

(b) Rules for recognising feminine gender
The following words are feminine.
   Words ending in **-ade, -aie, -aine, -aison, -ison, -ande, -ée, -ence, -esse, -ille, -ise, -sion, -tion, -te, -ure.** Also all words ending in **-ette** except for **le squelette** = *skeleton*; and all words ending in **-ie** except for **un incendie** = *fire* and **un parapluie** = *umbrella* Note also **le silence.**

(c) Rules for forming feminine nouns from masculine nouns
There are many cases where the feminine noun is formed from the masculine by adding a letter or changing an ending. These are the most common.
(i)   Masculine adds **-e (ami, amie).**
(ii)   Masculine **-en** and **-on** double the **n** and add **-e (lycéen, lycéenne; Breton, Bretonne).**
(iii)   Masculine **-ain** and **-in** add **-e (voisin, voisine).**
(iv)   Masculine **-at** and **-ot** add **-e (candidat, candidate).** Note the exception **chat, chatte.**
(v)   Masculine **-er** becomes **-ère (cuisinier, cuisinière).**
(vi)   Masculine **-x** changes to **-se (époux, épouse).**
(vii)   Masculine **-eur** becomes **-euse (danseur, danseuse; serveur, serveuse).**
(viii) Numerous masculine nouns ending in **-teur** change the ending to **-trice (inspecteur, inspectrice).**
(ix)   Some feminine forms end in **-esse (maître, maîtresse).**
(x)   Some words change the article to show whether the person is male or female, but there is no change in the word itself (**un élève, une élève; le touriste, la touriste**).

(xi)   Some words which look and sound the same have different genders (**un livre** = *a book*; **une livre** = *a pound*).

(d) Rules for forming the plural of nouns
Most English words form the plural by adding an *-s*, for example *school, schools; pupil, pupils*. French also forms most plurals by adding an **-s,** for example **école, écoles; élève, élèves.** Some words in English form their plural in a rather irregular way, for example *man, men; mouse, mice*. French also has some irregular plurals. The main ones are listed below:
(i)   Words ending in **-s, -x, -z** do not change in the plural (**un nez, deux nez; une croix, deux croix**).
(ii)   Words ending in **-al** form the plural in **-aux (un cheval, trois chevaux).** But note the exceptions: **un bal, des bals; un festival, beaucoup de festivals.**
(iii)   Words ending in **-au, -eau, -eu** add **x (un manteau, deux manteaux).** But note the exception: **un pneu, des pneus.**
(iv)   Words ending in **-ail** normally add **-s** in the plural (**détail, détails**). But note: **le travail, les travaux.**

2.   Articles

English has just two articles. These are the definite article, *the*, and the indefinite article, *a*, which becomes *an* before a vowel. In French these articles are as follows.
(a)   Definite Article
Masculine: **le** (or **l'** in front of a vowel): **le professeur, l'élève.**
Feminine: **la** (or **l'** in front of a vowel): **la femme, l'école.**
In the plural the definite article is always **les: les professeurs, les élèves, les femmes, les écoles.**
When it combines with the words **à** (*to* or *at*) and **de** (*of* or *from*), the definite article changes as follows: **à + le = au; à + les = aux; de + le = du; de + les = des.**
   Very often, the French definite article is used just like *the* in English. However, there are some cases in French where you use the definite article and do not use it in English:
(i)   When nouns are used in a general sense: **je n'aime pas les oeufs** − *I don't like eggs.*
(ii)   Very often with parts of the body: **mon père s'est cassé la jambe** (L45); **elle a les cheveux blonds et les yeux verts** (L2).
(iii)   Very often with days of the week, for example at the start of a letter: **le lundi 30 juin** = *Monday the 30th June.* Also when referring to a repeated action on a particular day: **on ne travaille pas le dimanche** = *we don't work on Sundays.*
(iv)   With units of weight or length, as you will hear when shopping: **deux francs le kilo** = *two francs a kilo.*
(v)   Before names of countries and provinces: **la France est un pays où on mange bien; la Normandie est la province que je préfère.** The article is *not* used after **en: je vais en France; il habite en Normandie.**

(b) Indefinite Article

Masculine **un: un garçon, un homme.**

Feminine **une: une femme, une table.**

In the plural, English often does not have a form of the indefinite article. The plural of *a boy* is just *boys*. In French you must use **des** as the plural of **un** and **une.** So the plural of **un garçon** is **des garçons.**

(c) Partitive Article

It is nearly always the case that there must be some sort of article in front of a French noun. In English you can say quite simply *butter, eggs, milk, bread.* But in French you must use a word to mean *some butter, some eggs, some milk, some bread.* This is called the partitive article. The forms are as follows.

Masculine – **du, de l', des.**

Feminine – **de la, de l', des.**

Note the following uses of the partitive article.

(i)   As explained above, it is used to express an unspecified amount of an object. If you were shopping you would say, **je voudrais du pain, de la farine, des oeufs et de l'ail.**

(ii) After expressions of quantity and containers, the partitive article becomes simply **de: beaucoup de pain; assez de farine; une douzaine d'oeufs; une bouteille de vin.**

(iv) The partitive article also takes the form **de** after a negative: **je ne bois pas de vin** (L40); **je ne veux pas de hors d'oeuvres** (L40).

3.   Adjectives

An adjective is a word which describes a noun, so words such as colours, and indications of size such as **grand, petit,** are all adjectives.

(a) Position of the adjective

In general, adjectives in French come *after* the noun they describe: for example, **avec les cheveux gris** (L2), **une barbe grise** (L2), **des chambres individuelles** (10E), **la frontière allemande** (L4).

However, a number of common adjectives come *before* the nouns they describe, in particular **grand, petit, joli, bon, mauvais, jeune, vieux.** Note these examples: **une petite maison** (L4), **une mauvaise idée** (L31).

When there are two adjectives describing the noun, it is possible for one to come in front of the noun and the other after: **une grande ville moderne.**

A small number of adjectives change their meaning depending on whether they are used before or after the noun: **le dernier jour des vacances** = *the last (= final) day of the holidays;* **la semaine dernière** = *last week.*

(b) Agreement of adjectives

Adjectives must agree with the noun if it is feminine or plural. Note the following rules.

(i)   The feminine form of the adjective is usually made by adding **-e** to the masculine: **un petit village** (L30); **une petite maison** (L4). Adjectives which already end in **-e** in the masculine form do not change: **Mlle Richard, qui est petite et mince** (L2); **une vue admirable** (L7).

(ii) Adding an **-e** sometimes causes changes in the spelling of the word. Adjectives ending in **-en** or **-on** double the **n: bon, bonne; ancien, ancienne.** The adjectives **bas, gras, gros** all double the **s: basse, grasse, grosse.** Note also **faux, fausse.**

(iii) Adjectives ending in **-er** change to **-ère: léger, légère.**

(iv) Adjectives ending in **-x** change to **-se: heureux, heureuse; doux, douce.**

(v)   Adjectives ending in **-f** change to **-ve: naïf, naïve.**

(vi) **blanc, franc, sec** change to **blanche, franche, sèche.**

(vii) **beau, nouveau, fou, mou** become **belle, nouvelle, folle, molle.**

(viii) **long** becomes **longue.**

(ix) Most adjectives ending in **-et** double the **t: muet, muette; net, nette.**

(x)   Almost all adjectives form the plural by adding **s** to the singular form. The only exceptions are: adjectives ending in **-s, -x** which do not change: **un homme heureux; des hommes heureux;** adjectives ending in **-eau** which add **x: les beaux jours;** adjectives ending in **al** which form the plural **-aux: loyal, loyaux.**

(c) Comparison of adjectives

(i)   In English, adjectives usually add *-er* when one thing is compared with another, for example *bigger, smaller, longer, shorter.* Another possibility in English, common with longer adjectives, is to use *more,* e.g. *more splendid, more magnificent.* It is in this way that comparisons are made in French, by using **plus,** for example **plus grand** = *bigger;* **plus petit** = *smaller;* **plus long** = *longer;* **plus court** = *shorter.* If you want to complete the comparison by saying *bigger than,* or *smaller than,* note the following examples:

> **mon frère est plus grand que moi** = *my brother is bigger than me;*
> **ma soeur est plus âgée que toi** = *my sister is older than you.*

(ii) There are two irregular comparatives for you to note in French: **bon – meilleur** *(better);* **mauvais – pire** *(worse).*

(iii) There are other sorts of comparisons which are made, besides those mentioned already. Here are some examples from English, with their French equivalents:

> *the bus is less expensive than the train* = **le bus est moins cher que le train;**
> *he comes to see me as often as possible* = **il vient me voir aussi souvent que possible.**

(iv) The superlative *(biggest, smallest, prettiest,* etc.) is formed in French by placing the definite article in front of the comparative form: **la journée la plus passionnante; les vacances les plus actives et les plus intéressantes que j'ai jamais passées** (10E). The two irregular comparatives mentioned above are also irregular in the superlative, for example **c'est le meilleur élève de la classe** = *he's the best pupil in the class.*

4. Possessives

In English, possession is shown by words such as *my, his, her, your,* etc. These words are called possessive adjectives. In French they are as follows.

	Singular masculine	*Singular feminine*	*Plural*
my	mon	ma	mes
your	ton	ta	tes
his	son	sa	ses
her	son	sa	ses
its	son	sa	ses
our	notre	notre	nos
your	votre	votre	vos
their	leur	leur	leurs

Note that when a feminine word begins with a vowel, the forms **mon, ton, son** are used in the singular instead of **ma, ta, sa,** for example **mon école.** The most important point to note about differences between French and English concerns the third-person singular forms. Consider these examples:

Paul va à l'ecole avec son frère et sa soeur.

Anne-Sophie aussi va avec son frère et sa soeur.

You see that, in English, the words *him* and *her* refer back to the *subject* of the sentence. (See paragraph 6(d) for a definition of *subject*.) So the above sentences would be: *Paul goes to school with his brother and his sister. Anne-Sophie also goes with her brother and her sister.* In French **son, sa, ses** can mean either *his* or *her* and change according to the gender and number of the word following. Another example (in L22) is **j'emprunte ses chemises** = I borrow his shirts.

Note also that **notre, votre, leur** are singular in form if the word following them is singular, and they take the plural form if the word following is in the plural: **n'oubliez pas notre rayon maison . . . nos frigidaires, nos transistors** (L44).

5. Demonstratives

In English, if you want to point out the position of something, you use the words *this*, for something close to you, and *that*, for something further away. This is called the demonstrative adjective.

In French the demonstrative adjective has the following forms:

Singular masculine: **ce** (**cet** before a word beginning with a vowel);
Singular feminine: **cette;**
Plural, all forms: **ces.**

Therefore, **cette assiette** (L43) = *this plate;* **cet appartement** (L7) = *this apartment;* **ce soir** (L15) = *this evening;* **ce collier** (L20) = *this necklace.* Usually, if you want to give the sense of the English word *that*, you say: **cette assiette-là; ce soir-là; cet appartement-là.**

6. Pronouns

There are various kinds of pronoun, but their main characteristic is that they stand in place of a noun or some other part of speech which has already been expressed. For example, if in one sentence you refer to *the teacher*, you can refer to him or her in the following sentence by the word *he* or *she*, which are third-person pronouns. (See table below.)

(i) The *subject* pronouns are the ones you use most often, whenever you say, for example, **je voudrais,** or **vous avez.** These are the weak forms of pronouns, and if you want to stress the pronoun, you can add the emphatic pronoun shown above, for example: **moi, je n'aime pas ça; toi, tu n'en sais rien!**

(ii) A very important little pronoun is **on. On** is often used instead of **nous,** if you want to refer to what you and your friends are doing. For example, in B10 you will find: **mon ami et moi, on voudrait beaucoup venir passer du temps en France** = *my friend and I would very much like to come and spend some time in France.* The writer of the letter could just as well have said **nous voudrions. . . .** If you look through that letter in B10, you will see that the writer uses **nous** or **on** with the same meaning: **on devait nettoyer les chambres . . . nous avons aussi aidé à servir. . . .** Another example is on p. 58, where you will find **on a parlé ensemble. . . .** Besides this use of **on,** it is also used to mean

(a) Personal pronouns

	First person masc & fem	Second person masc & fem	Third person masc	Third person fem
Singular				
Subject	je	tu	il	elle
Direct object	me	te	le	la
Indirect object	me	te	lui	lui
Emphatic	moi	toi	lui	elle
Plural				
Subject	nous	vous	ils	elles
Direct object	nous	vous	les	les
Indirect object	nous	vous	leur	leur
Emphatic	nous	vous	eux	elles

people, or *they* in a very general sense, like when you hear in English, *they say that . . .* or *people say that. . . .* In French this would be **on dit que. . . .** Finally, you can use it like the English *one,* for example: **on peut même voir la Suisse** = *one can even see Switzerland* (L5).

(iii) The direct object pronouns come immediately after the verb in English, as when you say: *they see me; I buy them; they like us.* In French, these object pronouns come before the verb: **ils me voient; je les achète; ils nous aiment.** The same is true of indirect object pronouns. This is the pronoun which, in English, can usually be recognised because of the use of the preposition *to,* as in this example: *we speak to him every day.* In French this would be **nous lui parlons tous les jours.** Some verbs, for example *to give,* may have both a direct and an indirect object, as in the sentence: *she gives the book* (direct object) *to her mother* (indirect object). If you use pronouns instead of nouns, this becomes *she gives it to her.* The problem in French is then to get the correct order of the pronouns in front of the verb: **elle le lui donne.** If ever you have two pronouns in one sentence, then there are quite strict rules for the order in which they come. This order is as follows.

me					
te	le	lui			
se					
nous	la	leur	y	en	VERB
vous	les				

(Notes on **y** and **en** are given in paragraphs (vi) and (vii) below.)

Here are some more examples of the order of pronouns in front of the verb.

Il m'envoie la lettre; il me l'envoie.

Elle explique les règles à ses amis; elle les leur explique.

In L29 you will find the question: **Est-ce que ça vous dérangerait de me les garder?** = *Would you mind looking after them for me?*

(iv) When a verb is in the Perfect or Pluperfect Tense, which is formed by an auxiliary verb (**être** or **avoir**) with a past participle, the pronouns come in front of the auxiliary: **il nous a envoyé la lettre.** When a pronoun object is feminine or plural and it comes before the auxiliary verb **avoir,** the past participle must agree with the preceding direct object, e.g. in L7, **la pièce . . . vous l'avez vue.** The feminine **-e** is added to the past participle **vu** because the preceding object refers to **la pièce.**

(v) In paragraph (i) above, we said that the emphatic forms of the pronouns are used to reinforce the subject pronoun, e.g. in 10A, **moi, j'ai travaillé dans un hôtel.** Another use of the emphatic pronouns is after prepositions, e.g. **pour moi** (L11); **autour d'eux** (10F).

(vi) The emphatic pronouns are also used to follow a verb used in the Imperative. That means when giving commands, e.g. **donnez-moi un quart**

de vin rouge (L38). Note that a hyphen is used to link the verb and the pronoun in this position. Note also that pronouns *follow* the Imperative when it is used to give a positive instruction like **donnez-moi; écoutez-lui; attends-moi.** When the imperative is *negative,* however, the pronouns come in front of the verb in the usual way: **ne me parlez pas de ça.**

(vi) Two common and important little pronouns are **y** and **en.** They usually refer to places, objects or abstract ideas. **En** is closely related in sense to the preposition **de,** and is therefore found as a pronoun object with verbs normally followed by **de.** For example, **penser de** means *to think about,* as in the question: **Qu'est-ce que vous pensez de ma nouvelle robe?** If a pronoun replaced the noun **ma robe,** this sentence would become: **Qu'est-ce que vous en pensez?** = *What do you think about it?* Another example might be **elle est sortie de la maison** = *she came out of the house.* With the pronoun, this becomes **elle en est sortie.**

A common use of **en** is when you are using numbers in French. If you are asked *How many lessons have you got today?* you might answer, *I've got six.* In French you would say **J'en ai six** = *I've got six (of them).*

(vii) The pronoun **y** corresponds to a construction with **à,** or with the use of a preposition such as **dans, en, sur, sous.** So if you have a verb like **aller à,** you will understand why you say, **j'y vais** = *I am going there.* Similarly, the sentence **il est entré dans la maison** becomes **il y est entré.** The most common use of **y** is in **il y a,** meaning *there is* or *there are.* In L5, where Michel is being shown round the flat, there are two examples of **il y a: il y a seulement deux chambres . . . il y a une vue magnifique sur les Alpes.** See 10G for an example in the Perfect Tense: **il y a eu un grand bruit.** The same passage has an example of the Imperfect Tense in the negative: **il n'y avait pas moyen de les faire sortir** = *there was no way to get them to go.*

(b) Possessive pronouns

In English, if you say *my book,* the word *my* is a possessive adjective. If you say *this book is mine,* the word *mine* is a possessive pronoun. Like the other pronouns we have discussed it stands for a noun, but in this case it also has the idea of belonging or possession. In the text for 10A, you will find the sentence, **ma mère est aussi comme la tienne** = *my mother is also like yours.* **La tienne** is an example of the French possessive pronoun. In the Listening text L3, you will find **les miens, ils veulent que je reste à la maison.** Here, **les miens** is the possessive pronoun standing for **mes parents.** Here are the complete forms of the possessive pronoun:

Singular	One object	Several objects	English
First person masculine	**le mien**	**les miens**	*mine*
feminine	**la mienne**	**les miennes**	*mine*
Second person masculine	**le tien**	**les tiens**	*yours*
feminine	**la tienne**	**les tiennes**	*yours*
Third person masculine	**le sien**	**les siens**	*his, hers, its*
feminine	**la sienne**	**les siennes**	*his, hers, its*
Plural			
First person masculine	**le nôtre**	**les nôtres**	*ours*
feminine	**la nôtre**	**les nôtres**	*ours*
Second person masculine	**le vôtre**	**les vôtres**	*yours*
feminine	**la vôtre**	**les vôtres**	*yours*
Third person masculine	**le leur**	**les leurs**	*theirs*
feminine	**la leur**	**les leurs**	*theirs*

(c) Demonstrative pronouns

You will remember that the demonstrative adjective in English is *this* or *that*, as in *this car; that bus.* If you asked someone, *Which is your car?* and they answered, *This one*, they are using a demonstrative pronoun. The forms of the French demonstrative pronoun are as follows:

	Masculine	*Feminine*
Singular	**celui**	**celle**
Plural	**ceux**	**celles**

(i) Here are some examples from the texts in the book of the way they are used: **la pièce dans laquelle nous étions . . . celle qui était sur les bords de la Seine** (L7) = *the room we were in . . . the one which was on the banks of the Seine.* **Celle** is the feminine singular form of the demonstrative pronoun, standing instead of **la pièce**.

Je préfère celle sans poches (L22) = *I prefer this one without pockets.* Here, **celle** refers to **une chemise**.

Sometimes the possessive pronoun is linked by a hyphen to **-ci** or **-là,** so that it adds a clearer idea of the object you mean, just as you say in English *this one here* or *that one over there.* **Et celui-là, là-bas . . . celui-ci aussi a un lecteur de disques** (L23) = *And that one over there . . . this one here also has a disc-drive.*

(ii) **Ce** is a form of the demonstrative pronoun which is the nearest thing in French to a neuter pronoun. It is very often used with the verb **être** as in **c'est important** (10A); **ce sera vraiment bien** (10A); **c'était un travail assez intéressant** (10C). Here it means very much the same as English *it*. It can also be used in this way negatively, e.g. **ça ce n'est pas vrai** (L6). Note that sometimes **ça** or **cela** are used to give more emphasis to **ce**.

(d) Relative pronouns

The English relative pronouns are *who, whom* or *which* in phrases such as: *the teacher who takes me for French; the book which I am reading at the moment.* The French words **qui** and **que** can both mean *who, whom* and *which*. The one you choose depends on the role played by the relative pronoun in the sentence. First, you need to understand how to recognise the subject and the object of a verb. The *subject* of a verb is the person or thing which performs the action. The *object* of the verb is the person or thing to which the action happens. Consider the sentence: *The man throws the ball.* The verb is *throws*. The person performing the action is *the man,* and that is therefore the subject. The action is happening to *the ball,* so that is the object. Now read further about subjects and objects in relative clauses.

(i) **qui** is the subject of the relative clause. What does this mean? Look at the following example. **C'est un travail** (main clause) **qui a duré presque tout le mois d'août** (relative clause) (10B). If you put your finger on the verb in the relative clause **(a duré)** and ask yourself where its subject is, you will see that the subject must be **qui,** which is a pronoun standing for **travail.** If you were very long-winded, you might write out in full: **C'est un travail. Le travail a duré. . . .** By using **qui** you avoid the need to repeat the noun, but **qui** still acts as the subject of the relative clause. In 10G you have the sentence: **C'étaient des types qui avaient déjà beaucoup bu.** Here, **qui** stands for the noun **des types,** and is the subject of the verb **avaient bu.**

(ii) **Que** is the direct object of the relative clause. If you look at the sentence **C'était un ancien manoir qu'on avait modernisé** (10F), you see that, written out in full, this sentence would be: **C'était un ancien manoir. On avait modernisé le manoir.** This shows you that the subject of the relative clause in this case is **on,** and the direct object is **le manoir** or the relative pronoun **que** which stands for **manoir.** In text 10G you have another sentence using **que: Une bande de jeunes est entrée qu'on ne connaissait pas du tout.** Here, **que** is a relative pronoun, object of the verb **connaissait.** Notice that **que** can be shortened to **qu'** before a vowel, but **qui** is never shortened.

(iii) Sometimes the relative clause may be introduced by a preposition, as when you say in English *the room in which he is standing.* In everyday English you might actually say *the room he is standing in,* but to get it right in French you need to recognise that this is really a relative clause. In sentences like this, French uses a combination of the preposition plus the appropriate form of **lequel, laquelle, lesquels, lesquelles,** depending on whether the word referred to is masculine or feminine, singular or plural. So in L7, you find: **la pièce dans laquelle nous étions,** where **laquelle** is feminine singular standing for **la pièce.**

7. Asking Questions

You will find some helpful hints about asking questions in Unit 1 (pp. 16–17). These notes are to give you a little more information.

(a) **Qui?** is used for people only (do *not* get confused with the relative pronoun where **qui** can mean *who* or *which*): **Tu étais avec qui?** = *Whom were you with?* Note that, as with the relative pronouns, **qui** is never shortened.

(b) **Que?** means *what?*, and refers to objects. **Que** is again shortened to **qu'** in front of a vowel: **Salut Christian, qu'as-tu fait ce matin?** (L11). This way of putting a question, where **que** is followed by the verb and then the subject, is regarded as rather formal in modern French, and it is much more common to ask the question *what?* by using **qu'est-ce que?** There is an example in the same Listening text as has just been quoted: **qu'est-ce que tu fais cet après-midi?** (L11). Later in the same passage, Christel asks Françoise, **qu'en penses-tu?** = *what do you think of that?* She could just as well have asked, **qu'est-ce que tu en penses?**

(c) **Quel** is an adjective, so it must always be used with a noun. It must agree with the noun that follows, so it has singular and plural forms in the masculine and feminine **(quel, quelle, quels, quelles).** It is equivalent in meaning to the English *what?* or *which?* Look at the following examples: **quelles sont tes matières préférées à l'école?** = *what are your favourite subjects at school?* (L11); **c'est à quel nom?** = *what name?* (L37).

This form is also used with the force of an exclamation: **quelle horreur!** = *how terrible!* (10F).

(d) **Quoi?** also means *what?*, and very often stands alone. You may often hear it in the phrase **quoi d'autre?** = *what else?*

8. Numbers and Quantities

There are two sorts of numbers to look at. Cardinal numbers are the straightforward numbers you hear when you count, or when you ask how much something costs or how many items there are. Ordinal numbers are those like *first, second, third,* etc., where you are thinking of objects coming in a particular order.

Most of the numbers between 70 and 100 are given below, because these are the ones which often prove difficult to remember. There are rules for the use of hyphens, and various other features of spelling, but we shall not go into explanations here. One point you might note is that **cent** shows the plural unless followed by another numeral. So you write **deux cents** (200), but **deux cent trois** (203). **Mille** never adds a plural **-s: trois mille** (3000).

(a) Cardinal numbers

1	**un, une**	21	**vingt et un**	83	**quatre-vingt-trois**
2	**deux**	22	**vingt-deux**	84	**quatre-vingt-quatre**
3	**trois**	23	**vingt-trois**	85	**quatre-vingt-cinq**
4	**quatre**	30	**trente**	86	**quatre-vingt-six**
5	**cinq**	40	**quarante**	87	**quatre-vingt-sept**
6	**six**	50	**cinquante**	88	**quatre-vingt-huit**
7	**sept**	60	**soixante**	89	**quatre-vingt-neuf**
8	**huit**	61	**soixante et un**	90	**quatre-vingt-dix**
9	**neuf**	70	**soixante-dix**	91	**quatre-vingt-onze**
10	**dix**	71	**soixante et onze**	92	**quatre-vingt-douze**
11	**onze**	72	**soixante-douze**	93	**quatre-vingt-treize**
12	**douze**	73	**soixante-treize**	100	**cent**
13	**treize**	74	**soixante-quatorze**	101	**cent un**
14	**quatorze**	75	**soixante-quinze**	102	**cent deux**
15	**quinze**	76	**soixante-seize**	110	**cent dix**
16	**seize**	77	**soixante-dix-sept**	182	**cent quatre-vingt-deux**
17	**dix-sept**	78	**soixante-dix-huit**	200	**deux cents**
18	**dix-huit**	79	**soixante-dix-neuf**	240	**deux cent quarante**
19	**dix-neuf**	80	**quatre-vingts**	500	**cinq cents**
20	**vingt**	81	**quatre-vingt-un**	1000	**mille**
		82	**quatre-vingt-deux**	2000	**deux mille**
				1,000,000	**un million**

Telephone numbers are usually given as groups of figures in French. In L47 you will find the number 61–92–03 = **soixante et un, quatre-vingt-douze, zéro trois.** (Normally 4 groups of 2 figures).

(b) Dates
French is different from English in that cardinal numbers are used for dates. In English you say, *my birthday is the 18th of July.* In French this would be, **mon anniversaire, c'est le dix-huit juillet.** Notice also how you write the date at the head of a letter: **le lundi 15 mars.** The only exception to this is for the 1st of the month: *1st May* = **le premier mai.**

When giving the year, it is usual in French to give the date in hundreds: 1990 = **dix-neuf cent quatre-vingt-dix.** Here are some more examples: 1974 = **dix-neuf cent soixante-quatorze;** 1982 = **dix-neuf cent quatre-vingt-deux.**

(c) Ordinal numbers
First = **premier/première.** Note that the ordinal number is an adjective, so it must agree with the noun: **la première fois que je vais faire du ski** (p. 57).
Second = **deuxième,** but **second** is also used sometimes. All the other ordinal numbers are formed by adding **-ième,** e.g. **troisième, dix-huitième, trente-quatrième,** etc.

(d) Quantities and amounts
There are a number of adjectives which express an idea of quantity or amount, even if the actual amount is a little vague, for example: **certain** = *a certain* number; **chaque** = *each, every;* **plusieurs** = *several;* **quelques** = *a few;* **tout** = *all.* Here are some examples: **certains employeurs** = *a certain number of employers* (L12); **chaque semaine** = *every week;* **plusieurs de nos amis** (10G) = *several of our friends.*

It is worth spending a little while looking at the uses of **tout.** As an adjective, **tout** agrees with the noun it refers to, e.g.: **toutes les deux** = *both of us girls* (10B); **toutes les matières** = *all subjects* (L12). It can be used in the singular to mean *every:* **tout automobiliste** = *every car-driver* (L32). There are a number of fixed expressions which use **tout** in this way: **tout seul** = *all alone;* **tout droit** = *straight ahead.* As a pronoun, **tout** in the singular is used to mean *everything:* **il a fallu tout expliquer** = *we had to explain everything* (10G).

9. Conjugation of Regular and Irregular Verbs

French verbs are constructed from a stem plus endings. If you look up a verb in the dictionary, the form you are given is called the *Infinitive.* From the Infinitive ending, you can form the rest of the verb, if it is regular. There are three sorts of regular verbs, which you can recognise from their Infinitive endings. By far the great majority of French verbs belong to the regular class of verbs whose Infinitive ends in **-er.** The forms of all the regular verbs, in the tenses you are most likely to need, are as follows. If you know the regular verbs it will help you to be sure about getting a lot of your written and spoken French right. More explanation about use of tenses is given later.

(a) Regular verbs

Example: **porter** = *to carry* or *to wear*

Present Tense	*Imperfect Tense*	*Future Tense*
je porte	**je portais**	**je porterai**
tu portes	**tu portais**	**tu porteras**
il/elle porte	**il/elle portait**	**il/elle portera**
on porte	**on portait**	**on portera**
nous portons	**nous portions**	**nous porterons**
vous portez	**vous portiez**	**vous porterez**
ils portent	**ils portaient**	**ils porteront**
elles portent	**elles portaient**	**elles porteront**

Perfect Tense	*Pluperfect Tense*	*Conditional*
j'ai porté	**j'avais porté**	**je porterais**
tu as porté	**tu avais porté**	**tu porterais**
il/elle a porté	**il/elle avait porté**	**il/elle porterait**
on a porté	**on avait porté**	**on porterait**
nous avons porté	**nous avions porté**	**nous porterions**
vous avez porté	**vous aviez porté**	**vous porteriez**
ils ont porté	**ils avaient porté**	**ils porteraient**
elles ont porté	**elles avaient porté**	**elles porteraient**

Imperative	*Present Participle*
porte!	**portant**
portez!	

Example: **finir** = *to finish*

Present Tense	*Imperfect Tense*	*Future Tense*
je finis	**je finissais**	**je finirai**
tu finis	**tu finissais**	**tu finiras**
il/elle/on finit	**il/elle/on finissait**	**il/elle/on finira**
nous finissons	**nous finissions**	**nous finirons**
vous finissez	**vous finissiez**	**vous finirez**
ils finissent	**ils finissaient**	**ils finiront**
elles finissent	**elles finissaient**	**elles finiront**

Perfect Tense	*Pluperfect Tense*	*Conditional*
j'ai fini	**j'avais fini**	**je finirais** etc.
Imperative	*Present Participle*	
finis!	**finissant**	
finissez!		

Example: **répondre** = *to reply*

Present Tense	*Imperfect Tense*	*Future Tense*
je réponds	**je répondais**	**je répondrai**
tu réponds	**tu répondais**	**tu répondras**
il/elle/on répond	**il/elle/on répondait**	**il/elle/on répondra**
nous répondons	**nous répondions**	**nous répondrons**
vous répondez	**vous répondiez**	**vous répondrez**
ils répondent	**ils répondaient**	**ils répondront**
elles répondent	**elles répondaient**	**elles répondront**

Perfect Tense	*Pluperfect Tense*	*Conditional*
j'ai répondu	**j'avais répondu**	**je répondrais** etc.
Imperative	*Present Participle*	
réponds!	**répondant**	
répondez!		

(b) Auxiliary Verbs

The verbs **être** = *to be* and **avoir** = *to have* are used a great deal as auxiliary verbs, that is to say they help to build up tenses such as Perfect, Pluperfect, etc. They are also the most common verbs in everyday use, so you must learn them and know them well.

être = *to be*

Present Tense	*Imperfect Tense*	*Future Tense*
je suis	**j'étais**	**je serai**
tu es	**tu étais**	**tu seras**
il/elle/on est	**il/elle/on était**	**il/elle/on sera**
nous sommes	**nous étions**	**nous serons**
vous êtes	**vous étiez**	**vous serez**
ils/elles sont	**ils/elles étaient**	**ils/elles seront**

Perfect Tense	*Pluperfect Tense*	*Conditional*
j'ai été	**j'avais été**	**je serais** etc.
Imperative	*Present Participle*	
sois!	**étant**	
soyez!		

avoir = *to have*

Present Tense	*Imperfect Tense*	*Future Tense*
j'ai	**j'avais**	**j'aurai**
tu as	**tu avais**	**tu auras**
il/elle/on a	**il/elle/on avait**	**il/elle/on aura**
nous avons	**nous avions**	**nous aurons**
vous avez	**vous aviez**	**vous aurez**
ils/elles ont	**ils/elles avaient**	**ils/elles auront**

Perfect Tense	*Pluperfect Tense*	*Conditional*
j'ai eu	**j'avais eu**	**j'aurais** etc.
Imperative	*Present Participle*	
aie!	**ayant**	
ayez!		

(c) Irregular Verbs

Here is a list of the most common irregular verbs which you will need to recognise and, perhaps, use. The verbs have been listed in family groups which all behave in the same sort of way. The verbs are listed according to whether their Infinitive ends in **-er, -ir, -re** or **-oir.** For each verb you are given the Present

Tense, the Past Participle (which helps you form the Perfect Tense), the Present Participle and the Future Tense.

(i) Irregular **-er** verbs

aller = *to go*   (one of the most important verbs you need to know)

Present	*Present Participle*	*Past Participle*	*Future*
je vais	**allant**	**allé**	**j'irai**
tu vas			**tu iras**
il/elle va			**il/elle ira**
nous allons			**nous irons**
vous allez			**vous irez**
ils vont			**ils/elles iront**

(ii) Irregular **-ir** verbs

courir = *to run*

je cours	**courant**	**couru**	**je courrai**
tu cours			
il court			
nous courons			
vous courez			
ils courent			

dormir = *to sleep*

je dors	**dormant**	**dormi**	**je dormirai**
tu dors			
il dort			
nous dormons			
vous dormez			
ils dorment			

ouvrir = *to open*

j'ouvre	**ouvrant**	**ouvert**	**j'ouvrirai**
tu ouvres			
il ouvre			
nous ouvrons			
vous ouvrez			
ils ouvrent			

partir = *to leave, set off*

je pars	**partant**	**parti**	**je partirai**
tu pars			
il part			
nous partons			
vous partez			
ils partent			

sortir = *to go out*

je sors	**sortant**	**sorti**	**je sortirai**
tu sors			
il sort			
nous sortons			
vous sortez			
ils sortent			

tenir = *to hold*

je tiens	**tenant**	**tenu**	**je tiendrai**
tu tiens			
il tient			
nous tenons			
vous tenez			
ils tiennent			

venir = *to come* (Same as **tenir**.)

Present	Present Participle	Past Participle	Future

(iii)   Irregular -re verbs

battre = *to beat*

Present	Present Participle	Past Participle	Future
je bats tu bats il bat nous battons vous battez ils battent	battant	battu	je battrai

boire = *to drink*

je bois tu bois il boit nous buvons vous buvez ils boivent	buvant	bu	je boirai

conduire = *to drive, to lead*

je conduis tu conduis il conduit nous conduisons vous conduisez ils conduisent	conduisant	conduit	je conduirai

connaître = *to know, to be acquainted with*

je connais tu connais il connaît nous connaissons vous connaissez ils connaissent	connaissant	connu	je connaîtrai

croire = *to believe*

je crois tu crois il croit nous croyons vous croyez ils croient	croyant	cru	je croirai

dire = *to say*

je dis tu dis il dit nous disons vous dites ils disent	disant	dit	je dirai

écrire = *to write*

j'écris tu écris il écrit nous écrivons vous écrivez ils écrivent	écrivant	écrit	j'écrirai

faire = *to make, to do*

je fais tu fais il fait nous faisons vous faites ils font	faisant	fait	je ferai

lire = *to read*

je lis tu lis il lit	lisant	lu	je lirai

Present	Present Participle	Past Participle	Future
nous lisons			
vous lisez			
ils lisent			

mettre = *to put*

Present	Present Participle	Past Participle	Future
je mets	mettant	mis	je mettrai
tu mets			
il met			
nous mettons			
vous mettez			
ils mettent			

plaire = *to please*

Present	Present Participle	Past Participle	Future
je plais	plaisant	plu	je plairai
tu plais			
il plaît			
nous plaisons			
vous plaisez			
ils plaisent			

prendre = *to take*

Present	Present Participle	Past Participle	Future
je prends	prenant	pris	je prendrai
tu prends			
il prend			
nous prenons			
vous prenez			
ils prennent			

rire = *to laugh*

Present	Present Participle	Past Participle	Future
je ris	riant	ri	je rirai
tu ris			
il rit			
nous rions			
vous riez			
ils rient			

suivre = *to follow*

Present	Present Participle	Past Participle	Future
je suis	suivant	suivi	je suivrai
tu suis			
il suit			
nous suivons			
vous suivez			
ils suivent			

vivre = *to live*

Present	Present Participle	Past Participle	Future
je vis	vivant	vécu	je vivrai
tu vis			
il vit			
nous vivons			
vous vivez			
ils vivent			

(iv)   Irregular **-oir** verbs

s'asseoir = *to sit down*

Present	Present Participle	Past Participle	Future
je m'assieds	s'asseyant	assis	je m'assiérai
tu t'assieds			
il s'assied			
nous nous asseyons			
vous vous asseyez			
ils s'asseyent			

devoir = *to owe* (also used with the sense of *must*)

Present	Present Participle	Past Participle	Future
je dois	devant	dû	je devrai
tu dois			
il doit			
nous devons			
vous devez			
ils doivent			

Present	Present Participle	Past Participle	Future
pouvoir = *to be able*			
je peux	**pouvant**	**pu**	**je pourrai**
tu peux			
il peut			
nous pouvons			
vous pouvez			
ils peuvent			
recevoir = *to receive*			
je reçois	**recevant**	**reçu**	**je recevrai**
tu reçois			
il reçoit			
nous recevons			
vous recevez			
ils reçoivent			
savoir = *to know*			
je sais	**sachant**	**su**	**je saurai**
tu sais			
il sait			
nous savons			
vous savez			
ils savent			
voir = *to see*			
je vois	**voyant**	**vu**	**je verrai**
tu vois			
il voit			
nous voyons			
vous voyez			
ils voient			
vouloir = *to want*			
je veux	**voulant**	**voulu**	**je voudrai**
tu veux			
il veut			
nous voulons			
vous voulez			
ils veulent			

There are a small number of irregular verbs for which you only need to know the one or two key forms which appear frequently. For example:

> **mourir** = *to die*. Past participle **mort: il est mort en 1989** = *he died in 1989.*
> **naître** = *to be born*. Past participle **né: je suis né en 1976** = *I was born in 1976.*

Notice also the verbs which can only be used impersonally, that is to say with the impersonal pronoun **il** as a subject:

> **falloir** = *to be necessary*. Present Tense: **il faut;** Perfect Tense: **il a fallu**; Future Tense: **il faudra.**
> **pleuvoir** = *to rain*. Present Tense: **il pleut;** Perfect Tense: **il a plu**; Future Tense: **il pleuvra.**

10.   Verbs and the Way They Are Used

You will find useful hints on the use of tenses in the Speaking section of Unit 4 (p. 58).

(a)   The *Present Tense* is the most important for you to learn. In English it has two forms, both of which are represented by the single Present Tense of French. Look at these two English examples: *The train leaves platform 2 every day at 9.0 a.m.; The train is leaving platform 2 at this moment.* Both these forms of the Present would be translated into French by the ordinary Present Tense: **Le train part tous les jours du quai numéro deux; Le train part maintenant du quai numéro deux.**

The Present Tense is used in French in constructions with **depuis,** such as the following: **nous sommes là depuis trente ans** = *we have been here for 30 years* (L7). In an expression where you talk about something you have done for some time, and *which you are still doing,* the French think it is more logical to use the Present Tense. The same sort of idea explains the French use of the Present in expressions of time using

ça fait. You will find an example in L43: **ça fait 15 minutes que j'attends ma soupe** = *I have been waiting 15 minutes for my soup.* The man is *still* waiting, so French uses the Present.

(b)   The *Perfect Tense* (**passé composé**) is the next most important for you to learn. It can best be understood if we first notice the way English works. English has two ways of saying that something happened in the past. There is a past definite way of describing an event which took place, and which is now finished and done with: *Last week he went to London.* There is also a tense which uses the verb *to have* as an auxiliary verb to describe something which is in the past but more recent: *He has gone to London this morning.* The important thing to remember is that the Perfect Tense in French does *both* these jobs. So the two sentences above would be translated: **Il est allé à Londres la semaine dernière; Il est allé à Londres ce matin.**

Look first at exercise 10G in the Key to Chapter 10. Most of this is written in the Perfect: **Les parents ont annoncé leur intention ... ils ont donné la permission ... tout a très bien commencé.** All this in English would be past definite: *The parents announced their intention ... they gave their permission ... everything began very well.* Now look at 10A, and towards the end of the letter you will find **je n'ai jamais voyagé seule à l'étranger** = *I have never travelled abroad on my own.*

In French, the Perfect Tense is one of a number of tenses called compound tenses, because they are made up of two parts, an auxiliary verb and a past participle. The auxiliary verb for the great majority of verbs is **avoir,** just as English uses *to have* as an auxiliary in the examples given above. There are also examples above from the French texts.

A number of verbs, mainly verbs of movement, take **être** as their auxiliary verb. The main ones are:

aller	monter	rentrer
arriver	mourir	rester
descendre	naître	retourner
devenir	partir	tomber
entrer	sortir	venir

Here are some examples from the texts in the book:
quand nous sommes arrivés dans cet appartement (L7);
l'homme et la femme sont ressortis ... la police est vite arrivée (10F).
une bande de jeunes ... est entrée chez Michel ... Plusieurs de nos amis sont partis (10G).
You will notice from these examples that when the auxiliary verb **être** is used, the past participle must agree with a feminine or plural subject, in the same way that adjectives have to agree with feminine and plural nouns.

Verbs which take **avoir** as an auxiliary do not agree in this way, except in one case. When a verb takes a direct object, it is sometimes possible for that object to come before the verb. When there is a preceding direct object of this kind, the past participle agrees with it even though the verb takes **avoir.** Look at the following examples: **Je vous remercie beaucoup de la**

lettre que vous avez écrite (10B). The relative pronoun **que** is a direct object, as was explained on p. 189. Here, it stands for **la lettre,** and it precedes the verb in the Perfect Tense, so the past participle **écrit** is given a feminine agreement.

Here is another example: **Je les ai regardés descendre la rue** (10F). In this case, the preceding direct object is the plural pronoun **les,** so the past participle **regardé** is given a plural **-s.**

(c)   The *Imperfect Tense* in French is used as follows.
(i)   To describe people and things as they were in the past: **ce quartier était quelque chose de délicieux ... il y avait un parfum de province ... c'était une rue extraordinaire** (L7).
(ii)   To describe some action that was done repeatedly in the past, like the way English says *we used to do that every day:* **je faisais de l'autostop quand j'étais plus jeune** (L32) = *I used to hitch when I was younger.*
(iii)   to describe continuous, unbroken action in the past: **un homme et une femme étaient en train d'ouvrir la porte** (10F). This usage is often equivalent to the English past continuous tense: *a man and a woman were opening the door.* Note also in 10G, **quelques-uns bavardaient, d'autres dansaient ou écoutaient de la musique** = *some were chatting, others were dancing or listening to music.*

(d)   The *Pluperfect Tense* refers to a past which is even more distant than the past. In English, you can recognise the Pluperfect by the auxiliary verb *had*, for example *the people had gone on holiday ... the noise had woken me.* The Pluperfect in French follows the same rules for **avoir** or **être** as auxiliaries which were given above, but this time the *Imperfect Tense* of the auxiliary verb is used with the past participle. In 10F you will find the examples just given in English: **les gens étaient partis en vacances ... c'était ce bruit-là qui m'avait réveillé.** Note also, in 10G, **la mère de Michel avait préparé à manger ... la soirée avait été un vrai désastre** = *Michael's mother had prepared some food ... the evening had been a real disaster.*

(e)   There are several ways of expressing *future* meaning in French.
(i)   Sometimes the Present Tense can be used to talk about the future. Look at the task on p. 38. **Je rentre vers 5 heures et quart ... elle passe l'examen d'anglais vendredi.** It is clear that this note is talking about things which will happen later this afternoon and even in a few days time, but the Present Tense can be used. Compare this with English, where you could say either *I am coming home at 5.15* or *I shall come home at 5.15.* And either *She is taking her English exam on Friday* or *She will be taking her English exam on Friday.* Note also the question in L11: **Qu'est-ce que tu fais cet après-midi?**
(ii)   A very common way of expressing the future, especially in conversation, is to use the appropriate part of the verb **aller,** followed by an Infinitive. This is a bit like the way English

sometimes uses *going to* instead of *shall* or *will*: **tu vas le faire tout de suite** (L6); **je vais vous parler du travail que j'ai fait** (10C).

(iii) You can always use **aller** + Infinitive in conversation and also in writing letters, but should also be able to recognise the Future Tense when you see it or hear it. Remember, the letter **-r** will always come immediately before the ending. With regular verbs, the Future Tense is formed by adding the Future endings on to the Infinitive of the verb, as you will see in the verb tables on pp. 191–196. Here are some examples of the Future Tense from the texts in the book:

> **Cet après-midi j'aurai un cours d'allemand** = *This afternoon I shall have a German lesson* (L11);
> **Samedi, en Normandie, il fera beau temps ... il pleuvra par contre en Bretagne ... dimanche, en Normandie, il y aura du vent et en Bretagne le temps sera couvert** (L13).

(f) The *Conditional* is recognised in English by the use of the auxiliary verb *would*, for example *I would like to go to France*. In French the conditional is formed by taking the Infinitive and then adding the endings of the Imperfect: **j'aimerais voir la chemise bleue** (L22). Note also the following examples of irregular verbs in the conditional: **il serait possible de faire des randonnées ... quelle sorte de travail est-ce qu'on pourrait faire?** (10B) = *it would be possible to go for walks . . . what sort of work would we be able to do?*

Sometimes the conditional is used to make a question sound more polite, just as *I would like . . .* is more polite than *I want. . . .* Note, for example, **je voudrais un kilo de tomates** (L38); **on voudrait beaucoup venir passer du temps en France** (10B). On p. 25, your French friend has left a note saying, **pourrais-tu mettre le couvert?** This is a polite way of saying *could you. . .?* or *would you mind. . .?*

(g) The *Imperative* is for giving commands. You will find the forms of the Imperative in the verb tables. Here are some examples: **donnez-moi un quart de vin rouge** (L41); **n'oubliez pas notre rayon maison ... achetez aujourd'hui ... allez au quatrième étage.** These are from L44, and mean, *don't forget our household department . . . buy today . . . go to the fourth floor.* There is a good example on p. 52 of Unit 4: **Inventez un jeu!** An example of the **tu** form of the Imperative is in L6: **écoute, Marie-Dominique.** Another example is in L31, **dis donc. . . .** This is quite a common way of starting off when you want to attract the attention of the person you are speaking to. In the text on p. 156 you will find **demande tout de suite à tes parents, puis écris-nous et dis-nous quand tu seras libre.** You will notice that when using the Imperative in a positive way, the pronoun objects *follow* the verb, and are the emphatic forms: **donnez-moi; dis-nous; écris-nous.** But if the Imperative is negative, the normal word order applies: **ne me donnez pas; ne l'écoutez pas.**

(h) To understand what is meant by *Passive Voice*, look at these two sentences: *John reads the book. The book is read by John.* They both mean exactly the same thing, but the idea is expressed differently. The first sentence is said to be in the *Active* Voice. The second is in the *Passive* Voice. If you understand the way the passive is formed in English, you will have no problems with French. The verb *to be* (or the verb **être**) is used as an auxiliary verb with the past participle. In French, the two sentences given above as examples would be: **Jean lit le livre. Le livre est lu par Jean.**

To make the Past and Future tenses of the Passive, you just use the tenses of the auxiliary verb, as in these examples:

Present: **Les enfants sont accueillis** (Text F p. 54)
The children are welcomed
Où est-ce que votre ferme est située? (10B)
Where is your farm located?

Perfect: **Une déviation a été mise en place** (L32)
A diversion has been set up

Imperfect: **Le travail était assez bien payé** (10C)
The work was quite well paid

11. Verbs: Reflexive and Impersonal

(a) Reflexive verbs
If you say, for example, *he washes himself*, you are using a reflexive verb, because the object pronoun *(himself)* refers back to the subject, or seems to 'reflect' the subject. In English, you can always recognise a reflexive verb because of the reflexive pronouns *himself, herself, myself,* etc.

In French, the reflexive pronouns are as follows:

me = *myself*		**nous** = *ourselves*	
te = *yourself*		**vous** = *yourselves*	
se = *himself/herself*		**se** = *themselves*	

The Infinitive of a French reflexive verb is the part given in dictionaries and vocabulary lists, e.g. **se laver; se réveiller.** The tenses are formed just like the tenses of other verbs, but you must never forget to use the reflexive pronoun, e.g. **je me lave; il s'est assis; elles se sont habillées.** Note the following uses of reflexive verbs:

(i) They are used just as in English, to talk about something you do to yourself. If you are describing your daily routine you might say **je me lave ... je m'habille ...** etc. = *I wash myself . . . I dress myself.*

(ii) Very often you will find that verbs may be reflexive in French but you translate them into English without using an English reflexive verb. In text 10D you will find **je me lève à sept heures ... je me repose un peu. . . .** In English you would say *I get up at 7 o'clock . . . I have a bit of a rest. . . .*

(iii) When you are using reflexive verbs in Past and Future tenses, they behave just like other verbs, except that they *always* keep the reflexive pronoun. Note also that reflexive verbs *always* take the verb **être** as an auxiliary when you are forming the Perfect and Pluperfect tenses. The following examples are in text 10F: **Je m'étais presque endormi ... je me suis réveillé ... la porte s'est ouverte lentement ... je me suis décidé à agir.** You will notice that none of these is translated by an English reflexive verb: *I had almost fallen asleep ... I woke up ... the door opened slowly. ... I decided to act.*

(b) Impersonal verbs

The subject of impersonal verbs is always **il,** and the verb is always singular. Verbs which describe weather are examples: **il pleut; il neige; il fait du vent,** etc. Other important impersonal verbs to notice are:

(i)   **Il faut** = *it is necessary:* **il faut dire que la vie comme interne ne me plaît pas du tout** (L12). Note that the English version of this would be *I must say that. ...* Similarly, in L37 you will find **il faut la faire sur place,** meaning *you must get it done on the spot.* In text 10C there is an example of the Perfect Tense: **il a fallu écrire une lettre** = *I had to write a letter.*

(ii) **Il y a** means *there is* or *there are,* and you will find many examples in the book: **il y a beaucoup de courrier** (10C); **il y a une carte internationale qui est valable dans tous les pays où il y a des Auberges de Jeunesse** (L37). You will find several examples of the Imperfect Tense: **il y avait aussi des jeux d'équipe** (10E); **il y avait de petits commerces** (L7). Note that in expressions of time, **il y a** means *ago:* **il y a trois ans** = *three years ago.*

(iii) **Il est** is always used when you are giving the time o'clock: **il est midi; il est trois heures.** You will also find **il est** in some other positions, e.g. **il est à noter que ...** = *it is to be noted that. ...*

(iv) There are quite a number of impersonal expressions which consist of **il est** plus an adjective, e.g. **il est possible de trouver du travail** (10A). Very often in modern French **ce** is used instead of **il** in such expressions. You will find examples in the same text, 10A: **c'est important de pouvoir gagner un peu d'argent ... ce sera bien d'aller ensemble.** As you can see, whether **il** or **ce** is used in French, they are both translated as *it* in English: *it is possible to find work ... it is important to be able to earn some money ... it will be good to go together.*

12.   Infinitives and Participles

(a) The Infinitive

You have already seen in the verb tables that the Infinitive is the part of the verb which you find in dictionaries, and which is often given when you want to refer to a verb without naming all the parts. You will often find the Infinitive of the verb used in French constructions. Here is a brief summary of the uses.

(i)   Some verbs form a construction where they are followed directly by an Infinitive. Because the Infinitive works so closely with the other verb, it is called a dependent Infinitive in this position: **je vais commencer; j'aime aller; mes parents me laisseraient partir** (all from 10A); **qu'est-ce qu'on pourrait faire?; on devait surtout nettoyer les chambres** (both from 10B). You can see from this last example that the Infinitive can sometimes be separated from the other verb, but it is still 'dependent'. You could begin to make a list of verbs which are followed directly by an Infinitive. Here you have the Infinitive after **aimer, aller, devoir, laisser,** and you could also add verbs of seeing and feeling like **voir, entendre, sentir, regarder,** and other common verbs like **vouloir, savoir,** e.g.: **je les ai regardés descendre la rue** (10F); **je voudrais faire des études** (L12); **je ne savais pas quoi faire** (10F).

(ii) It is worth saying a little more about **devoir,** which occurred in one of the examples above. You have already met **il faut,** which is one of the ways in which you can say that something is necessary, or translate the idea of *must.* The verb **devoir** also has the idea of *must:* **je dois aller le voir à l'hôpital** = *I must go and see him in the hospital* (L46). In English the past tense of *must* is *had to,* so in the example above, **on devait surtout nettoyer les chambres** means *above all we had to clean the bedrooms.* Note the Future Tense: **les voyageurs devront faire attention** = *travellers will have to take care* (L32).

(iii) A large number of verbs take **de** before the following Infinitive: **il est possible de trouver** (10A); **je vous prie d'accepter** (10B).

(iv) Another group of verbs takes **à** before the following Infinitive: **nous avons aidé à servir** (10B); **je n'arrive pas à me concentrer** (L12); **on commence à préparer** (Text H, p. 135).

(v)   The words **pour** and **sans** are both followed by the Infinitive form of the verb. Look at the text on p. 41: **pour découvrir l'histoire de notre pays ... pour mieux parler notre langage ... pour apprendre à vivre ensemble.** You will see that **pour** means *in order to.* In the text about fast-food restaurants on p. 135, you will find several more examples of **pour** (**pour le savoir ... pour rincer ... pour laver**). There is also an example of **sans: sans même avoir le temps** = *without even having the time.* See also L32: **sans bien regarder** = *without having a good look.*

(vi) A construction which you will find particularly with the verb **demander** is the following: **je vais demander à mes parents de me laisser partir** = *I shall ask my parents to let me go.* Here there is **à** with an indirect object and **de** with a dependent Infinitive.

(vii) Sometimes, particularly in recipes, the Infinitive is used to give a command or instruction: **mettre dans une casserole ... verser ce liquide ... laisser reposer** = *put into a saucepan ... pour in this liquid ... leave it to stand* (see text pp. 133–134).

(viii) There are other occasions when you might find the Infinitive standing alone, and this is usually rendered into English by the form of the verb ending -ing, e.g.: **vivre dans un cadre comme ça, c'est vraiment beaucoup de chance** = *living in a setting like that is really lucky* (L7).

(b) The perfect Infinitive
After **après** you will find a part of the verb called the perfect Infinitive: **après avoir vu sept médecins** = *after seeing seven doctors* (text I, p. 148). Note that the form of the perfect Infinitive depends on the auxiliary verb. You have just had an example with **avoir**; here is one with **être: après être rentré** (10D).

(c) The present participle
This is the form ending in **-ant,** such as **allant, venant,** equivalent to the English forms *going; coming,* e.g. **voici les détails sur les trains desservant Rouen aujourd'hui** = *here are the details about trains going to Rouen today* (L26). Very often, the present participle is used with **en,** as in the following example: **Ils avaient entendu la musique en passant . . . en entrant ils ont bousculé des gens** = *they had heard the music as they went by . . . as they came in, they bumped into people.*

Very frequently, as in English, the present participle is used just like an ordinary adjective, e.g.: **une chaise pliante . . . c'était surprenant** = *a folding chair . . . it was surprising* (10F).

Note that the present participle is not as much used in French as in English, particularly in the way many verbs are used. English says *I like reading,* but French uses the Infinitive and says **j'aime lire.**

(d) The past participle
This is used to form the compound tenses such as the Perfect and Pluperfect, as already explained in part 10 of the Grammar Section.

13. Adverbs

Adverbs form a large group of words which are sometimes difficult to classify. The following section gives a selection of adverbs and some examples of their use.

(a) Adverbs of manner
These include all those adverbs which end in **-ment,** like **extrêmement, vraiment, lentement, calmement.** You will see that these adverbs are equivalent to English adverbs ending in *-ly,* such as *extremely, slowly, calmly,* and they either add some meaning to a verb, e.g. **parlez lentement** = *speak slowly,* or they are used with an adjective, e.g. **extrêmement vivant** = *extremely lively* (L7); **vraiment idéal** = *really ideal* (10E). Another common adverb in this group is **bien** = *well:* **ça ira bien avec la chemise** = *it will go well with the shirt* (L22). Note also **vite** *(quickly):* **il allait trop vite** (L48); **mal** *(badly).*

(b) Adverbs of quantity
These include **assez, aussi, beaucoup, moins, plus, tant, très, trop.** Here are some examples of use: **elle est très stricte** = *she is very strict* (L2); **une assez petite ville** = *a quite small town* (L4); **moi aussi** = *me too* (L7); **on a beaucoup trop de devoirs** = *we have far too much work* (L11); **il fait trop chaud** = *it's too hot* (L31); **beaucoup de devoirs** = *a lot of homework* (10D); **je ne mange pas beaucoup** = *I don't eat much*

(10D); **il y avait aussi des jeux d'équipe** = *there were also team games* (10E).

(c) Adverbs of time
These include **après, avant, bientôt, déjà, depuis, enfin, jamais, maintenant, puis, quelquefois, souvent, toujours.** For the use of **depuis** see Section 10(a) of the Grammar Summary.

(d) Superlative and comparative of adverbs
These are formed in the same way as with adjectives (see Section 3(c): **allez plus vite** = *go faster.* Note that the forms for **bien** are **mieux** (comparative) and **le mieux** (superlative).

14. Negatives

The most common way of forming the negative in French is to use the **ne . . . pas** construction, as in the following example: **je ne mange pas beaucoup** = *I don't eat much* (10D). As you can see, **ne** precedes the verb and **pas** follows. In the case of a compound tense or Passive Voice, **ne** and **pas** come before and after the auxiliary verb: **il n'est pas blessé** (L48). If there is a pronoun object before the verb, the **ne** comes before the pronoun: **tu ne l'as pas vu venir?** (L47); **il n'y avait pas moyen de les faire sortir** (10G). When **ne . . . pas** is used to make an Infinitive negative, the two words come together before the Infinitive: **la police conseille à tout automobiliste de ne pas dépasser . . .** (L32). There are also occasions on which **pas** may stand alone. See the answer to task L in Unit 7: **une liste d'hôtels . . . pas trop chers.**

If you want to give the negative more force, you can say **pas du tout,** meaning *not at all:* **la vie comme interne ne me plaît pas du tout** (L12).

The following are the other most commonly used forms of negative expression: **ne . . . jamais** = *never:* **je n'ai jamais voyagé seule à l'étranger** = *I have never travelled abroad alone* (10A); **ne . . . rien** = *nothing:* **ça ne me dit rien de . . .** (10D). This is an idiom, meaning *I don't at all like. . . .* **Rien** can be used as the subject of the verb, but do not forget the **ne: rien ne bouge** = *nothing moves* (10F). Note that **jamais** and **rien** can both be used alone, without a verb. So in answer to the question **Est-ce que vous êtes déjà allé en France?** you might answer, **Jamais!** or **Non, jamais.** Similarly, you might hear the question **Qu'est-ce que vous faites ce soir?** and answer, **Rien!**

Ne . . . aucun is an emphatic negative, as in **comme je n'obtenais aucune satisfaction** = *as I didn't get any satisfaction at all* (L12). **Aucun** may also be found used separately from a verb, e.g. in L32: **sans aucun doute** = *without any doubt at all.*

Ne . . . personne = *nobody:* **je ne connais personne** = *I don't know anybody.*

Ne . . . plus = *no more,* or *no longer:* **je n'en peux plus** = *I can't manage any more* (L12); **le système ne fonctionne plus** = *the system doesn't work any more* (L46).

Ne . . . que = *only:* **il n'y a que moi ici** = *I'm the only one here.* See L45: **les bureaux ne sont ouverts au public que de neuf heures à douze heures** = *the offices are open to the public only from 9 till 12.*

15. Prepositions

The job of prepositions is usually to show the position of something (*on, under, near*), or the relationship between parts of a sentence. Prepositions are often the most difficult words to get right in learning a foreign language, because they seem to do so many different jobs. If you looked up the preposition **à** in a dictionary, you would find that it can mean *at, to, in,* and several other things as well. So the dictionary is not much help for prepositions, and the important thing is to note how they are used when you read French or when you hear it spoken. The notes below provide some guidance to the use of the most common prepositions.

(a)   **à** is used to indicate place, particularly when using the names of towns: **un lycée à Poitiers** (L12); **je ne vais pas exactement à Poitiers** (L30); **arrive à Rouen** (L26). It indicates place in other ways, rather like the English preposition *at,* e.g. **à la Gare Maritime** (L26). The word **à** is also used with time: **demain à 8h30 on a Mme Lambert ... à 9h30 il y a maths** (L2). It is used when you want to talk about the distance between two things: **nous sommes à 50 mètres de la plage, à 200 mètres du grand supermarché** = *we are 50 metres from the beach, 200 metres from the big supermarket* (L33). Finally in this short summary, **à** is used with prices: **il est en solde à 75 francs** = *it is in the sale for 75 francs* (L20); **nos belles tomates à dix francs le kilo** (L21). Note the use of **à** in the expression **à l'étranger** = *abroad* (10A). The preposition **jusqu'à** means *until* or *as far as:* **jusqu'à la fin septembre** (L33).

(b)   **de** is mainly concerned with the idea of belonging, often giving the English idea in *of, from.* For example, English uses the apostrophe *'s* to show possession, as in *Michael's parents.* French says **les parents de Michel** = *the parents of Michael* (10G). You often find **de** in French where there is no preposition at all in English, which expresses the idea in a different combination of words. Here are some examples: **jobs d'été** = *summer jobs* (L12); **lecteur de disquettes** = *disc drive* (L23); **un service de wagon-restaurant** = *a restaurant-car service* (L26); **une salle de jeux** = *a games room* (L33); **Auberge de Jeunesse** = *Youth Hostel* (L37). You will find many other examples in the texts.

When talking about places, **de** has the same meaning as *from* in English: **je ne vais pas exactement à Poitiers mais à huit kilomètres de là** = *I am not exactly going to Poitiers but 8 kilometres from there* (L30). For this reason, **de** is always used after the verb **sortir**, meaning *to come out from:* **qui est sorti de la rue Gros Horloge** = *who came out from the rue Gros Horloge* (L47). The preposition **près de** means *near to:* **près de Montélimar** (L32).

(c)   **dans** and **en** may both mean *in,* depending on the context. You use **dans** to refer to being inside something like a room or a building: **dans des restaurants ... dans un hôtel** (10A). **En** is not as specific as **dans,** and is practically never followed by the definite or indefinite article. Use it particularly with the names of countries: **passer du temps en France** (10B); **j'ai envie d'aller en Espagne ... même en Suisse ... ça te dirait d'aller en Italie?** (L31). It is also used with the French regions: **samedi, en Normandie, il fera beau temps ... il pleuvra en Bretagne** (L13). **En** is also used with the seasons of the year: **en été; en automne; en hiver.** Note that *spring* is the exception: **au printemps.** It is used with all forms of transport: **en auto; en train; en vélo.** The exceptions here are if you are *on foot,* which is **à pied,** or *on horseback,* which is **à cheval.** There are a large number of expressions formed with **en,** such as **en vacances; en ville; en général.**

(d)   **chez** means *at the house of:* **chez lui** = *at his place* (10G); **chez moi** (Unit 2, answer to Exercise H). It is also used with the names of shops: **chez le boucher** = *at the butcher's;* **chez l'épicier** = *at the grocer's.* It is also used in such expressions as **chez le dentiste** = *at the dentist's.*

16. The Grammar of Spoken French

As in all languages, there are some differences between the spoken and written forms of French. Note the following points.

(a) Forming questions
The written language makes much more use of inversion, that is changing the order of subject and verb. For example, **il se passe** means *it happens.* In text H on p. 135 you find the opening question: **Que se passe-t-il?** = *What is happening?* This is an example of inversion. Inversion is sometimes found in speech, e.g. in L11: **Qu'as-tu fait ce matin ... qu'en penses-tu?** It is more normal in speech to use **est-ce que ...** and avoid the inversion: **Qu'est-ce que tu fais cet après-midi?** (L11). It is common to use an even more direct word-order, for example in L3: **Tu étais avec qui?** It would have been possible to say **Avec qui est-ce que tu étais?** and even (but very unlikely in conversation) **Avec qui étais-tu?** You will hear many examples in the Listening texts where the only indication of a question is in the change of intonation of the sentence. In L7, for example, **il vous appartient** (*does it belong to you?*) could be a plain statement, but it is made into a question by the question mark in the written version of the text, and by the rising question tone when spoken. Note these examples also: **Tu penses qu'on a trop de travail?** (L11); **Vous désirez, monsieur?** (L22); **Tu es d'accord?** (L31).

(b) Use of ça
This is very common in the spoken language, often as an all-purpose subject or object: **Ça te dirait d'aller en Italie?** (L31); **ça dépend de votre âge ... ça va donc de 40 à 58 francs** (L37). When talking about likes and dislikes, you might often say **j'adore ça** or **je n'aime pas ça.** This little word can also be used to give emphasis to something being said: **Ça, ce n'est pas vrai** (L6).

(c) Use of interjections
Conversation is full of interjections and exclamations, such as **dis donc** (L31); **eh bien** (L40); **ça alors!** (L46); **bon ...** (L40); **voyons ...** (L40). Also very

common is **alors,** used like English *well* as a way of filling a possible gap while you choose your words: **alors, voilà jeune homme** = *well, there you are young man* (L44). Here are some more examples: **oui, alors, pour commencer . . .** (L40); **alors, pour les 18 à 26 ans . . .** (L37); **alors, vous voyez . . .** (L30).

*(d)   Omission of negative **ne***

Conversation frequently omits the first part of the negative, e.g. **je sais pas; il vient jamais,** but this is not regarded as correct written French. Note the example in L46: **il a pas pu s'arrêter à temps.**

Index to Grammar Section

The numbers in this Index refer to paragraphs of the Grammar Section.

Bibliography and Sources of Information

(a) *Dictionaries*
Harrap's Concise French and English Dictionary (Harrap, London)
Collins Robert French and English Dictionary (Collins, London)
Oxford Concise French and English Dictionary (Clarendon Press, Oxford)

(b) *Grammars*
J.E. Mansion, *A Grammar of Present Day French* (Harrap, London)
H. Ferrar, *A French Reference Grammar* (Clarendon Press, Oxford)

(c) *Opportunities for Hearing French*
Radio broacasts from France (for example, **France Inter** and **Europe 1**) provide an opportunity for listening practice, although the speed of delivery makes such broadcasts difficult for English students. The best source of opportunities for hearing French is the BBC, with programmes intended for adult listeners and for schools. ITV also broadcasts TV French programmes for schools.

(d) *Other Sources of Information about France and the French Language*
Institut Français, Queensberry Place, South Kensington, London SW7.
French Government Tourist Office, Piccadilly, London.
French Railways, Piccadilly, London.

First published 1986 by
THE MACMILLAN PRESS LTD
Houndmills, Basingstoke, Hampshire RG21 2XS
and London
Companies and representatives
throughout the world

ISBN 0–333–53475–1

A catalogue record for this book is available
from the British Library.

Printed and bound by Unwin Brothers Ltd.,
The Gresham Press, Old Woking, Surrey GU22 9LH
A Member of the Martins Printing Group

First edition reprinted (with corrections) once
Second edition 1987
Reprinted three times
Third edition 1990
10   9   8   7   6   5   4   3   2
00 99 98 97 96 95 94 93 92

P.S. Don't forget to buy your Work Out French cassette!

You see, in addition to this Work Out book, you, as a GCSE student, are offered extra help in French with the Work Out French Cassette.

The approach for using cassettes is based on a view that sees languages best learnt when encountered in an interesting and real context. By using such methods you will find it much easier to learn and revise French – and therefore much easier to get the grade you want in your French GCSE.

The Work Out GCSE French cassette is priced at just £12.99 and you can buy it from any good bookshop.

Bonne chance!

In case of difficulty tear off the form below and return it to
John Darvill
Macmillan
Houndmills
Basingstoke
HANTS RG21 2XS

or telephone 0256 29242

- - - - - - ✂ -

Please send me my copy of the **Work Out French cassette** 0 333 53890 0

I enclose a cheque/postal order for £12.99 (cassette price, including VAT)

As a special offer students who have already bought the Work Out GCSE French book are entitled to receive their Work Out French Cassette asbsolutely free of postage and packing charges.

NAME _____

ADDRESS _____

_____

_____ POSTCODE _____